# Fundamentals
## of
# Social Intervention

# Fundamentals
## of
# Social Intervention

## core concepts and skills
## for social work practice

## F. M. Loewenberg

**Columbia University Press · New York · 1977**

Library of Congress Cataloging in Publication Data

Loewenberg, Frank M
    Fundamentals of social intervention.

    Bibliography: p.
    1. Social service.  2. Social workers.  I. Title.
HV40.L814          361          76-23290
ISBN 0-231-03611-6


                Columbia University Press
        New York          Guildford, Surrey

# Preface

In every age society looks for those who can extricate it from the problems which it faces, particularly from those problems which have defied conventional solutions. Once priests and medicine men filled this role. Next came medical doctors and, still later, scientists. But none of these was able to free society from its problems. In fact, many feel that nowadays things are worse than ever.

Today many turn to psychiatrists, social workers, and others in the helping professions. Yet the workers in these professions are the first to admit that they are no miracle workers and that there are many problems for which they do not have the answers. But there are other problems where their intervention can be helpful. How to intervene most effectively, and in what problem areas such intervention is most appropriate for social workers, is the subject of this book.

Traditionally, social work practice, like Caesar's Gaul, was divided into three parts or methods: casework, group work, and community organization. And the traditional social work curriculum followed this tripartite division. But the recognition that the method label may be misleading or even false has been growing in the last decade. In practice, as well as in education, increasing emphasis is being placed on the core elements of social work practice and not on those things which focus on the differences. This emphasis is especially important in the beginning phase of the learning process, in the first course, when the novice student is first introduced to social work.

The common base of social work practice has been recognized by many. Harriett Bartlett, in her seminal monograph (1970), calls for "integrative thinking" and for "concepts and hypotheses that promote synthesis" in order to deal with the critical problems facing today's social workers. Helen Perlman (1966:177) had observed earlier,

Maybe the way we go about identifying social work practice activities is not within the traditional boundaries of casework, group work, and community work at all, but across lines, by asking ourselves what kinds of problems call for what kinds of services and actions.

Placing emphasis on the common base of social work practice does not necessarily deny that there is room for specializations in social work. But the operative assumption is that practice specializations require a common professional base. While there is need for different techniques, suited to the type of problem and the number of people in the target system, the holistic view of man requires the development of a common basic approach to man and his problems. This common base, called here *social work practice,* is the foundation upon which all later social work specializations are built. And in preparing students, especially in their first course in social work practice, it is the common base rather than any specialization which will provide the most fruitful and the most rewarding learning experiences. This is the approach adopted here.

We have called the basic approach to social work practice *social intervention.* The theory and practice of social intervention can later serve as the base for more advanced and perhaps more specialized practice modalities. While we recognize that no social worker will become an expert in working with individuals, groups, and communities, just as no social worker will become an expert in working with every type of risk population, we believe, nevertheless, that every social worker must have a beginning competence in a wide variety of interventive techniques.

Skill in working with individuals is perhaps the first skill which every social work student must learn, no matter whether he will ultimately specialize in practice with individuals, groups, or communities. Though a family is more than the sum of its members and a group more than the total of the people who participate, the basic unit of direct social work practice is the individual. The social worker who cannot help an individual cannot help a larger collectivity. This is the reason that we have emphasized in this book work with individuals. Though the discussion and the examples often deal with groups, families, and neighborhoods, the emphasis has been placed on work with individuals because this represents the basic step in social work education.

This book has been written for college students who want to prepare for a career in social work practice. Basic concepts for social work intervention in contemporary social and human problems are identified and developed. Effective modes of service, skills, values, attitudes, and knowledge needed by social workers, working in a wide variety of community and human service settings, are explored. Opportunities are provided to help students become acquainted with and explore social intervention strategies in a wide variety of traditional as well as innovative settings. Exemplars and vignettes of practice and problems requiring social intervention are presented in Part Three. These same exemplars and vignettes frequently serve as illustrations in the earlier parts of the book. When so used, they are identified by SMALL CAPITALS.

When it comes to social intervention practice, good intentions and basic knowledge are important but not sufficient. Social workers are judged by what they do and what they achieve, not by what they know or what they plan to do. The outcome of the social intervention is what counts. Knowledge and intentions must be supplemented by skills. But these skills must be linked to knowledge and values. If a student learns skills without the theories on which they are based, he may become an expert technician who can undertake specific operations at a certain agency, but he will not be equipped to function when new circumstances demand responses other than those learned.

In this world of rapid changes, the learning of skills which are not related to knowledge and values will be dysfunctional both for the learner and for the society. As the world changes, the nature and scope of problems also change. Persons who possess only technical skills will not be able to cope with all of the new problems which will arise in the coming decades. To understand the world of the 1980s and 1990s will require social workers with a sound base of knowledge, values, and skills.

These are the thoughts that have guided the writing of this book. Our purpose was not to prepare students for work in any specific agency or in any one field of practice. No attempt has been made to train students for their first job or to teach them specific, job-oriented skills, unrelated to theory and values. Instead, every effort has been made to involve students in the basic theory and practice of social intervention in order to prepare them for a lifetime of practice and continued learning. This is the only way in which we can help students get ready for life and work in a world which does not yet exist and whose shape no one today can predict.

# Acknowledgments

Writing a book is a demanding task. The present book was written over six years in many different parts of the world, stretching from Hawaii to Jerusalem. And in these six years the world has changed more than one realizes. Peace and war, prosperity and depression, Vietnam and Watergate—these are some of the events which undoubtedly had an impact on the writing of this book. Had they not occurred, this book would have been a different one.

Yet more than geography and events, it was the people who influenced me in writing this book. Though the author alone is responsible for what he wrote, many people participated in the process of developing this book, often without being aware that they participated. Among those who in a very real sense were partners are:

My students at Adelphi University, New York University, Tel-Aviv University, and Bar-Ilan University; these were my best teachers and their willingness to sit with me provided me the opportunity to test the ideas found in these pages.

My colleagues at these universities and at the Council on Social Work Education, who were always ready to listen and share their thoughts.

The hundreds of social work educators in the United States, Canada, England, Holland, and Israel who shared with me the problems which they faced as teachers.

The anonymous reviewers whose critiques and suggestions made this a better and more useful textbook.

My editors, John D. Moore and Mrs. Dorothy M. Swart, who always encouraged me to continue.

My daughter, Mrs. Naomi Baum, who critically read an earlier draft of the manuscript while she served as a National Service social worker in the Bet She'an Valley.

Dr. Ralph Dolgoff, Mrs. Florence Mittwoch, and Mrs. Judith Sadeh, colleagues and friends, whose wise counsel saved me from many pitfalls.

My wife, Chaya, and our children, Joel, Naomi, Chaim, and Alisa, who for too long put up with a part-time husband and father.

To all of them go my sincerest thanks.

F. M. L.

# Contents

**PART TWO: CORE SKILLS**

## PART THREE: EXEMPLARS AND VIGNETTES

# Fundamentals
## of
# Social Intervention

# Prologue

Betty and Jim KING, together with their three young children, live in a cold-water flat in a dilapidated building near the center of the city. Jim is twenty-six years old and has been working fairly regularly at various unskilled jobs since he dropped out of school in the eighth grade. For the past three years he worked at the vegetable counter of a local supermarket. Betty is five years younger than Jim; she quit school in the ninth grade when she and Jim eloped. For a time Betty worked in a department store, but since the birth of her oldest daughter, three years ago, she has been staying at home to take care of her children.

While the Kings never had enough money to do all the things they wanted to do, they managed to get along on their own until Jim was suddenly hospitalized three weeks ago. Betty does not know exactly what is wrong with her husband, but the doctor has told her that he may not be able to work again. With no income and no insurance money, Betty has been borrowing from her sister to buy food and pay the rent. But she knows that she cannot go on like this for long because her sister is not rich. She realizes that she will have to go to work very soon but does not know how she can do this with three babies at home, the youngest less than a year old.

This is the story which Betty King told the social worker at the County Welfare Department where she had gone after a friend had told her that this was the place where people like her could get help. Mrs. King had no real idea how a social worker would help, but she was hoping that here she would find an answer to her problems. Her story did not come out all at once; the social worker realized that Mrs. King found it difficult to talk about her problem. She had never before asked a complete stranger for help. The social worker listened to her attentively, asked questions to clarify some unclear points, urged Mrs. King to tell her story, and . . .

How should the social worker respond to Mrs. King's request for help? How can he help Mrs. King, whose request is typical of many which social workers receive every day? [1] In the following chapters we will discuss some of the elements which will enable students and beginning workers to find answers to these questions.

1. Some social workers are men, some are women. In this book "he" will always be used for the social worker.

# Part One
# Basic Concepts

Part One
Basic Concepts

# chapter one

# Social Intervention and Social Work: an Introduction

It is difficult to produce a short, yet useful definition of social work. A good definition should describe a thing clearly and indicate what is unique or distinctive about it. A definition of a practice field, such as social work, should include information about its area of competence (that is, its target problems), its value base, the desired outcomes, and the skills and techniques utilized by the practitioners. No one-sentence definition can handle all this, particularly for a field as complex as social work. No wonder that those authors who have attempted to present a short definition of social work usually have required many additional pages to explain their definition. Nevertheless, the beginning student who wants to know what he will be studying is entitled to an answer.

One of the difficulties in formulating a useful definition is that the field of social work is not easily distinguishable from other professional fields; and what social workers do, does not appear to be too different from what laymen generally do when they help others. Social workers do not use special tools or appliances, nor do they wear a white coat or some other easily identifiable uniform. Many others deal with the same kind of problems; marriage counselors, psychologists, community developers, and people of good will without any particular training also seem to be doing what social workers are doing. "The giving of help is by no means a social work monopoly," observed Katherine Kendal (1958:30). Yet a meaningful definition of social work must establish clear boundary lines if it is to be informative and helpful.

## Social Work: Definitions

Instead of developing an original definition of social work, we will cite several short definitions which have found wide acceptance over the years. To be sure, there are other formulations of social work and social work practice which differ from these presented here. However, the definitions cited below have been widely used in the social work literature, and they do converge on the approach to practice which we will develop in this book. After citing these definitions, we will examine them, noting both commonalities and gaps. In a larger sense, this entire book will serve as our attempt to define the field of social work and social intervention practice.

Helen Perlman once wrote that "to attempt to define social casework takes courage or foolhardiness or perhaps a bit of both" (1957:3). But a page later she defined social casework, the earliest of the social work "methods," in this way:

Social casework is a process used by certain human welfare agencies to help individuals to cope more effectively with their problems in social functioning.

Gisela Konopka proposed the following definition for social group work (1963:20):

Social group work is a method of social work which helps individuals to enhance their social functioning through purposeful group experiences and to cope more effectively with their personal, group, or community problems.

The definition of social work developed by Werner Boehm for the Council on Social Work Education Curriculum Study is well-known and has been cited by many (1959:45):

Social work seeks to enhance the social functioning of individuals, singly and in groups, by activities focused upon their social relationships which constitute the interaction between man and his environment. These activities can be grouped into three functions: restoration of impaired capacity, provision of individual and social resources, and prevention of social dysfunction.

All three definitions use the phrase "social functioning," but evidently the same phrase serves different purposes. Perlman uses "social functioning" to designate the problem area for which social workers are uniquely competent while Konopka and Boehm identify the enhancement of social functioning as a desired outcome of the social worker's activity. All three suggest, implicitly or explicitly, that the area of social work's competence is the problems that are likely to occur at the point where individuals and their environment interpenetrate. However, none of the definitions addresses itself to the value base of social work and only Konopka mentions in general terms the methodology used to achieve the desired outcome. And none reveals what it is that is unique or distinctive about social work. Perhaps, as William Gordon (1965) points out, the distinctiveness of social work lies in its values and its knowledge base and not in its techniques, purposes, functions, or methods. But about these, the three definitions also remain silent. Nevertheless, these definitions do offer an introduction to the concepts of social work and social work practice.

## The Concept of Social Intervention

*Social intervention* is the term that social workers increasingly use to describe what they do. The term, as we use it here, is not merely a synonym for therapy or treatment but goes beyond these in several important ways, as we will discuss in the following chapters. Social intervention emphasizes the active, purposeful, and planned participation of both client and worker in all phases of the social intervention process. It describes those activities which are initiated in response to a specific problem condition (or to prevent its further development), at the request of, and in partnership with, a client or with someone or some group that carries responsibility for the resulting condition or for the population at risk. These activities are based on a strategy especially designed to achieve a specified goal, namely, to cope with, eliminate, or prevent the particular problem. Intervention, as the concept is used by social workers, does not give license to meddle with other people's affairs; instead, it sanctions activities which are "directed to purposes and guided by values, knowledge and techniques which are collectively unique, acknowledged by and identified with the social work profession" (Gordon, 1962:11).

The adjective *social* modifies *intervention* in order to emphasize the primary area of social work practice, as well as its over-all goals. The "turf" of social work, as noted, is located at the interface of the person system and the environment system, at the point where individuals interact with their environment. The problematic consequences of this interaction constitute the target problems of social work, regardless whether these are located in the person or in the environment or, as happens most often, in a combination of person and environment. The concept of target problem will be examined in greater detail below and again in chapter 3. The purpose and goal of the social intervention are social in the Weberian sense that "action is social insofar as, by virtue of the subjective meaning attached to it by the acting individual (or individuals), it takes account of the behavior of others and is thereby oriented in its course" (Weber, 1947:68). Social workers claim that theirs is the most socially oriented of all the helping professions; they attempt to use their skill and knowledge to help people achieve socially desirable objectives. The question of *who* defines societal goals and *how* these are related to social work goals will be examined in chapters 2 and 4.

*Social intervention,* as we use the term, is a generic term which includes social work activities on various levels. It can be used to describe work with individuals, groups, neighborhoods, communities, and even larger social systems. It includes activities intended to modify or eliminate problem-causing or stress-producing conditions in the environment, as well as activities which are planned to help people learn how to cope more effectively with their problems. At times social intervention is used in an attempt to prevent the increase of a problem in severity or scope. At other times, the purpose is to prevent a problem from developing. And at still other times the objective is to help people fulfill themselves and maximize their potentials. Students and beginning workers generally work with individuals, families, small groups, and neighborhood groups rather than with communities and larger social systems. This is why our emphasis in this book will be largely on the former rather than on the latter collectivities.

Social intervention is indicated whenever it is believed that certain worker and client activities will make a difference. Social intervention, by definition, is time-limited and will end when the specified goal has been achieved (or earlier, when one of the participants withdraws). When the problem is an ongoing one, arising out of the social arrangements which characterize modern industrialized societies, public social utilities rather than social intervention should be made available. While social intervention is time-limited, public social utilities are not time-limited (Kahn, 1973). The provision of financial assistance for the unemployed, for example, should be a function of a public social utility; but helping people regain their independence and rejoin the labor force is a task for social intervention. In this book the focus will be on social intervention and not on social utilities.

A review of MRS. KING's situation will illustrate various types of social intervention activities. While listening to her, the social worker noted some of the immediate problems which might require intervention. His tentative list included: (1) lack of income; (2) need for child-care arrangements; (3) need for information about Mr. King's medical condition and a more precise prognosis; (4) Mrs. King's uncertainty about her new role as head of the family. Various social intervention activities are appropriate for each of these problems. The selection of a specific set of activities will depend not only on a greater knowledge of the facts than are presently available to us, but more especially on Mrs. King's wishes and interests. Nevertheless, it may be helpful to present a preliminary sketch of possible social intervention activities for each of the identified problem areas.

1. With the family's sole wage earner in the hospital, Mrs. King must now feed her family, pay the rent, and take care of all the other things which a family requires. She may also have to pay for her husband's hospitalization and recuperation. Is "going to work" the only solution? Is it the best solution? How much can an unskilled and inexperienced person earn? The social worker must find a way to help Mrs. King cope with these questions. He should provide her with information about possible alternative solutions (for example, child-care center, training program, AFDC, and so on) so that she can select the one she feels is best for her. She will also need information about available resources and how to obtain access to these resources. If there are no provisions for people like Mrs. King or if these arrangements are inadequate, the worker must alert the community to this situation and help it develop the necessary services. The social worker's interventive activities may range from data collection and interpretation to interorganizational planning and coordination in order to secure the resources which Mrs. King and others like her need. The worker may carry direct responsibility for community social intervention, or there may be other workers in his agency who take responsibility for this level of intervention activities.

2. If Mrs. King finally decides to go to work, she will need information about available child-care facilities or other types of child-care arrangements. If there are no such arrangements in this community, social intervention with the

community is indicated; careful consideration must be given to the question whether the most effective target for securing child-care services is the community's public system or some other system. In some cities, factories are providing child-care services for the children of their employees; under certain circumstances, social intervention with prospective employers may produce more effective and more efficient results than intervention with city hall. But since Mrs. King cannot wait until the community has decided to rectify the lack of services, the worker may play an active role in helping her recruit other mothers for a cooperative child-care program.

3. Accurate information about Mr. King's present condition and the medical prognosis is essential before Mrs. King can make any long-range plans. There may be various reasons for her inability to secure this information, and at a later time the worker may want to explore these with her. But the immediate problem is to secure the necessary information. The worker can either help Mrs. King obtain this information by advising her whom she should approach, what she should ask, and how she should ask for it—or he can secure the information himself after obtaining her consent. Mrs. King's strengths, as well as her preferences in this matter, will determine which method of data collection will be employed. But the objective at this point is to obtain the information and not to help Mrs. King develop general interpersonal skills or to help the hospital overcome its public relations problems.

Some months later, this worker learned at a staff meeting that Mrs. King's problem with the hospital was not unique; many relatives of hospitalized patients had encountered the same kind of difficulty in obtaining information. It now became clear that intervention in the hospital social system was appropriate since the problem was obviously there. Consequently, the worker developed an approach to the hospital administration which included planning a staff self-study of the hospital's patient information service. By functioning as a consultant to the self-study staff, the worker was able to play a crucial role in changing the hospital's information services. But all this happened months after Mrs. King had need for the information. While working with her, the worker focused on obtaining the information for her and not on changing the hospital.

4. For the time being, the King family is a one-parent family. Mrs. King does not appear entirely sure about her new role as head of the family. Here the worker can provide clarification of what society expects of her, provide feedback on her performance, and offer emotional support as she faces new and undoubtedly difficult situations. If there are other women in Mrs. King's neighborhood who face similar problems, the worker can help them organize a self-help group. Often it is easier to face problems and learn how to cope with them if there is an opportunity to share one's concerns and fears in a group. Later, when Mrs. King's invalid husband returns home, he will need help in adjusting to his new role of being dependent upon his wife; again the worker can play a supportive role.

These examples are only illustrative. Even though here the beneficiary is always Mrs. King, various modalities of intervention have been suggested. Whether the intervention activity will focus on the individual, the group, or the community should depend on the problem, the objectives, and the situation—and not on some predetermined formula. The actual selection of activities and strategies does not depend on the worker alone but is a cooperative activity between the worker and Mrs. King. As they learn more about the problems and as they identify goals and objectives, various types of intervention activities may appear feasible. The purpose of this preliminary analysis of the potential problems and possible activities is to illustrate that for most problems there is a wide variety of intervention techniques and a multiplicity of targets. Skill in developing these is one of the hallmarks of the competent social worker.

## Propositions and Assumptions

One social worker assumes that weak ego strengths can explain his client's chronic unemployment; his colleague thinks that the uncertain economic situation is responsible for pockets of chronic unemployment. These two social workers, in an attempt to be helpful to their unemployed clients, will develop different social intervention strategies. In this example, as in practically every instance, the assumptions which social workers bring along have a definite impact of their practice. Yet these assumptions are often ignored or taken for granted. Just as social workers rarely talk about their assumptions, so many writers have neglected to mention the assumptions which have guided their approach to social work practice. Probably they thought that everybody was aware of and accepted their particular set of assumptions. But there is neither full awareness nor general acceptance of the specific assumptions which provide the base for social work practice. An explicit examination of these assumptions is therefore appropriate.

In the philosophy of science, an *assumption* is a statement which is more or less self-evident and which is used without proof as to its validity merely because some sort of agreement is necessary in order to communicate with others. A *proposition,* on the other hand, is a statement whose truth is supported by convincing objective evidence. Several of our assumptions are potential propositions, but since they have not yet been established by objective evidence they are, for the time being, only assumptions.

The following five assumptions guide our approach to social intervention practice:

1. Human and social conditions are responsive to social intervention.

2. Problems may result from environmental flaws, from individual inadequacies, or from a combination of both.

3. Problems are dynamic.

4. The societal context in which social work is practiced affects problem definition, goal-setting, and strategy development.

5. Social intervention is a practice modality particularly relevant for problems that result from the faulty interaction of persons and environment.

Because these assumptions are important, we will discuss them in some detail.

1. *Human and social conditions are responsive to social intervention.* Until modern times most people thought that they could not or should not interfere with "nature" or with the divine plan for the world. Supernatural forces were believed to cause problems, and man could not change what was inevitable or preordained. The revolutionary assumption that the world is amenable to intervention is based on the belief of man's capacity to understand what is happening to him and his world. Man's ability to control his world and to change it is the key assumption which distinguishes modern civilization from the medieval world of magic and superstition. The evolution of social work practice from charitable acts to planned social intervention became possible only with the acceptance of this key assumption. There is no place for modern social work in a culture which rejects this assumption. The somewhat uncertain status of American social work may be due in part to the fact that this assumption has not yet been fully accepted by everybody in our society.

2. *Problems may result from environmental flaws, from individual inadequacies, or from a combination of both.* The belief that problems are always caused by personality defects is a popular one and one which has guided many of the helping professions well into the twentieth century. Such an assumption may have fit a society more traditional than ours, but it hardly suits the contemporary world. When black and Chicano teen-agers cannot find jobs because they are not white, it is almost besides the point to suggest that they use more initiative in order to overcome their disadvantage. Neither is it realistic to attribute

to "character disorders" the dire poverty of a retired couple whose pension benefits have all but disappeared in the face of double-digit inflation.

Social workers tend to pay more attention to modifying human behavior than to changing the environment, but there has been a gradual change in the way in which they approach the world. Early social workers, especially those practicing in the years prior to World War I, had assumed that if only people would live and work in adequate physical surroundings, their social functioning and coping capacities would automatically improve; public housing, slum clearance, fair labor laws, and similar projects were an expression of this assumption. In the 1920s social workers realized the inadequacies of these efforts and began to direct their attention to psychiatric conditions within the individual. Disregarding the larger environment and its impact on the individual, social work treatment focused on personality defects. Even the cataclysmic events of the great depression in the 1930s did not greatly affect the psychiatric thrust within social work. But in more recent decades, particularly in the years after World War II, social workers once again shifted their attention to the social environment. However, the concept of environment as currently used in social work practice differs somewhat from its earlier namesake. At first social workers began to look at the environment through their clients' eyes, but more recently they have used "the telescopic lens of the environment" to understand their clients and their problems (N. E. Cohen, 1964:362). The environment, once in the background of social work practice, has moved to center stage! This renewed focus on the environment fits our assumption that problem causes are sometimes located in the individual, sometimes in the environment, and most often in a combination of individual and environment.

3. *Problems are dynamic.* Scientists working in a laboratory can say with a good deal of certainty that the addition of a given chemical to a solution in a test tube will cause a specified

reaction. Scientists can perform the same experiment in two laboratories, thousands of miles apart, and report identical results. In a laboratory it is possible to speak of one cause as necessary and sufficient to produce a change; this possibility exists because the scientist can control the test-tube environment. But in the real world it is all but impossible to achieve identical results when applying the same intervention in two "identical" situations; neither is it possible to identify a single cause as necessary and sufficient for most human problems. For one thing, it is not possible to duplicate a situation; the same event will affect different people in different ways—the loss of a job may be a traumatic experience for one person, a challenge for another, and an inconsequential nuisance for a third. Social workers cannot duplicate scientific procedures, because a person is never exposed to one influence only; instead, a person constantly reacts to a large number of stimuli, and it is difficult, if not impossible, to assign cause and effect to any one factor when it comes to human beings. A large number of factors give meaning to an experience such as losing a job. The person's general mental health, his economic situation, the availability of other jobs, the reasons for losing this job, and a multitude of other factors must be considered before one can fully understand the significance of losing a job for this person. While the experimental scientist can introduce one and only one change factor, in real life persons are never exposed to only one factor. This multiplicity of impinging factors makes it difficult to speak of *the* problem. A problem does not stand still but continues to develop and change as the person continues to be exposed to various other influences. The problem changes even while the social intervention process unfolds. The problems that Mrs. King faces today are different from those she faced yesterday and still different from those she will face tomorrow.

Just as there is almost never only one problem, so is there rarely only a single cause. Single-cause explanations for individual and social problems may make good slogans, but they usually do not provide an effective data base for planning social intervention. Assigning single causes to complex and dynamic problems tends to result in simplistic intervention strategies which are often inappropriate and of little effect.[1] The dynamic nature of problems also suggests that there is a reciprocal interaction between people and problems. Far from being inert or passive receivers of whatever fate has in store for them, people react to every stimulus and attempt to cope with every problem which comes their way. Just as problems affect and change people, so people's reactions to problems and people's attempts to cope with the problems change the nature of the problems. When a mother is angry with her child, her behavior is shaped, in part, by the child's reaction to her anger. And his reaction, in turn, will depend to some extent on how his mother reacts to his responses. A single incident has never created a tense neighborhood situation; rather a succession of events and the reactions of various community groups to these events and to each other may result in the gradual evolution of a neighborhood crisis.

4. *The societal context in which social work is practiced affects problem definition, goal-setting, and strategy development.* Social work, like other helping professions, reflects the value system and the social structure of the society in which it is practiced. Though the personality and practice style of each worker play a role in influencing the specific mode of intervention, the alternatives are limited to those permitted by the society. Furthermore, the same objective condition will be defined in different ways by various societies. One society places a high value on the individual while another places greater emphasis on the common good. Behaviors classified as deviant in one society may not be so labeled in another. Intervention techniques which are appropriate in one cultural setting may be out of place in a second. The societal emphasis on individual

1. C. Wright Mills (1943) presented an opposite view since he believed that the acceptance of the principle of multiple causation implied a denial of the possibility of making radical changes in the social structure.

rights has led American social workers to develop a primary commitment to individualism, as expressed in the theories of classical democracy. Their preference for avoiding institutional placements for children can best be understood in the light of this value commitment since other societies, with different values, do not frown on placing children in institutions of various kinds (Wolins, 1969).

The institutional network of any given society provides the opportunities and resources for social intervention but also sets limits to what is possible. Becoming an unwed mother has different meanings and results in different types of problems in various societies. Not only do values about illegitimacy and motherhood differ, but some communities are structured to help "girls in trouble," while others provide a wide variety of services to all pregnant women, married or not, and still others do not provide any services but delegate this responsibility to the family or the clan. Different types of intervention strategies are possible in each of these communities.

The priorities of a society will influence social work practice. Racism, for example, became a problem for priority attention for social workers only when it became an important issue in the larger society (Briar, 1971:108). To be sure, social workers do not always follow and react; often they take the lead and alert society to those critical problems which require priority attention. Many social workers took an early lead in calling attention to the debilitating consequences of institutional racism. However, social work practice cannot for long be out of step with the general thrust of the society in which it is practiced.

5. *Social intervention is a practice modality particularly relevant for problems which result from the faulty interaction of persons and environment.* Helen Perlman (1957:27) once wrote that "there is probably no problem in human living that has not been brought to social workers." Yet we should suspect any claim which suggests that social intervention is a panacea for every kind of problem. So long as practitioners are unable to specify

the target areas for which social intervention can be effective, they are likely to devote their energies to helping people with problems for which others may be able to offer more skillful help. Knowledge-building and theory development will also be handicapped unless social workers identify their area of competence and concern more precisely; otherwise their efforts will be scattered in a dozen directions. By focusing on the person/environment interface we want to suggest that social intervention is relevant for problems arising out of social relations and relations with formal organizations. We shall avoid talking about personality problems and environmental problems as two distinct problem areas because social work's competence is precisely at the point where person and environment meet; dealing with one without the other is not social intervention. This definition of problem area will be discussed at length in chapter 3; it is mentioned here because our definition is based on an assumption with which not everybody may agree.

## Model for Social Intervention Practice

There is danger that social workers will substitute skills and techniques for purposeful and thoughtful activities if they fail to understand that their practice requires more than expertise and skill in a number of intervention modalities. We will develop a model for social intervention practice in order to minimize this danger. This model, like all models in science, will attempt to clarify the complexities of the social intervention process by selecting a small number of key components and showing how these serve crucial functions. A model is not intended to reflect reality accurately but is only a simulation constructed to help explain what happens in the real world. In chemistry, for example, the physical model used to explain the structural organization of molecules uses red and green balls to simulate oxygen and hydrogen atoms without paying attention to the relative size of these colored balls. In a similar way our model of the social intervention process will not accurately reflect the actual process but only simulate certain key components of that process. While the model should be helpful in gaining a better understanding of the field of social work and in providing a general approach to social intervention practice, it is not designed to offer a specific set of directions of what practitioners are expected to do.[2]

Our model includes five elements: *values, problems, goals, participants,* and *strategy.* There is no special significance to the order in which these elements have been enumerated and no linear sequence of activities is intended. The five elements will be explored in depth in later chapters; here we will define them in a preliminary way, indicating how each fits into the practice model and demonstrating how each is related to every other element. This discussion will be followed by a preliminary analysis of social intervention practice.

1. *Values* are those culture-bound ideas and societal beliefs which serve as criteria for preferring or choosing one course of action rather than another. Values are a key element in the societal context and as such affect problem definition, goal-setting, and strategy development. Values also play an important role in determining who should participate in the social intervention activities. In a patriarchal society, the father of the family, whether or not he suffers from the problem, must become a participant if the social intervention is to be effective. Whether an unwed father is included in making plans for his child depends in the first instance on how the society in which he lives values marriage and parenthood. The antipoverty programs provide another example; poor people will be invited to participate in developing and designing antipoverty strategies only in societies which value self-determination

---

2. Some have used models in other ways. Reid and Epstein (1927:7), for example, say that "a model is a coherent set of directions which state how a given kind of treatment is to be carried out. . . . It usually states what the practitioner is expected to do or what practitioners customarily do under given circumstances." Our use of models follows Carlo Lastrucci (1963) and others.

highly. The relationship between values and the other elements of our model is not always unidirectional; over time the impact of other elements will result in marked value changes. When a problem becomes widespread, value changes often follow. Thus, some values about drug addiction changed when that problem surfaced in American society.

2. The focal point of the social intervention process is the *problem.* A problem is defined as an intolerable condition which requires intervention for its elimination or modification. Problems for which social intervention is relevant are those which occur at the interface of the person system and the social system. The impact of values on problem definition has been noted. Goals also play an important part in problem definition; unless the problem definer is aware that a more desirable or less problematic condition is possible, he will not identify the current situation as a problem. Various participants may identify different problems or define the same problem in various ways. The client may ask for help with one problem, the social worker may recognize another, and in the course of working together the participants may agree to focus on still another problem.

3. Social intervention is a focused process, designed to achieve specified *goals.* The desired outcome should be stated in specific terms so that it can guide the participants in developing and later in implementing the social intervention strategy. Goal is a dynamic concept. As the social intervention process unfolds, each short-range goal or objective becomes a milestone on the road toward achieving further goals. Relevant goals are deduced from the problems identified by the client and the worker. All goals, even short-range objectives, should be connected to the problem. Whether social work goals should include personality changes or societal changes or whether they should be limited to more modest environmental modifications and behavior adaptations will be explored in chapter 4. The answer to these questions is determined in large measure by the societal value system which

impinges on goal-setting as it does on every other component part of the model.

4. In the prehistory of modern social work, the social worker (or friendly vistor, as he was often called) made all the decisions for the client. Later, much later, Gordon Hamilton and other social work teachers introduced the notion that it was up to the social worker to engage the client as an active *participant* in decision-making. Today there is recognition that many different factors and people affect the problem evolution and influence the achievement of the desired goal; as a consequence of this recognition the circle of participants in the social intervention process has been widened and often includes other people in addition to client and worker. Potential participants, though not necessarily in every phase of the social intervention, include the applicant, client, target, and beneficiary, as well as others who are related to the problem cause or problem solution. In addition, the social worker and the social agency participate actively in the social intervention process.

Applicant, client, target, and beneficiary are four positions which are sometimes occupied by one person and at other times by different people. The person (or persons) who brings the problem to the social worker and requests help is the *applicant*. Once an applicant has entered into a formal, goal-focused relationship with a social worker, he becomes a *client*.[3] Becoming a client implies that there is a contractual

---

3. Some social workers no longer use the term *client* since they feel that it conveys an unfavorable evaluation of the person so labeled (Tropp, 1974). Since other terms, such as *recipient* and *consumer,* have not found general acceptance, we will continue to use *client* to designate those who participate, together with a social worker, in a formal, goal-focused relationship. Mary Richmond's comment (1917:38) on her use of the term *client* may be of interest:

Those with whom social workers are dealing are called many names—applicants, inmates, cases, children, families, probationers, patients are only a few of them. One word will be used for all, usually, in this volume—the word client. Its history is one of advancement from low estate to higher. First it meant a suitor, a dependent. Later it meant one who listens to advice, and later still one who employs a professional service of any kind. The more expert the service, the more appropriate the word. . . .

relationship between that person (or persons) and the worker, defining the problem, goal, strategy, and the tasks for which each is responsible. The *target* is the person(s) or institution which must be modified in order to achieve the desired goal. Often, but not always, the target is or will become the client; this is especially true if the goal includes personality changes or behavior modification. The *beneficiary* is the person(s) who will benefit from successful goal achievement. The beneficiary may but need not be the client or target. If he is neither, his participation is usually only indirect. But this list does not exhaust the possible participants. Anyone cannected with a problem situation may be invited to participate in the social intervention process. When working with Ben, a member of the CAREY FAMILY, his parents and siblings became important participants; in one phase his teachers and principal were recruited as participants, and later on a neighborhood storekeeper who could offer part-time employment became a potential participant. In social intervention the focus often shifts from the solitary client or the specific small group to the social systems in which the client participates. All those active in these social systems are potential participants in the social intervention process.

5. The plan which the worker and client together develop to cope with the problem condition is called the *strategy*. This plan identifies the taks necessary to achieve the desired goals and the persons responsible for completing each task. The strategy serves as a bridge, connecting problem identification and goal-setting with the implementation phase of social intervention practice. When a strategy is based on a specific problem and goal, there is less danger that the intervention activity will be derived from the professional ideology or preferred methodology of the agency or worker. In developing an intervention strategy, thoughtful consideration must be given to identification of the problem situation, determination of the desired outcomes, selection of the most effective points of intervention, and choice of the most efficient intervention methodology. The use of such terms as "selection" and

"choice" implies that various strategies and targets are possible and that conscious decision-making is a crucial part of the social intervention process.

## The Social Intervention Process

"Study-diagnosis-treatment" has been one popular way to describe the social intervention process. This formulation was borrowed from the field of medical practice and, like any borrowed concept, does not give an entirely accurate portrait of the social intervention process.[4] We think it is desirable to examine the process once more in order to obtain a more complete and perhaps a more accurate picture.

Our outline of the component processes will be derived from social work practice in many different functional fields. We will try to incorporate social intervention practice with individuals, groups, neighborhoods, and communities. We will speak of component processes rather than of sequential phases because we have found that these are not steps in a linear sequence, one always following the other, but rather dynamic processes, many of which continue to occur throughout the social intervention process. Some component processes logically occur before others, but they can also reoccur at a later stage. Thus, recognition of a problem or a potential problem is a prerequisite for social intervention, but as the process unfolds, new problems become indentified. Similarly, contract negotiations are not a one-time event but a process which starts at the very first encounter between worker and client and then continues, more or less actively, throughout all subsequent encounters until the very last meeting.

1. *Problem recognition.* An undesirable situation must be

4. The study-diagnosis-treatment formulation, though widely but not universally accepted, has meant different things to different social workers. The current preference for "assessment" in place of "diagnosis" is more than a mere change of name. For one thing, it suggests an ongoing process rather than a distinct, one-time phase (see Simon, 1970:374-77).

recognized as a problem before anything can be done about it. It may be recognized by those who suffer from the problem, by those who are responsible for the victim of the problem (a parent or a guardian, for example), by those who "cause" the problem, or by a community group responsible for the general welfare of the community. Even though a problem is not always accurately identified at this stage, it is necessary that someone or some group feel sufficiently strong about the condition to want to do something about it.

Sometimes a social worker recognizes a problem which others have not yet recognized. Yet in most situations he cannot intervene until his help has been requested, even if he believes that harm will occur without his intervention. But the social worker need not sit in his office and wait until he is called. He can take the initiative and help individuals and communities identify and recognize problems which face them.

2. *Request for help.* Social intervention requires that someone requests the help of a social worker. The request may come from the persons or group or community which suffers from the problem (problem carrier or victim), from one who has specific or general responsibility for the problem carrier (parents, police, protective agency), or from a group which is in a position to do something about the situation (neighborhood association, community council, mayor's office, and so forth). The only general requirement is that those who request help should be willing to participate appropriately in the social intervention process. When the initial contact with the social worker is not "voluntary," the actual social intervention will commence only after there has been a voluntary request and a freely determined decision to participate. But if the police or the court requests the social worker to meet with a prisoner or parolee who does not want to participate, the social intervention process is not applicable and the social worker can only function in some other role.

3. *Preliminary assessment.* The applicant and the worker

together will assess the problem and the request for help to determine if social intervention is appropriate. Prior to this determination, the applicant should have a reasonable understanding of the social worker's way of intervening and of his own role as a potential participant in the social intervention. The social worker should obtain a preliminary understanding of the problem. He should also be able to make a tentative assessment of the strengths and limitations of the applicant in order to determine how the applicant can best participate. This preliminary assessment requires the sharing of information between the applicant and the worker, as well as a joint decision regarding continuation.

4. *Problem assessment and goal identification.* In order to designate an intervention goal (outcome) and to locate the most effective point of intervention, more precise problem identification and assessment are necessary even after the problem has been recognized and even after it has been determined that the problem is appropriate for social intervention. Often the nature of the problem or its focus changes at this time. As client and worker clarify the dimensions of the problem and its relation to other problems they will select a specific part of the larger problem for immediate attention. During the assessment process the worker and the client will examine all elements which might impinge on the problem, including appropriate elements from the personality system and the societal system.

5. *Strategy development.* Social intervention practice has not yet reached the stage of development where accurate assessment leads directly to one and only one intervention strategy. That day may come, but in the meantime worker and client must consider and develop alternate strategies and estimate the effectiveness, cost, and risk of each. Only after comparing the available options can client and worker select the strategy which will serve as a map and guide for the intervention activity. Feedback from the implementation, as well as identification of new problems and the availability of additional infor-

mation, requires that strategy development remain an ongoing process.

6. *Contract negotiation.* Contract negotiation is an essential component of the social intervention process, even in those social agencies which do not use a formal written document to confirm the rights and obligations of client and worker. By definition, a contract is an agreement between two or more people which spells out what everyone is expected to do.[5] In the social work contract, every participant needs to agree to the goals and to the strategy. Every participant must also know what he is expected to do. This contractual relationship, freely arrived at, is the essence of the social intervention relationship. The contract negotiation process starts during the first encounter between worker and client and continues until termination. The client or the worker has the right, at any time, to reopen the contract for review and renegotiation.

7. *Implementation of strategy.* After choosing the strategy the worker and client must recruit the necessary resources, material and human, to implement the strategy in the most effective and most efficient way. Sometimes the resources are already at hand and implementation can start at once, but at other times recruitment of resources becomes a protracted process in which the worker frequently takes a more active role than the client. Once the resources are available, the full sequence of planned intervention activities follows.

8. *Feedback and evaluation.* Evaluation is an ongoing process, not a one-time activity at the end of the social intervention. Continuous feedback, based on a continuing evaluation, enables client and worker to make modifications and improvements while there is still time and opportunity to make changes. When client and worker agree to end the social inter-

---

5. Strictly speaking, the social work contract is between the social agency and all participants other than the social worker. The worker's contract with the agency is an employment contract which implicitly or explicitly spells out the limits under which the worker operates. In the contract negotiations with participants, the social worker represents the agency or acts as its agent.

vention, the final evaluation should identify the results achieved.

9. *Termination*. Worker and client may agree from the very begining to end the social intervention after a certain number of weeks; in this time-limited approach the worker will remind the client periodically that they are approaching the agreed-to termination point. Alternately, the intervention may be continued until the goal has been achieved or as long as there is progress toward the goal. Either approach, time-limited or goal-focused, is based on the assumption that the intervention is for a specific purpose and that it is not a life-time project. Since the success of the intervention will be eva-luated, in part, by the client's ability to cope with problems without the worker's help, termination is an integral and cru-cial part of the entire process.

The phrases "ongoing process" and "not a one-time activ-ity" have occurred several times in this outline of component processes in order to remind the reader that we are not de-scribing a series of successive events. Though the enumeration of distinct component processes is necessary for analytical pur-poses, in practice these fuse into one.

## Onward !

This is the introduction to social intervention practice. What follows is built on this foundation. We will now examine in greater detail each of the elements of the social intervention model. And in the second part of this book we will focus on some of the core skills used by social workers in social inter-vention practice.

# chapter two

# Values: the Societal Context of Social Intervention

Values influence the basic orientations and institutions of the social system and, at the same time, guide the activities of all who work and live in that society. This makes values a key element of social intervention practice. Values affect the social structure and the personality structure of both client and worker. Without understanding the value component of behavior, a social worker will find it difficult to assess problems and people, and he will find it all but impossible to plan effective social intervention strategies. How can a social worker understand MRS. KING's problems if he does not take into consideration the societal context in which these problems occurred? What is the social origin of Mrs. King's desire to go to work? Why did Mrs. King turn to her sister for emergency help and not to a welfare agency? Would she have required help had she lived in another country with different structural arrangements and different values? Can the worker suggest solutions to Mrs. King's problems which are not approved by this society?

Not only does the society provide the background in which the social intervention takes place, but it may itself be a problem "cause" and also a key component in the social intervention process. Identical objective conditions will create a problem in one society but not in another, where that condition is considered normal or where there are institutional arrangements to cope with that situation. Lengthy hospitalization of the family breadwinner almost always results in serious problems in America, but in societies where extended family patterns or collective living arrangements (such as the Israeli kibbutz) prevail, Mrs. King would have avoided many of her current problems. This is due, in great part, to different structural and institutional arrangements which flow from different value systems. In America, lengthy hospitalization usually results in economic problems because no alternate income-maintenance arrangements have been developed, but elsewhere this particular problem may be unknown because adequate alternate arrangements have been established. Again, the reason for a particular social structural arrangement can be found in the values of any given society. Wherever individualism is considered a supreme value, one type of structural arrangement will follow, but where other values are of greater importance, other structural arrangements will evolve. And these structural arrangements change as values change. Thus, the recent debates about more adequate income-maintenance programs and various national health insurance schemes reflect evolving changes in the American value pattern.[1]

Societal value patterns serve as criteria for client behavior and for problem definition. At the same time, they give direction to social work practice. While values do not specify directly the activities in which a social worker should engage, they do more or less clearly indicate the situations in which social intervention is appropriate, the types of intervention activities which are acceptable, and the extent of change which a society will tolerate. Gordon Hamilton (1958:xi) recognized the impact of values both on clients and on social workers:

Each client collectively incorporates and exemplifies the cultural environment. Every treatment objective is a value judgment, culturally

1. Values are components of the cultural system. However, since they have a direct bearing on social structural arrangements, they also bear consideration in any analysis of the social system. See Parsons (1970).

shaped. Cultural patterns influence the kind and amount of self-expression and life satisfactions. It is too easy to forget that every treatment goal, just as every kind of community planning, is influenced by our value system.

Gordon Hamilton's terminology and practice formulation are somewhat different from ours, but her recognition of the critical importance of values for social intervention practice coincides with the view presented in this chapter. There are some who have questioned whether societal values do exert such an impact on social work. Charles Levy (1973), for example, argues that social work values are autonomous and "cannot be regarded as conditioned by societal or even religious values." But many others, including the present writer, agree with Harold Wilensky and Charles Lebeaux (1958:13):

American social work is part and product of the larger social and cultural setting in which it lives. While it helps to shape the larger society, social work reflects more than it determines the nature of the whole. It cannot be understood apart from its social context.

American social work practice differs from social work practice in France, Holland, and some South American countries; these differences did not just happen but reflect different societal contexts and varying value constellations. (For a description and analysis of various patterns of social work practice in different countries see Kendall, 1973.) Similarly, the failure to understand variations in value patterns within American society and the subsequent failure to adapt social work practice to these variations may account for some of the problems that some social workers have encountered in recent years. A service based on middle-class, Protestant-ethic values may not be appropriate when working with lower-class groups from varied ethnic backgrounds.

It is difficult to think of a social work situation that is not affected by values. CYNTHIA BENNET, a recently deserted mother, wanted to stay at home so that she could continue to be a full-time mother. But her worker urged her to go to work so that she could support her family. The social worker defined the problem and the desirable solution in terms of what he thought were generally accepted values without realizing that Mrs. Bennet grew up in an environment where other values received priority. The members of the YOUNG ADULT HIKING CLUB correctly understood the high value that their society places on marriage; in another value context, arranged marriages might have been a preferred solution to their dilemma but here they needed to invest in socially accepted activities which would permit them to meet girls in a controlled situation.

## Value Base for Social Work Practice

What are values and what is their specific importance for social work practice? Social workers generally follow the philosophic tradition of John Dewey when they define *value* in terms of appraisal and preference. Muriel Pumphrey (1959:23) notes that the word "value" suggests "a usual preference for certain means, ends, and conditions of life. . . . The meaning attached to values is of such impelling emotional quality that individuals who hold them often make personal sacrifices and work hard to maintain them." And according to William Gordon (1965:33), "to 'value' something is to 'prefer' it." Values, in other words, serve as guides for behavior. Robin Williams, Jr. (1967:23) defines values as "those conceptions of desirable states of affairs that are utilized in selective conduct for preference or choice or as justification for proposed or actual behavior."

In social work, terms such as *values, norms,* and *goals* are often used interchangeably, but they are not identical. *Values* can serve as guides or criteria for behavior. *Goals,* on the other hand, define the specific outcome of social intervention activity. Goals may be based on values, but they are much more specific and precise. Finding a job which will enable CYNTHIA BENNET to earn an adequate income is a goal which may be based on the value of societal responsibility for every individual's basic needs. *Norms* are directives which set the limits within which every person (or group) can do as he sees fit. Norms are based on, or derived from, values. They vary from those strictly sanctioned to those which are little more than suggestive. Some norms, such as those describing the responsibility of parents for their young children, are enforced by laws while others, such as those about style of dress, are neither clearly defined nor rigidly enforced. In times of rapid social change a gap may occur between values and norms, since the latter change more rapidly than the former. Or there may be a conflict between the old and the new norm which for a while may exist side by side. Changing norms regarding sexual behavior in our times illustrate both situations.

One of the problems in discussing values is the difficulty in identifying or observing them. It is far from easy to determine clear, yet meaningful indicators which identify the more abstract values. Most often values are inferred from observed behavior, but here there is a risk of identifying certain behaviors as values even though they are not really held by the person or the society being observed. There is the further danger of circularity; that is, of inferring values from observing behavior and then identifying the same behavior as a consequence of this value. A number of research studies, for example, have shown that many needy families do not receive public welfare assistance even though they probably are eligible; their failure to request welfare help has often been attributed to the high value which these families place on independence and self-reliance. But more recent studies have found that ignorance of the availability of financial aid and misunderstanding about eligibility requirements and not values about self-reliance account for the failure of as many as two thirds of the eligible poor families to apply for welfare assistance (Greenleigh Associates, 1965; Moles, Hess, and Fascione, 1968; Piven and Cloward, 1971). This is a blatant example of erroneously deducing a value (self-reliance) from observed behavior (failure to apply for welfare assistance) and then attributing that behavior to the value when actually other factors (ignorance and misunderstanding) explain the behavior.

## Societal Values, Group Values, Individual Values

Values occur at varying levels of generality. The more generalized and abstract a value, the greater the likelihood of its acceptance by all groups of the population. Highly generalized values, such as honesty and happiness, are often accepted by groups which hold diametrically opposite points of view. Thus, the sacredness of life was claimed as a value both by the supporters and the opponents of the Vietnam war. It is not uncommon that people who share the same generalized value have sharp differences about the goals and strategies necessary to implement them.

*Societal values.* A further problem is that values appear at different levels of the social system. We must differentiate among societal values, group values, and individual values. Although values at these different levels can contradict each other, most often they are complimentary or reciprocal. In most societies overt value conflicts are relatively infrequent. This may be due to the fact that most people, most of the time, accept the same generalized values, though they may arrange them differently, interpret them in different ways, and accept them with varying degrees of intensity.[2] Thus most Americans accept success as a desirable value, but they may disagree about the legitimate ways of achieving it. Muzafer Sherif (Sherif and Sherif, 1964:199) reports that all American youths hold values which indicate their acceptance of the com-

2. This value consistency also holds over time. A number of studies have shown that on the most generalized level there has been remarkably little change in the American value system over the past few centuries even though actual behavior has changed markedly. See Coleman (1941), Kluckhohn (1958), and Lipset (1961).

mon "American ideology of success"; all, even those coming
from the most depressed neighborhoods, want to possess the
tangible symbols of that success. Almost all teen-agers want to
drive a car. Those who can borrow the family car have no
problem; but those who come from families without a car face
a dilemma: whether to "borrow" a car without the owner's
permission (that is, to use illegitimate means in order to acquire the symbol of success), or whether to value honesty but
admit that the tangible symbols of success are, at least for the
present, out of reach. However, individual teen-agers usually
are guided by the values of the group to which they belong,
thus obviating the individual dilemma.

The identical societal value is often given various interpretations by different groups, just as group values are
given private interpretations by individuals. This process of
individualization sometimes makes it appear that individuals
hold personally distinctive values when in fact they subscribe
to group values. An individual generally supports the values
of his peer group, but he may at times follow more rigorous
or a less rigorous set of values, so long as his values are compatible with those of his group. Talcott Parsons (1960:193) observes that "every subsystem has a value system of its own
which is a differentiated and specialized version of the general
value system, limited by the level and function of the subsystem in the whole." Problems and conflict arise when the value
orientation of one level is inconsistent with that of the next
higher level. For example, the youth culture, though different
from the general adult culture, did not pose any problem so
long as the values of teen-agers were consistent with those of
adult society. But when teens accepted and acted according to
values which ran counter to those of the adult community,
there was immediate concern about the generation gap, about
juvenile delinquency, and about the crisis in child-parent relationships.

*Group values.* These values are generally complementary
to societal values even though different groups develop and

maintain what appear to be unique value patterns. This is why value conflicts may occur between groups even when both groups derive their values from the same societal value set. One group may approve occupations that a second group proscribes; both groups subscribe to the societal success value, but one honors the successful racketeer while the other attempts to put him behind bars. In a simpler society with few subgroups, the problem of value conflicts usually does not occur, but when a society becomes more complex and contains many different groups, value conflict can become an acute problem, both for society and for individuals. This problem of value conflict becomes a very real threat for individuals who live in societies characterized by high rates of mobility. Since the advent of television, the values of the majority culture have been transmitted to groups that previously lived in more or less isolation; access to or knowledge about, competing value constellations has created new types of problems for many. And these are often the kinds of problems with which social workers are asked to help.

Differences in group values do not just happen but usually develop in response to different life experiences. Melvin Kohn's research (1963) showed how work requirements influence the values which guide parental child-rearing activities. Since middle-class jobs usually demand a great deal of self-direction, child-rearing patterns of middle-class parents generally are based on values which stress autonomy and self-direction. Working-class parents, on the other hand, follow more authoritarian child-rearing practices since their work experience is generally with jobs that demand strict adherence to rules and instructions.

*Individual values.* It must be recognized that individual behavior is not always consistent with societal values, with group values, or even with a person's own personal values. Values act as screens against which behavior preferences are filtered. Even though there is a tendency toward behavior that is consistent with values held, an individual's behavior does not always follow his value orientations. People do "wrong" even when they know what is "right." Juvenile delinquency experts have noted that juvenile offenders are rarely ignorant of the societal values which proscribe delinquent behavior. They often admit that their behavior is inconsistent even with their own values (Berelson and Steiner, 1964:576; Glueck and Glueck, 1950). Various explanations for these inconsistencies have been offered. Some have pointed to irresistible impulses and threads of infantilism as explanations (Allport, 1955:77). Others have suggested that lack of access to the means to achieve socially desirable goals is a cause for this inconsistency (Cloward and Ohlin, 1960). Social workers must consider both internal (psychosocial) and external (environmental) factors in trying to understand people whose values and behaviors are inconsistent. But far more important than any discrepancy is the fact that, by and large, there is a consistency between values and behaviors. Even criminals and deviants behave most of the time in ways consistent with societal values.

Sometimes attachment to one value results in behaviors that do violence to another value. Jenny, a fifteen-year-old high school sophomore, was picked up by the police on a charge of prostitution. During the pretrial investigation the juvenile court social worker learned that Jenny came from a family of illiterates who did not want her to stay in school. Yet Jenny had developed a love of learning and desperately wanted to continue her education. But she needed money to buy clothes and all the other things a teen-age girl requires. Working as a part-time prostitute on Friday and Saturday evenings was the only way she could balance her budget. She rationalized her behavior (which she knew was "wrong") by giving priority to what she considered a superior value (education). In this example, as in so many others, there is no need for the social worker to effect value changes. Jenny does need help in finding a way in which she can continue to go to school, properly dressed, without having to resort to prostitution.

## Value Orientations of American Society

One should not assume that there is only one set of values on which all Americans agree. It is probably true that there is widespread agreement about values at the most generalized level, but these are not the values that have a direct impact on the choice of actual behaviors. All mothers value happiness and honesty, but there are basic differences when it comes to applying these generalized values to child-rearing and other activities. The difference in actual behavior are due to the fact that people also adhere to less generalized values, and here differences do occur. Thus, middle-class mothers value self-control and pleasure postponement, while working-class mothers give much higher valuation to conformity and obedience (Kohn, 1969).

Despite the apparent consensus it is an oversimplification to speak of a single societal value set, even at the most generalized level. Instead, at least in America, a value and its countervalue frequently occur simultaneously and both seem to enjoy wide acceptance. It has been suggested that a value and its countervalue identify the two polar positions along a range of possible value options, with any point between the two polar positions available as a possible value alternative.[3] This may account for the heterogeneity in American values which has aroused the comment of many foreign observers, starting with de Tocqueville. Some of the more significant value dimensions which have been identified in American society include the following:

3. The idea that there is a countervalue for each value was first called to my attention by Kluckhohn's reference to Kaspar Naegele's paper, "From De Tocqueville to Myrdal: a Research Memorandum on Selected Studies of American Values" (Kluckhohn, 1958:152–54). The concepts developed in this chapter are based on Naegele's scheme but differ from his in several respects. For a slightly different list of value dimensions, abstracted from the social work literature, see McLeod and Meyer (1967).

Importance of individual—importance of group
Autonomy—interdependence
Self-help—cooperation
Self-determination—decision by experts
Freedom—limits
Personal liberty—social control
Heterogeneity—homogeneity
Progress—stability
Activism—fatalism.

Attempts have been made to attribute one dimension of each pair to specific historical periods (such as the Western frontier) or to certain groups (such as immigrants, slaves). While there may be some merit in this effort, more important is the fact that both the value and its countervalue represent acceptable value positions in contemporary America. The simultaneous occurrence of a value and its countervalue has both functional and dysfunctional consequences. It permits the expression of many different value positions. But this, in turn, can result in societal problems and in individual strain. An individual may be pressured by different role opposites to utilize at the same time both a value and a countervalue as criteria for his behavior. A probation officer may receive cues from his colleagues, urging him to give priority to protecting the rights of prisoners, while his judicial superiors may assign a priority value to setting limits. Societal problems will result when one group subscribes to a value and another, equally powerful group follows the countervalue. The varying responses to the current efforts to create a racial balance in public schools are based on just such a dilemma.

Value heterogeneity is itself a value of American society, one unique to our society. This lack of uniformity arose out of the cultural and racial diversity of our population. But it is not at all clear whether this heterogeneity in values represents a strength of our social system since it is not possible to specify the degree of diversity which is desirable. Nor is it possible to identify the point at which disunity becomes a threat to the maintenance of society. There are, therefore, those who reject heterogeneity as a value and prefer instead the countervalue, homogeneity and uniformity. Yet we should remember that the availability of heterogeneity and its companion value of change has made this a relatively open society with the potential for social change without revolution or riot.

The reader may ask how values can serve as guides for behavior if the value orientations of American society are as heterogeneous as has been suggested. Two answers can be given to this question. There is a basic unity in the value constellation of the American society. Though there exists a great deal of diversity on the operational level, almost all Americans support the same values on the most generalized level. Thus, Talcott Parsons (1970:195) says that "at the highest level of generality . . . there is, and for some time has been, a single relatively well integrated and fully institutionalized system of values in American society . . ." But we noted earlier that abstract values do not serve as guides for behavior; instead, the more specific and more concrete lower-level values provide the criteria for behavioral choices. And on this operational level there is no unitary value set. However (and this is the second answer), individuals do not chose operational values on a random basis, nor do groups freely select between competing values. Instead, for any given group or subgroup there is a consistent and fairly permanent value set, and it is these values that serve as behavioral guides for the members of that group. Only when individuals change groups or when they stand on the interface between two groups do they have any real choice of values. At other times, the individual has little choice in selecting values despite the diversity of values which characterizes American society.

Social workers, as well as teachers, nurses, and other helpers, at times fail to understand the values of those with whom they work, particularly if their clients come from the working class or from ethnic groups whose value sets differ from those of the worker. But such an understanding is essential for effective social intervention practice. When a social worker bases his practice on the assumption that there is only a single, unitary value set he fails to come to grips with the realities of contemporary life in America. He must recognize the diverse value orientations and he must take these into consideration when identifying problems, setting goals, and planning the intervention strategy. In fact, it is all but impossible to identify a problem accurately without recognizing the specific societal context in which that problem condition developed.

Cheryl CAREY and Mary MCPHERSON are both young teenagers and both are pregnant; but, despite their identical physical condition, they face different problems because of the differing societal contexts in which the condition is situated. Cheryl lives in an upper-middle-class suburban community where illegitimacy is severely proscribed while in Mary's neighborhood it is not uncommon to find young girls who are pregnant. The social worker who would overlook these differences cannot be effective. In a similar way, the social worker who talked with MRS. KING must understand the value base which led her to delay her request for help from the county welfare department. Her preferred solution, going to work, also reflects a powerful value orientation. The social worker who takes cognizance only of the general values of our society or of his own values will most likely misunderstand Mrs. King and her problem. In developing the intervention strategy, the worker not only must recognize Mrs. King's value commitments, but he will want to utilize these as strengths upon which an effective intervention activity can be based.

## Basic Social Work Values

Social work takes its basic values from those held by the general society, but as Werner Boehm (1958) has noted, the value sets selected by the profession "are not necessarily or altogether those universally or predominantly held or practiced in society." While the social work values and practice modalities which are derived from these values must be compatible with the values held by the society, there may also be differences, and these can result in various problems, including value conflicts. By selecting and emphasizing certain values, while attaching less emphasis to others, social workers have at times adopted unpopular or marginal positions. Gordon Allport (1955:211) observes in this connection that the relatively low status of social work may be due to the emphasis which social workers have given to cooperation, a value representing a minority viewpoint in a society, which places a high value on competition and aggressiveness in order to obtain the material rewards which everyone desires.

There is relatively little disagreement about the basic value orientations of social work. Though specific lists of values differ, most social workers can agree with what Boehm (1958) identifies as the "minimum commitment for social work": the worth of the individual, the inherent dignity of the human person, society's responsibility for the individual's welfare, and the individual's responsibility for contributing to the common good. Differences and problems begin to occur when an attempt is made to operationalize and implement these generalized and abstract value positions. Disagreements are rarely about generalized values but occur most often about priorities, specific objectives, and the means to achieve these. Some have argued that adherence to the "inherent dignity of the individual" value requires the social worker to give priority to activities which are designed to strengthen a person's independence and autonomy, even when this strategy fails to assure desperately needed physical necessities; but other social workers maintain that the priority should be reversed.

KEVIN MINTON's social worker is in a quandary. He knows that Mr. Minton, who was recently released from prison, needs a job, both to assure regular family income and to restore his self-confidence. He also knows that the best way to restore this self-confidence is for Mr. Minton to find a job by himself; it would be much less satisfactory for the worker to arrange a job placement because this would only serve to emphasize Kevin's dependence on the worker. But the worker also realizes that ex-convicts, such as Kevin Minton, find it very difficult to locate a job. The dilemma is one of conflicting values, and the resolution of the dilemma will affect every member of the Minton family.

A number of value positions which social workers once accepted without any question have come under scrutiny and critical examination. The right of a client to make his own decision has been called "a basic premise, a key concept, a foundation stone" of social work practice; and "it would be difficult to imagine how its value could be assessed any higher" (Biestek, 1957:103–4). Yet contemporary social workers have raised many questions about the implementation of self-determination, without abandoning the theoretical basis of the value itself. Saul Bernstein (1960) concludes a critical examination of this value by noting that "while self-determination is not supreme, it is supremely important." This conclusion suggests that there are situations where other values take precedence over client self-determination. And according to Helen Perlman (1965), "self-determination is nine-tenths illusion, one-tenth reality . . . but [it] is one of the 'grand illusions' basic to human development and human dignity and human freedom." She notes that blind adherence to client self-determination has often resulted in worker overpassivity. The ritual implementation of self-determination may result in the observance of the form without the substance; this has not helped clients become more effective, more identified, or more responsible. Social workers have become aware that blind impulses or prejudices or habit determine choices when people are ignorant of alternatives; whenever people are not aware of the resources which are available or when they are unable to evaluate properly the risks involved in following a given course of action, they do not really have a free choice and cannot make a meaningful decision. Under these circumstances, self-determination becomes an empty exercise or ritual.

The HERMANS knew what they wanted for their retarded daughter—at least they thought that they knew; but accepting their request for an institutional placement without knowing the advantages and disadvantages of this and other options is hardly a good example of self-determination. The social worker who fails to help the Hermans learn about institutionalization and other alternatives for retarded children is hardly promoting the implementation of true self-determination, the very value which he claims as his guide.

Lack of information is one factor which limits the efficacy of self-determination as a value guide for behavior. The far-reaching social and technological changes which characterize our society are another limiting factor. SOPHIE LEFFERT never liked the idea that her mother moved in with them after her father died three years ago, but there was no other choice since the elderly mother had no resources. At one time three generations under one roof may not have been particularly problematic, but in today's nuclear family (and in the housing designed for that family) there is literally no room and no function for the older generation. KEVIN MINTON was ready to work, but today's mechanized production lines, many of which are computer controlled, have made unskilled labor almost obsolescent.

These examples and the preceding discussion were not meant to serve as an argument for abandoning the social work value of self-determination but rather to suggest that every value needs to be examined critically. Otherwise, empty ritual may take the place of effective social intervention. This is what Eileen Younghusband (1958:53) had in mind when she wrote:

Respect for the uniqueness of every human being and for his right to decide how he wishes to order his life, within the limits of other people's rights, are the basic tenets of social work, though their expression may differ in different cultures. It is easy to pay lip service to these tenets but really to practice them so that they become settled attitudes of mind makes tremendous demands.

And this applies no matter whether the social worker intervenes with individuals, with groups, or with communities.

## Summary

Values affect every element of the social intervention process. They impress themselves on the social structure and on the personality structure of every participant. They have an impact on problem definition, goal-setting, and strategy selection. The effective worker must be cognizant of the value sets which affect his client's functioning and his practice.

Values, especially societal values, serve as guides or criteria for behavior. Societal values tend to be accepted by most social groups though different groups may operationalize the identical value in a variety of ways. Most values have been stable over time, but there have been changes in the ways in which some of these values have been expressed.

There is a general consistency between societal values, group values, and individual values. Yet at times there are differences between these different levels of values. Conflict tends to occur when these differences become pronounced or acute.

Persons tend to behave in ways which are consistent with the values they hold, but exceptions to this generalization do occur. When values and behaviors diverge, problems may occur. As society becomes more open, opportunities for these divergences multiply.

It may be an oversimplification to speak of one set of societal values for the American society, a society which recognizes a countervalue for every value. In fact, value heterogeneity is itself a value of the American society, a value unique to this society.

# chapter three

# Problems for
# Social Intervention

People who come to a social agency with a problem often expect that they can sit by passively while the social worker takes
their problems away and solves them. This is a far cry from
what actually happens in social intervention where both client
and worker must participate actively. But active participation
can occur only when both worker and client recognize, acknowledge, and understand the problem. It was not enough
that the social worker thought that MRS. KING had a problem
in functioning as the head of a family. The worker's recognition was no more than a first tentative step. Unless and until
Mrs. King acknowledged that this new role was a problem for
her and that she needed help in coping with it, intervention
around this problem would have been irrelevant. The social
worker, of course, can and should help actively in this recognition process.

Both client and worker must recognize and understand a
problem before social intervention can be effective—yet their
understanding need not be identical. The social worker, because of his training and experience with similar problems,
may have greater insight, but his understanding of the problem will necessarily differ from that of a person who experiences it firsthand. However, both must recognize and understand the problem if the social intervention is to be successful.

In this chapter we will discuss a number of aspects of the
problem concept from the worker's perspective. In later

chapters we will examine how the problem appears to the client and what a worker can do to help a client gain a better understanding of his problem. Here, after briefly examining the assumptions underlying the problem label, we will identify more specifically the type of problems with which social workers are best equipped to deal. Following this we will consider the problem identification process and the relationships between problems, causes, and goals.

## Assumptions

*Problem* is one of those simple words which are used without much thought since everyone believes that its meaning is self-evident. The dictionary definition of the term is apparently clear and noncontroversial: (1) a question proposed for solution or consideration; (2) a question, matter, situation, or person that is perplexing or difficult. Yet behind this simple definition hide several assumptions that have significant implications for social intervention strategies and goals. These assumptions relate to the nature of problems, as well as to their causes and solutions. The two major assumptions about the nature of problems are often left unstated, but they should be examined: (1) One assumption suggests that a problem is similar to a cancerous growth which has invaded the body of a healthy person. The best way to help the sufferer is to cut away the festering problem. And once the problem has been removed, the person again will be in perfect condition. (2) The second assumption holds that almost all problems are symptomatic of (or caused by) personality defects; therefore, personality changes are necessary for problem resolution.

There are many problems to which one or the other assumption applies. But the uncritical application of these assumptions to every kind of problem in much of current social work practice has not been productive. For one thing, it has led workers to concentrate on those problems which fit these assumptions, while disregarding other problems, such as those arising out of healthy, even desirable, situations. Life-cycle problems, for example, generally are not "cancerous" nor are they the consequence of a pathological personality. Such problems are apt to occur at times of significant status changes in the normal life cycle of every person. Becoming an adolescent, entering college, getting married, or becoming a mother are life-cycle changes which are often accompanied by stress. At times a person cannot cope with the consequent problems without somebody's help. Social intervention with this type of problem cannot aim at cutting out the "problem," nor are basic personality changes usually indicated. Instead, the intervention activity will focus on helping this person over the difficulty by providing additional support or by making environmental adjustments so that he can fulfill himself and resume functioning at his maximum capacity. With this kind of problem, as with some others, neither of the two assumptions about the nature of problems applies.

When these assumptions, particularly the second one, guide practice, there is frequently a shift of focus away from the problem toward the client. There are many situations where the client is *not* the problem but only the problem carrier or the victim. Yet when the client becomes the problem, the focus of the social intervention is shifted away from the core concern of social work, away from the person/environment interface. Treating the client as the problem often leads to specifying personality changes as the desired goal—if only the client would change, the problem would go away. But when the problem is elsewhere, a change in the client will not make the problem disappear. Under these circumstances, a change in the client's personality at best will reconcile him to accept the condition and to cope with it in a more adequate manner, but the problem will remain. To be sure, there are many times when the situation defies any quick solution, and the only immediate assistance that the social worker can provide is to help the client learn how to live with the problem. But when this becomes the goal, it should be selected because of the nature of the problem and not because it is thought that changing the client will lead to problem resolution. MRS. KING, for example, faces many different problems, but few of these will be alleviated by a change in her personality even if such a change could be effected in a short time (and it cannot). Changes in personality take a long time, while many of the problems brought to the social worker's attention need relatively quick handling.

Another dysfunctional consequence of the two assumptions is that they limit attention to basic problems and ultimate goals instead of including consideration of the more pressing immediate problems and the more readily achievable goals. MRS. KING may have a personality problem, but she would receive little help with her immediate problems if the social worker were to concentrate on helping her work through her feelings about authority figures. Even with respect to her problem of filling the role of head of the family Mrs. King needs more immediate and more practical help. It may be that the worker will never get to the point where he can help her with some of her basic problems, but the urgency of the present situation directs where the priorities should be placed.

The two assumptions also tend to dichotomize all problems into social (environmental) and individual (personality) problems when in fact there is a social aspect and an individual aspect to every problem. The dichotomy leads to specialization and to separate groups of social workers, often typed by the "method" in which they have been trained. Caseworkers, it is said, deal with personality problems and community workers, with social problems. A focus on the total problem, on the other hand, will require workers who are comfortable in working with individuals, groups, and neighborhoods, who are knowledgeable about both the personality and the social environment, and who are ready to participate in social intervention activities which are focused on the total problem.

While we reject the universal application of these two assumptions, our use of the term *problem* is also based on a number of assumptions and propositions (in addition to those listed earlier in chapter 1). Our assumptions include the following:

1. Problems are "normal." There are no people without problems. Most people, most of the time, can cope with their problems, but occasionally some people need help.

2. Problems result from normal, everyday situations. Life-cycle episodes which involve changes in status are a particularly common source of problems.

3. Problems become perilous when they are denied by the people who happen to be the victims or the carriers.

4. There is an individual (personality) and a social (environmental) aspect to every problem. Together these two aspects make up the total problem.

5. Priority attention must be given to the most pressing and immediate problems even when these are not the basic cause of the problem condition.

## Target Problems

Target problems are those for which social intervention is most relevant and most effective. A clear and precise identification of these problems will greatly increase the effectiveness of social workers. It may be presumptuous to talk about increasing the effectiveness of social work intervention when a number of studies have shown that such intervention efforts have little or no effect on people's lives.[1] If, nevertheless, we write about the potential effectiveness of social intervention and continue to teach social work practice, it is because we believe that social work can give a good account of itself. Because of its failure or its unwillingness to define its areas of competence it has not yet proved itself successful. Overselling the abilities of social workers ("they can help with

1. Mullen and Dumpson (1972) and Fischer (1973) critically review a large number of evaluation studies.

all kinds of problems") has resulted in using potentially effective intervention techniques for many inappropriate problems. Should success be expected under these conditions?

Better definitions of target problems will serve as guides for both clients and workers. Scarce social work manpower can be directed to problems where social intervention can be effective, while leaving other problems to personnel with different skills. Once social workers are clearer about their areas of competence, people with problems also will be in a better position to know when to go to a social worker and when to turn to someone else.

There are those who have warned against any attempt to specify in detail the areas in which social workers are competent. What is needed in this complicated world, they argue, is a social worker who is ready to engage in solving all kinds of problems. People with problems are not diagnosticians and cannot be expected to determine to whom to turn for the kind of help they need. Professionalization has already resulted in too much specialization. Persons with problems are often sent from office to office without finding the right address where they can be helped. Or one problem is carved up into so many subproblems that workers from different specializations almost fall over each other, each trying to do his "thing"—and in the end no one helps. I once knew a family which received service from twelve different social workers in one week! The list of agencies represented by these workers sounded like a registry of social work: welfare department, public housing, employment service, hospital social service, probation department, school social work, old age insurance, community worker, family service agency, public health department, community center, and church charity organization. Instead of helping, these specialists complicated an already complex situation by working at cross purposes. However, overpartialization in this case was the result of bureaucratic policy decisions and not of specification of competence. Efforts to reverse the

Balkanization of much of contemporary social work deserve support. But attempts to specify the target area of social work will arrest, not encourage, further specialization and partialization.

*Social component.* Traditionally, social workers have been vague about identifying target problems. For example, Florence Hollis (1970) indicated that the psychosocial approach to casework is effective with all types of character disorders and especially with neurotics. Speaking at the same symposium, Ruth Smalley (1970) made an even broader claim for the functional approach, suggesting that it could be effective with every type of social problem. Harriett Bartlett (1970) observed that this lack of clarity is not a new problem in social work. She noted that practitioners have never been able to agree on their area of responsibility and expertise. Some are concerned with broad social problems, others prefer to identify with the methods and processes they use, and still others specialize in specific fields of practice, such as child welfare, medical social work, or corrections. At least since the 1920s, when social workers embraced the teachings of Freudian psychology, the major focus has been on individuals and their inner problems. At times, social workers were hard-pressed to differentiate their practice area from that of other other nearby disciplines. Some social workers began to practice psychotherapy and, perhaps facetiously, considered themselves junior psychiatrists. Yet there were other social workers who all along sought to establish a different identity. Medical social workers, decades ago, identified as their target the social problems created by illness and hospitalization. Other social workers picked up this formulation and indicated that they were competent to intervene in the social component of every problem.

*Social interaction.* In time, social workers identified two major areas of concern: (1) problems of the individual, particularly personality problems; and (2) problems in the social environment which affected the individual or the group. Social workers, it was suggested, needed to have competence to work with both problem sets. This formulation represented a giant step forward but was not yet sufficiently specific and clear to improve practice effectiveness. A further refinement, formalized by Werner Boehm (1958), directs attention to social interaction as the target for social work practice. The nature of any problem in the social interaction area is determined by a person's capacity for relationships, as well as by the resources available to him. Boehm (1959) points out that "the social worker's activities are directed both to relationships among individuals and to relationships between individuals and the organized social resources of the community." This formulation does way with the dichotomy between the individual and his environment which heretofore had been accepted by many social workers. Instead, it suggests that social work intervention is particularly relevant for problems that arise out of the interaction between a person and his environment. This formulation also prevents the partialization among prevention, problem-solving, enhancement, and therapy. It does identify the area where the problems for which social workers have competence are most likely to occur but it does not limit the type of intervention strategies or the timing of the intervention to any one schema. On the contrary, the assumption here is that intervention may occur before the problem arises, after it has arisen but before it has caused serious damage, or after serious damage has been caused. The choice of strategy, given this formulation, depends on the resources of the person and of the environment, on the nature of the problem, and on the goals expected from the social intervention.

Some further specification of the types of problems which occur at the person/environment interface may be desirable. A preliminary typology of problems for which social intervention is particularly relevant includes the following:

1. *Interpersonal relationships:* problems arising out of a
   person's (or a group's) interaction with other people.

2. *Formal relationships:* problems arising out of a person's (or group's) interaction with formal organizations and bureaucratic agencies.
3. *Role transition:* problems arising out of abrupt or drastic changes in a person's (or group's) role or position.

Any useful typology will separate those problems for which social intervention is appropriate from other problems for which other types of intervention are indicated. A typology based on the applicant's characteristics or on the applicant's initial request for service does not screen problems sufficiently to serve as an effective guide. On the other hand, a typology based on target problems, as proposed here, appears to hold greater promise.[2] It may be helpful to discuss the proposed typology in somewhat greater detail.

1. *Interpersonal relationships.* This type of problem arises out of the relationship between client(s) and other people. The problematic interaction may be between two people (such as a husband and wife, employer and employee, two lovers), between an individual and a group (such as a teen-age gang, a work group), or between two collectivities (such as a minority group and a majority group). The nature of the problem may involve open conflict, dissatisfaction with the existing relationship, questions or doubts about meeting role expectations, or the need for support to develop and strengthen interpersonal relationships. Illustrative examples of this type of problem which come to the attention of social workers include: a husband and wife constantly quarrel; a mother wants help in

2. Our discussion of target problems was especially stimulated by Reid and Epstein (1972) but departs in several respects from their typology, which classifies problems "as the individual defines them." Our typology is based on client problems as viewed and classified by the worker. Consequently, we have not listed "reactive emotional distress" as a separate problem category since we define this as a possible consequence of other problems rather than as a separate problem.

controlling her children; a young man wonders why he has difficulties in talking with girls; a foreman has been accused of prejudiced behavior by the workers in his department; a group of fifth graders is afraid to play in the park because the Jets gang has warned it to stay away.

2. *Formal relationships.* The multiplicity of formal organizations and bureaucratic agencies is a characteristic of contemporary life. From the moment of birth most people are dependent upon such organizations. Those who do not develop skill in relating to schools, government offices, employers, and so forth, are handicapped and disadvantaged. This problem may be especially acute for those who are also disadvantaged in other ways (by ethnicity, poverty, physical handicap), since they are even more dependent on formal organizations than those not so disadvantaged. The problem may involve: (*a*) *lack of information*—people need to know that there is a formal organization which has responsibility for a certain area of need or which provides a desired service; (*b*) *lack of access*—people may not know how or where to obtain the desired service; (*c*) *blocked communications*—people need to know how to talk with bureaucratic officials and how to understand them; (*d*) *inequality and/or powerlessness*—the overpowering position of bureaucrats makes for problems in relationships with those who are powerless, such as lower-class people. A particular problem may, of course, extend over several problem areas. Illustrative examples of formal relations problems which social workers have noted include:

Mrs. King cannot obtain information about her husband from the hospital.

The parents of a brain-damaged infant do not know where they can receive help for their child.

A mother believes that her child has been mistreated in school but doesn't know what she can do about it.

An elderly factory worker stopped working six months ago but has not yet received his first Social Security check.

An unemployed war veteran in desperate economic circumstances and poor physical condition is not aware of the rights to which he is entitled nor does he know how to obtain those veteran services that he is eligible to receive.

The tenants of the Kennedy Houses have been unable to obtain many necessary repairs.

The local chapter of the Welfare Rights Organization wants its members to receive credit in department stores.

3. *Role transition.* Life-cycle changes or drastic changes in personal status are typical causes of role transition problems, but other emergencies may also cause this type of problem. The problem may occur before the abrupt change (when a person is afraid of the immediate future) or after the change (when the person realizes that he is unprepared for the new situation in which he finds himself). Illustrative examples are the problems which occur to the retired worker who never knew what it was to sit with idle hands, the new army recruit who never before had been away from home, the immigrant family which suddenly finds itself transplanted into a strange environment, and the young wife who has just been notified that her husband was killed in an industrial accident. This type of problem is often aggravated by the discontinuities which characterize our society. Problems like these become acute because we have institutionalized relatively few ways of helping people when their role or position changes. The problem is not necessarily one of a problematic interaction with specific persons but rather of interaction with society generally. These are the types of problems which can and do occur to everybody. Most people, most of the time, can cope more or less adequately with role transition problems, but some will need help. Even those who do cope on a minimal level could function more adequately if social workers anticipated these problems and offered timely preventive services.

Many of the problems which are brought to a social worker can be classified under more than one rubric. Cheryl CAREY, the pregnant teen-ager, faces a status change but also has interpersonal problems. KEVIN MINTON, the unemployed ex-convict, has problems in all three areas. Worker and client together must clarify which problem or which aspect of a problem is most pressing and most urgent. The fact that a problem can be classified in more that one category does not invalidate this preliminary problem typology since its major purpose is to identify those problems which are appropriate for social intervention. Those problems that fit one or more categories are problems which are suitable, while problems that do not fit any of these categories are best handled by other types of intervention, that is, by helpers other than social workers.

If the typology is effective in screening *in* some problems, it will necessarily screen *out* others. Our definition and the problem typology based on that definition exclude those problems that are wholly within the person, as well as those problems that are entirely within the environment and affect the person only indirectly. Excluding these categories does not mean that social intervention cannot be used, for example, with people who have personality disturbances, such as psychotics; it does indicate that social workers should not attempt to treat the psychiatric problems of these people but instead should focus on the person/environment interface problems which they might present. A resolution of the person/environment interface problem often results in a general reduction of tension, and this may lead to a resolution of a client's basic personality problem. This is a desirable by-product of social intervention but should not be viewed as the primary goal. Similarly, there are environmental problems which affect people's functioning. Many have noted the stultifying impact of the mechanized assembly line where the impersonal machine controls the worker. Social workers are not competent to change production methods or to engineer new assembly procedures, but they can advise management on the effect of current procedures and provide consultation on the impact that any proposed mechanical change might have on the interpersonal and formal relations of the workers.

There are some social workers who employ a much broader definition of target problems and of social work activity. Some social workers engage in psychotherapy. Others specialize in working with clients who have psychiatric problems, while still others are ready to tackle almost any problem brought to them. But there is some indication that people who come to social agencies rather than to mental health clinics locate their problems in the environment or in interaction with others.[3] Yet it is no secret that most people (especially those who have never been in contact with a social worker) are still uncertain about the purpose and function of social work. This lack of clarity will change only as social workers become more precise and more consistent in defining the target areas for which they claim competence.

## Problem Identification

Thus far we have discussed the general areas for which social intervention is appropriate. But social intervention can be effective only if a specific problem has been identified. The clearer and more precise the specific problem identification, the greater the chances for successful results. No social worker can act on the basis of the statement the "Mrs. King has a formal relationship problem." And the information that "the Carey family has a problem" or that "something is wrong with Julian Rios" does not provide sufficient data for developing a social intervention strategy. At best such statements mark the entry point or the beginning of problem identification.

We will consider the question of who should participate in the identification of the specific problem before we examine the three components of this phase of the social intervention process: recognition, definition, and specification. But first we

3. Ripple and Alexander (1956) report that more than 80 percent of the 351 clients they studied defined their problem in this way. Perlman (1970:147) cited their finding to support her own contention that problems in social role transaction are central to social work.

must repeat that problem identification is a continuous and ongoing activity throughout the social intervention process. Though this activity is particularly important in the beginning, it is a mistake to consider it completed once the next phase has started. Instead, worker and client are continually engaged in examining and reexamining, defining and redefining, specifying and respecifying the problem of concern. While the intensity of the activity will vary from time to time, problem identification is never final.

*Participation.* Who participates? Few social workers today would admit agreement with Max Weber's statement that "I should think myself a very poor bureaucrat indeed if I did not believe myself to know better than these blockheads what is really good for them" (Michels, 1959:230n.). More acceptable is Everett Hughes's formulation (1963) that professions "profess to know better than others the nature of certain matters and to know better than their clients what ails them or their affairs." And indeed the professional activities of some social workers suggest that they do think that they have greater expertise and more insight than their clients and that this fact gives them certain rights and obligations. Some workers believe that clients cannot possibly be aware of their real reason for asking for help. Others assume that a generalized goal, such as positive mental health or assured economic security, is more important than any one specific problem brought by the client. Social workers who follow these assumptions will not go out of their way to seek active client participation in problem identification.

A contrary approach suggests that only the applicant or client can identify his problem. Some assert that the client knows his problem better than anyone else; he has lived with it, suffered from it, identified it before he came to the social agency, and now is asking the social worker to help. Other social workers are not prepared to accept the assumption that the client always knows best, but they argue that the client is prepared to work only on those problems which he has identified, even if these are not the most crucial ones. Social workers who act on the basis of either of these two premises will remain relatively passive in the problem identification phase.

A third viewpoint on the question of participation in problem identification combines elements of the previous two approaches. This position suggest that both worker and client must take an active part in problem identification. The social worker, it is to be hoped, does have more experience and greater insight, but at the same time he must recognize that the client is not only the problem-carrier but also the problem-solver. Successful intervention requires that the client participate actively in every part of the social intervention process. Identification should start with the problem which the client brings, but an early objective is to sharpen and clarify the worker's and client's understanding of this problem. Whether the client is an individual or a group, the worker through questions and comments obtains details about the problem which hurts or bothers the client so that both can understand it better. The nature and scope of the problem may change in the course of this examination, but changing the problem, that is, redefining it, is not the objective of the identification activity. The worker may take a more active role during problem identification if this is required, but unless the client also participates the social intervention process will flounder almost as soon as it starts. By starting with the problem that the client presents and by accepting this as a real problem, the worker demonstrates from the very beginning that in social intervention there is a partnership relation between client and worker. It may be "easier" for the worker to define the problem alone, but this will not lead to effective social intervention.

This partnership approach to problem identification applies no matter whether the client is an individual, a family, a group, or a neighborhood. MRS. BENNET's worker had had a great deal of experience in working with mothers of young children who had been deserted by their husbands. He thought that there was little need to go through the bother of involving Mrs. Bennet in problem identification since he knew better than she possibly could what her problem was. The worker's error became apparent before the end of the first month when Mrs. Bennet stopped participating in the plan he had arranged. The social worker assigned to the YOUNG ADULT HIKING CLUB could have defined the group's problem alone because it was fairly obvious what ailed these young people. He could have saved time if he had done so but since he believed that group participation in problem definition is crucial to the success of a group, he refrained from doing it himself.

*Involuntary clients.* At times social workers find themselves in situations where involvement of the client in problem identification seems impossible. A prisoner will lose privileges and forfeit early release from jail unless he cooperates with the prison social worker. The parolee is required to report every week to the parole social worker or face return to prison. So long as the involuntary client does not have a realistic choice, he may be going through the motions without really participating. He may manufacture problems in order to keep the social worker happy or in order to avoid the need to reveal his real problems. Social intervention, on the other hand, requires the free and active participation of the client in problem definition and in every other phase of the process. Therefore, the first task of the social worker who works with an involuntary client is to help him understand what social intervention is and what is required of him. Next, worker and client should identify meaningful alternatives so that the involuntary client can choose between continuing as a real participant and rejecting participation. An additional year in jail may not be a realistic alternative, but the availability of various options, such as social intervention, pastoral counseling, or occupational therapy, may lead to a voluntary choice of one or the other option. The same procedure is followed with voluntary clients who have no understanding of what social intervention involves. But in the case of involuntary clients there is one additional step: the social worker must involve the prison authorities or the courts to arrange for alternative correctional and protective services. This will be easier if the social worker himself is clear about the target problems for which social intervention is relevant.

Infants and children also cannot participate fully in problem identification. Brought to the social agency by their parents or their guardians, they may not even be aware that they have a problem. In a way the situation of children resembles that of adults who do not know that they have a problem. As we indicated earlier, the social worker need not wait until a person has identified a problem but may reach out and help him become aware of this problem. A child's participation in problem identification will differ from that of an adult, but his active participation on a level appropriate to his age is as crucial as the adult's participation. More troubling is the question of infants whose seeming inability to participate in problem identification would indicate that social intervention is not relevant for this group. However, Martha Warfield's provocative report (1972) on her work with a two-year-old in preparation for adoption suggests that with certain modifications social intervention is feasible even with infants.

*Recognition.* An objective fact does not become a problem unless a person or group of persons recogizes it as a problem. A stranger may recognize a certain family as an "empty-shell family" (a family whose members continue to live together but who no longer have any meaningful interaction or communication) even though the family members do not know that they have a problem. A wife recognizes that something is not right between herself and her husband, while the husband, who faces the same objective situation, prides himself on the ideal relationship between himself and his wife. Regardless of the facts, people do not have a problem unless they recognize it as such. The first step in problem identification, therefore, is to recognize the problem. A clear and precise definition of the problem or its causes is not necessary for problem recognition. What is required is: (1) a more or less vague feeling that the present situation is not desirable or that something threatens to upset a desirable situation; (2) an impression that the present situation is not inevitable and that there must be ways to change it; and (3) a feeling that the cost of recognition will not exceed the cost of continued denial of the problem.

Problem recognition does not depend solely on the person and his feelings of discomfort since in different ways the larger society facilitates problem recognition or makes it more difficult. By stigmatizing some problem situations, the cost of recognition is often made excessively high. A father may refuse to recognize that he is unable to provide for his family because he does not want to be labeled incompetent. The way a group defines its norms will determine in large measure what is and what is not a problem. Among the families of professional sailors and soldiers a father's long-time absence from home is commonplace even though most other population groups consider such prolonged absences as problematic. The availability of services to deal with problems also makes it easier for a person to recognize that he has a problem. When a person knows that there are socially sanctioned helpers who can assist him with his problem, he will be less hesitant to admit that he has a problem. The HERMANS might not have acknowledged that their daughter was retarded if the community in which they lived had not provided several services for retarded children.

Sometimes a person or a group has a vague feeling that something is amiss but does not believe that anything can be done about the situation. This is particularly apt to happen among people who believe that they are the victims rather than the masters of their fate. When this is so, people will accept whatever happens as inevitable, and discomfort will not lead to problem recognition unless a social worker or other helper can help in transforming the "half-problem" into a full problem. MRS. JOHANSEN knew that she was poor, that their housing was entirely inadequate, and that her son was not doing well in school. But until she talked with a social worker she did not realize that things did not have to be this way. Most of the residents of the KENNEDY HOUSES had long ago given up hope for any improvements in their situation. They knew that things were not right but they felt completely powerless to do anything to improve their lot. Only the few people who participated in the tenants' council were still willing to do something to help themselves. The worker's task in both instances was to transform the half-problem into a full problem by helping the potential participants realize that their problem was not inevitable.

*Definition.* Problem recognition is a necessary first step, but it is not sufficient for problem identification. Before social intervention can be effective a clear and precise definition of the problem to be worked on is required. Without such a definition, neither worker nor client will have sufficient information or direction for strategy development or implementation.

Every person perceives objective situations in his own individual way and develops his definition on the basis of his own perception. Different people will derive different problem definitions from the identical facts. A boy's imminent expulsion from school may be defined by some as the boy's problem (his laziness, lack of intelligence, lack of interest, lack of discipline, and so forth); by others, as the school's problem (lack of relevance, poor teachers, prejudice toward certain ethnic groups); and by still others, as the parents' problem (excessive demands, lack of love and acceptance). Yet in actual practice, problem definition is not a personal matter but a social activity which follows the general rules of social interaction. Thus, lower-class persons tend to define their problems in physical terms while middle-class people more often use psychological definitions for their problems even when the facts appear to be the same (Bart, 1968; MacMahon, 1964). This difference of approach to problem definition may cause conflict between client and worker if they come from different social classes.

Defining the problem is one of the most crucial steps in problem identification since it sets in motion processes which determine or influence the selection of the intervention strategy. It will make a difference whether an addict is defined as a sick person or a criminal, whether a homosexual is classified as sick or deviant. Problem definition requires a degree of specificity about the problem—what is its nature and why is it a problem. A statement about the problem-free condition, the goal of the social intervention, should also be a part of every problem definition. A problem definition which defines the problem in terms of an intervention technique or strategy is less useful than one which contrasts the current situation with the desired outcome. If we define the problem of unemployment as "finding jobs," we have limited the intervention strategy to just that activity even though job location may not be the most effective or most efficient way to cope with this particular problem. For an unemployed teen-ager without any skills, providing opportunities for education and training may be a more effective intervention technique, even when the presenting problem is unemployment.

The emphasis on problem recognition and definition is not meant to divert attention from the problem which the client has brought. His problem is important and requires immediate attention. This response by the worker is indicated even when the client defines his problem incorrectly and even when he presents a problem which clearly is not the central problem. By starting with the problem which the client brings and by treating it as real, the worker almost automatically provides some reduction of the stress and discomfort which motivated the client to come to the agency. By starting in this way the worker has also taken the first step in involving the client in the social intervention. The worker must understand, however, that the client's perception or verbalization of the problem is not always entirely accurate. The client may exaggerate his problem out of anxiety or fear, he may overestimate or underestimate his problem in order to impress the worker, or he may not be aware of the full implication of his problem. One recent study of public welfare recipients found that these clients seemed to be underestimating their difficulties systematically. The authors concluded that "assistance based entirely on client demand resulted in underserving client need" (Gummer, Kronick, and Perlmutter, 1972). The worker must also be alert to the possibility that the problem presented by the client is not his only problem and that others will be identified in the course of the social intervention process.

Some workers have found it useful to distinguish between *trigger problems* and *basic problems*. The loss of a job may be the event which triggered an applicant's request for help, but a more basic problem may be his inability to work with others. For MRS. CAREY the trigger problem was her inability to deal with her son's petty thievery, but before long it became apparent that the son's behavior was only symptomatic of a number of more basic problems of the Carey family. MRS. HERMAN'S trigger problem was a clear one—she wanted help in finding a good institution for her retarded daughter. But it turned out that the real problem was one of inadequate community resources since there were no suitable institutions for young retarded children in their state.

The jobless person is helped to find a job, but at the same time work is started on coping with some of his other problems. Mrs. Carey must receive help in dealing with her son Ben, but in the course of her contacts with the social worker she learned that there were other problems for which she could receive help. Mrs. Herman found that the social worker accepted her definition and understood her problem; he did not try to talk her into some other, more readily available solution. At the same time, she accepted his invitation to explore ways of approaching the community problem in order to develop a strategy which would permit her to achieve her goal. In each case the worker started with the immediate or trigger problem which the person brought. Since one of the objectives of the identification activity is to sharpen and clarify the client's and the worker's understanding of various aspects of the problem, it may happen that at this or a later point attention shifts to other problems, perhaps to the basic problem. But this shift of focus is not the worker's primary objective during the identification and assessment stage of the social intervention process.

*Specification.* Problems generally come in sets. Ludwig Geismar (1973) found that when families had problems, these were usually not limited to one or a few selected life areas but were in evidence everywhere. Even "ordinary" persons who come to a social agency with a relatively simple problem often will be found to have a chain of other problems. "Treating the whole person" and helping him cope with all of his problems may be an attractive precept, but experience has shown that this is neither practical nor feasible. The worker who tries to deal with everything at once often ends up without doing anything.

The immensity and complexity of many problems tend to overwhelm both client and worker. At times even an experienced social worker will become immobilized because he does not know where to start when a client comes with so many different problems. In the face of a complex problem or set of problems it is essential to partialize and specify which part of the problem to attack first. Client and worker together should specify which part of the problem is most pressing, most important, and most accessible to social intervention. In specification, consideration must be given to what is possible and realistic in terms of the problem, the client's capacities and desires, and the resources which can be secured. Dividing big problems into smaller parts not only makes them more manageable, but also permits earlier feedback and assessment. If a complex problem is treated as a single unit, it may be months or even years before client and worker can assess the effectiveness of their efforts. By that time it may be too late to attempt an alternative strategy. But when the big problem is divided into smaller, more manageable problems, earlier feedback will be possible. At the same time, dividing the big problem and specifying parts of the problem will prevent an increase in the anxiety and frustration which often result from uncertainty about outcomes.

A retarded child, such as TOOTSIE HERMAN, is a big problem or a series of big problems for her family. Specification requires that early in the identification process parents and worker together select those specific problems for which social intervention is suitable. At the same time, specification will identify other problems for which other types of help are more appropriate. When client and worker can agree on a specific problem as the focus of the social intervention they avoid working on problems which are not amenable to social intervention or which the client considers unimportant. Failure can be expected when client and worker cannot agree on the specific problem on which the social intervention should focus.

Recognition, definition, and specification are the three components of the identification process, but they do not always occur in a neat and orderly sequence as the presentation here has suggested. Often these activities occur simultaneously. If the feedback is real and effective, new problems will be identified from time to time, old problems will be redefined, and specifications will be adjusted and changed in the light of the constantly evolving situation. The social worker will not stop everything to undertake "problem definition." Despite the proposition that effective social intervention requires precise problem identification, the social intervention process does not hang in suspense until the problem has been defined and specified. This points to one of the crucial differences between medical practice and social work practice. The medical doctor delays treatment until he has completed his diagnostic studies, unless he is dealing with a matter of life and death. The social worker, on the other hand, engages the client from the very first contact in the social intervention process. Medical diagnosis precedes treatment, while problem identification is an integral part of social intervention.

There are some models of social work practice that prescribe a diagnosis or study phase before the start of the intervention or treatment. If everything depended on the worker's knowledge and insight, such a procedure might be justified, but in our model the worker is only one of several active participants. Delaying intervention in order to engage in a prolonged study of causes may increase the problem and almost certainly will increase the client's anxiety and stress.

## Problem Causes

Knowing something about the causes of a problem will be helpful in developing an appropriate intervention strategy. If the strategy is based only on symptoms and hunches (and not on an analysis of the causes), chances for success are limited. How much worker and client need to know about causes depends on the type of problem. When an unemployed worker asks for help in finding a job it may be important to know something about the causes of his unemployment. Did he lose his last job because of the current economic situation? Or has he never had a regular job because he lacks useful skills? Was his job eliminated by a new machine? Or was he the victim of racial discrimination? The intervention strategy will depend to some extent on the cause of his present predicament. On the other hand, there may be additional causes, more distant in time and perhaps more basic in terms of personality, which are not crucial for intervening with the current problem. Information on whether his mother breastfed him may point to a causal factor in personality development but is probably quite unimportant for developing a suitable intervention strategy that deals with the current problem of unemployment. When a husband and wife want help in dealing with a marital problem, it may be of some importance that they understand what triggered their present difficulty, but will it help resolve their current problem if they unravel the problems that they had with their parents twenty and thirty years ago? Nor will a better understanding of the eighteenth- and nineteenth-century origins of discrimination against blacks and other ethnic groups help resolve present-day racial antagonism. Causes, especially the immediate causes of trigger problems, are important for strategy development, but a prolonged study of the causes of underlying problems may be dysfunctional even when these add some new knowledge about the present situation. For social workers, the only criterion for accumulating additional information should be its usefulness in facilitating practice and in achieving the desired goals.

Probing for causal factors—any causal factors—is viewed as nonrelevant by many client groups who attribute all problems to external causes or who consider behavior as fundamentally immutable. Lower-class persons often do not understand why social workers probe for problem causes. They expect the worker's active intervention and become impatient with social workers who follow different models of problem-solving (Mayer and Timms, 1970). Nevertheless, there is need for some exploration of problem causes, particularly the more immediate causes. Without an understanding of these the social intervention activity will be impaired from the very beginning. Even when the client expects to be passive it is important to involve him in problem definition and exploration of problem causes. Perhaps there will be less verbal activity and more doing when the client is not accustomed to verbalize freely, but this is a question of more-or-less, not of either-or.

## Goals

A full problem statement includes three parts: description of the current situation, statement of immediate causes, and identification of goals. We noted earlier that a condition is not recognized as a problem unless there is some vague feeling that things could be different. This vague feeling may be sufficient for recognizing a problem, but a more specific identification of the desired outcome is necessary for the kind of problem definition which can serve as guide for the subsequent steps in the social intervention process. The tenants of the KENNEDY HOUSES may be disgusted with the way their housing project looks, but unless they have some idea of what they want, it will be impossible to move them to become involved in the social intervention activity. The worker need not sit by passively until the tenants have identified a goal. Indeed, he should play an active role in this step of the process, as in all other steps. But unless goals have been identified, the social intervention will be less than successful.

ALICE SAMORA, thirty-two years old and paralyzed from the waist down, has led an almost entirely passive life. Except for her attempted suicide five years ago, she has let others make all decisions for her. The new rehabilitation worker did not come in response to a specific request by Alice or her parents (though at some earlier time Alice's parents did apply for welfare assistance). His first attempts to involve Alice in defining her problem were unsuccessful. He thought that she was unhappy just sitting in the house all day long, watching television. The worker did not explore events of five or ten years ago but limited his study to the present and the immediate past. On the basis of his conversation with Alice and her parents he identified several problems which could serve as first steps in Alice's rehabilitation program. For the most part Alice's participation was nonverbal, but when he heard her say something about "making money," he assumed that this was a specific request for help and acted upon it, even before he had a clear idea about the social intervention goals.

Goals will be discussed in greater detail in the next chapter. Here we mentioned goals to point out that problem definition and goal-setting are not separate sequential phases but elements of the social intervention process which happen more or less simultaneously.

## Summary

*Problems* are a key concept in social intervention. Problems are common. Everybody has problems. Most people, most of the time, can cope with their problems alone. But occasionally people do need help in coping with their problems. Social workers are equipped to help with problems that arise out of faulty interaction between persons and their environment, such as problems of interpersonal relations, formal relations, and role transition.

The full participation of the applicant or client in problem identification is essential to assure the success of the social intervention activity. Problem identification includes recognition, definition, and specification. The full problem statement describes the current situation, the immediate causes of the problem, and the goals to be achieved by the social intervention activity.

# chapter four

# Identifying
# Social Intervention
# Goals

Alice, in her travels in Wonderland, asked the cat, "Would you tell me, please, which way I ought to go from here?" And the cat replied, "That depends a good deal on where you want to go."

"Where you want to go" has much to do with the way one travels and how one gets there. It is difficult, if not impossible, to make travel plans without knowing the destination. The social worker too must know the destination of the social intervention in order to prepare. Unless a client and his worker can specify what it is they want to achieve, the social intervention activity will be routine, aimless, and probably nonproductive.

In social work practice the goal indicates where one wants to go and suggests how one can get there. The social intervention goal is a statement of the changes desired in the client or in the situation. It should indicate not only the desired state of affairs but also what needs to be changed in order to attain the outcome. This goal serves as a link between the problem and the strategy.

Goals are not identical with outcomes. Outcomes reflect the actual changes which have occurred as a result of the social intervention. They describe the condition of the client or the neighborhood after the intervention. Goals define the intentions or desires prior to the commencement of the intervention activity. A comparison of goals and outcomes will reveal the degree of success achieved. Unanticipated consequences may result in an outcome far different from the one identified by the goal. Sometimes a wrong strategy is used or the correct strategy is poorly implemented so that the outcome does not resemble the desired goal. These problems will be discussed in this and subsequent chapters. Even though there are problems in formulating and applying goals, there is little question about the desirability of goals. Without goals, happenstance replaces planned social intervention. The best of good intentions is no substitute for a carefully defined goal.

In this chapter we will first examine goals which are characteristic of social work generally. Then we will explore various types of goals which are relevant to the social intervention process. Finally we will discuss a number of problems which social workers are apt to encounter in goal-setting.

## Social Work Goals

Social work intervention has always been directed toward preventing or reducing stress and suffering, toward helping resolve problems, and toward strengthening the social functioning capacities of individuals, groups, and communities. All of the participants in a major symposium on casework theory agreed on these goals, no matter what their differences in theoretical approaches to practice. Florence Hollis (1970:57) stated that social work goals include "alleviating the client's distress and decreasing the malfunctioning in the person-situation system. . . . to enhance the client's comfort, satisfaction, and self-reliance." Helen Perlman (1970:138) suggested that the goal was "to help people achieve socially constructive and individually satisfying lives." Bernece Simon (1970:378) noted in the summary presentation that "all treatment approaches have a goal of change, modification, or improvement in relation to the situations that come to the attention of caseworkers." These goal statements, and others like them, are formulated at the most generalized level so that they can be applied to all kinds of problems. Though originally formulated for casework practice, they are sufficiently general to be appropriate for almost any type of social work modality. Such statements are intended to give general direction to social intervention and are not meant to take the place of more specific goal statements which are needed for each individual problem.

Even on a generalized level, goal statements should be sufficiently informative to indicate to practitioners and to the general public what social work is all about and what it is that social workers want to achieve. The "Working Definition of Social Work Practice" (NASW, 1958:6), considered by many as the professional charter of social work, identified three purposes:

1. To assist individuals and groups to identify and resolve or minimize problems arising out of disequilibrium between themselves and their environment
2. To identify potential areas of disequilibrium between individuals or groups and the environment in order to prevent the occurrence of disequilibrium
3. In addition to the curative and preventative aims, to seek out, identify, and strengthen the maximum potential in individuals, groups, and communities.

These purposes can serve as goals if it is agreed that disequilibrium is an undesirable state and that equilibrium is desirable. These purposes or goals relate directly to the profession's primary areas of concern, its target problems. While the statement does not specify the methods used to achieve these goals (this is done in another section of the "Working Definition"), it does indicate, at least in relation to the first purpose, that the social worker does not engage in whatever he does do by himself but "assists" other individuals and groups to achieve the desired goals.

However, this statement, useful as it is, is still a generalized one. It requires further specification before it can serve as a guide for social intervention activities. Two other types of goal statement are needed in addition to a generalized statement. There is need for a *middle-level goal statement* which focuses more specifically on intervention activities but which is still sufficiently general that it can apply to all situations which come to the attention of a social worker. And we require a *differential goal statement* which identifies specific operational goals or objectives for every given situation.

The goals [1] proposed by the federal government for state social service programs are examples of middle-level goals:

1. *Self-support:* to help individuals achieve financial and social independence, primarily through employment and education
2. *Self-care:* to secure and maintain maximum personal independence and self-determination
3. *Alternative care:* to help individuals maintain themselves in the community but not under their own care (for example, foster home, halfway house)
4. *Institutional care:* to obtain appropriate institutional care for individuals for whom other goals are not feasible.

Middle-level goal statements begin to provide social workers with guides about practice which are useful as the social intervention process evolves. Workers have a general idea what is expected of them, but for any given problem situation, more specific goals will be needed.

## Differential Goals

Generalized goals and middle-level goal statements are not sufficiently informative to link a particular problem to a spe-

1. Based on "Goal-oriented Social Services (GOSS)," *Federal Register,* February 16, 1973, p. 32. Both voluntary and public agencies attacked these goals because it was believed that they would limit the types of services that could be provided. Subsequently, the federal regulations were modified and GOSS was not made mandatory in 1973, as planned. However, emphasis on the first two goals has been widely accepted by public agencies. See Rosenberg and Brody (1974).

cific intervention strategy. One study found that social workers who work with mentally disabled clients often identify as
goals, activities which are universally beneficial (such as employment and recreation) rather than goals which are specifically indicated for a particular client (Segal, 1970). A differential goal means a specific goal for each problem and for each
person. Such specific goals are necessary if the intervention
strategy is to be effective. The desire to do "something" about
a pressing problem is not sufficiently clear or precise a goal to
give directions. The new social worker often finds himself in
situations where he wants to do something quickly, but this
desire is not enough for purposeful social intervention. Instead, a specific goal (or goals) is necessary in order to identify
suitable intervention strategies. If, for example, a section of
the differential goal statement for KEVEN MINTON read, "to
locate, within thirty miles of his home, a job with a monthly
salary of at least $700 and to enable Kevin Minton to work
steadily at this job for a period of at least six months," the intervention strategy would focus on job-finding, job-training,
and related services rather than on providing relief payments
or finding foster-home placements for his children. Without a
differential goal statement, workers tend to use routine intervention procedures. When the problem involves tenants and
landlords, some workers will invariably rush to organize a
picket line or a rent strike; had they taken the effort to develop a differential goal statement, they might have discovered another, more suitable strategy (Ecklein and Lauffer,
1972:298–300). ALICE SAMORA's worker routinely arranges
homework for his paralyzed clients. Such a strategy may be
generally desirable, but a differential goal statement for Alice
would clearly indicate the need for another strategy because
the priority goal here is not a job.

An unfortunate consequence of intervening without first
specifying differential goals is a tendency to become overcon-
cerned with emergencies and to neglect other problems which,
though serious in the long run, do not appear critical at this

time. The social worker who wants to help a particular family but who has neglected to identify differential goals often responds to one emergency after another, all the time being so busy that he fails to help this family get back on its own feet. The worker assigned to the MCPHERSON family encountered so many emergencies which required immediate handling that he never found time to assist them to function in a more autonomous manner. But if autonomy is one of the middle-level goals, it is crucial that relevant differential goals be established in order that the many emergencies be met within a framework of goal-focused services. Another social worker is trying to arrange foster family placements for teen-age girls who have been involved in sexual delinquencies. If this worker does not identify differential goals for each one of the girls referred to him, his intervention may be less than effective, for he may place a girl in a foster home when a different strategy would have been more desirable. Standard goals and standardized strategies are always second-best.

*Evaluation.* Neither client nor social worker will be able to evaluate the effectiveness of the intervention if differential goals were not specified in advance. Goals, of course, can be changed and modified as the social intervention process unfolds and as more information and feedback become available. But unless differential goals are specified in advance, nobody will really know whether and when success was achieved. Neither client nor worker will be certain when to terminate the intervention since either one may feel that continuing just a little while longer may result in even more progress—but progress toward what? And unless specific goals were identified in advance, almost anything the social worker does can be assessed as beneficial. If the goal was phrased only in vague and general terms, such as "to promote good mental health," then almost everything a social worker does can be considered as contributing toward the goal even if major mental health problems remain. It can always be argued that things would have been worse without the intervention.

When differential goals are not specified, success is often measured by whether a client or a group returns to the agency regularly, but this is a misleading indicator. A client may stop returning long before the social worker thinks he is "ready." Though the social worker may talk about "premature termination," that is, withdrawing before the intervention has been completed officially, the client may already have achieved *his* goal. Perhaps he only wanted to find a sympathetic ear to listen to his troubles or he only wanted information on where to obtain a certain service. Since the client had no indication that the worker had other goals, he stopped coming when he achieved his own goals (Mayer and Timms, 1970:22). On the other hand, when a former client returns for additional help three months or a year after his case has been "closed," the worker need not take this as an indicator of failure. This client may seek help for a new problem, or the old problem may have recurred. Just as a medical doctor does not consider it a failure if a discharged patient returns whenever he is sick, so a social worker should not feel discouraged when a former client returns for more help. The differential goals provide the real criteria for success. When the goals have been achieved we can speak of success; when they have not been achieved, we must examine the reasons for failure.

A differential goal statement must address itself to: (1) the problem; (2) the person or persons participating in the social intervention; and (3) the social situation in which the problem has occurred. A statement which omits consideration of any one of these three elements may mislead rather than aid the social intervention.

*Problem.* Consideration of the problem in the goal statement is necessary since the desired outcome is a problem-free or problem-reduced situation. Whenever the specific goal does not relate to the problem, there probably was faulty or careless problem identification, or insufficient efforts were devoted to goal formulation. When workers use generalized, nondifferential goals, such as "better mental health" or "more effective social functioning," the goal statement may be too far removed from the actual problem to be of much help in planning the intervention strategy.

*Person.* The person in the differential goal statement refers to the problem-carrier (the person who has the problem or who suffers from the problem situation), the client, the target of the intervention (if he is not identical with the problem-carrier), and the problem-solver (always the client, often the problem-carrier, and sometimes the target). The strengths and limitations of these persons should form an important consideration in setting realistic differential goals. The "same" problem will require different goals when the readiness and abilities of the participants differ. The death of a husband may in one instance require various arrangements which will permit the widow to continue to operate the family business, while in another situation the goal might be to devise a financial plan which will guarantee an adequate income for the widow and her children. In the first instance, intervention strategies may include arranging for child-care, household help, business consultations, and so forth, while in the second situation expert advice will be needed on when and how to sell the business and, subsequently, where and how to invest the proceeds. In both of these situations, the social worker's function will be to help clarify the problem, participate in goal-setting, and arrange for the various kind of services which professionals other than the social worker will provide. The consideration here has been limited to formal relationship problems faced by two recent widows; additional problems, especially role-transition problems, may also require the worker's attention.

*Social situation.* The choice of differential goals depends not only on the problem and the person(s) but also on the social situation. At times the social situation will make a greater difference for goal-setting than the personal characteristics of the participants. The financial situation of the recent widow will be as important for goal-setting as her strengths and interests; if the late husband did not leave any assets, the goal choices will be far more limited than otherwise. The type of goal which is appropriate for any given problem will depend in many ways on the social situation and on the cultural setting in which the participants are located.

The goal statement must be phrased in terms of the client's problem and social situation and not in terms of some abstract principles. Neither should the goals be stated in terms of some other system, even if the intervention target is located in that system. One of MRS. KING's problems was obtaining information from the hospital about the condition of her husband. Since Mrs. King had this problem, the goal statement should specify, "getting information for Mrs. King." The goal statement should not deal with the hospital's problem and its ineptitude in dealing with the relatives of patients even though the strategy, now or later, may include inducing changes in the hospital's information system.

Sometimes it is difficult to specify detailed differential goals because not enough is known about the problem or the person with the problem. While there is always need for "more information," sometimes so little is known that further assessment must precede goal formulation. Generally, however, it is possible to develop at least a preliminary statement of differential goals which can guide the social intervention activity until a corrected and more updated version is possible.

## Change Objectives

Some social workers favor goals which call for changes in the personality of their clients; others show a preference for goals which seek to change the society which may have caused the problem. For many years the major thrust in social work (in casework as well as in group work) was directed toward achieving personality changes which would enable the person with the problem to cope better with it. An earlier social work tradition which identified social change and social reform as the major professional objectives lay dormant for many years and became influential again only in the last two decades. But throughout the years the debate between social workers who favored personality changes and those who pursued societal changes has continued. The controversy is not only about principles and theories but also involves daily practice concerns. What, for example, is a social worker's responsibility toward children with learning difficulties? Should he help these children acquire better study habits, help them resolve their psychological conflicts, provide stimulation, and strengthen their sense of self-identity—or should he direct his efforts to effecting changes in the home and in the school in order to create a more suitable learning environment? [2]

But personality changes and societal changes may not be as far apart as they appear to be at first glance. Before deciding whether these goals are contradictory or complimentary, we must ask two types of questions. There are the ethical questions: What right do social workers have to change either personality or society? And there are the practical questions: Is personality change possible in adults? Is societal change really possible? Can one type of change be effective without the other?

*Societal sanctions.* Social workers' sanctions to engage in change activities come from a variety of sources: the larger society which authorizes social workers to practice; the social agencies which employ them; the professional association which provides general supervision and encouragement to professional practice; and the clients who engage the worker's services. Society defines more or less clearly the range of permissible norms and authorizes social workers (and other control agents) to attempt to make changes in the behavior of those who deviate overly from these norms. Society also empowers social workers to engage in preventive activities which

2. Jones (1969) brings an example of a social worker who followed the latter approach; see also Neugeboren (1970).

are designed to keep people in the high-risk population groups from violating these norms. This is not the only way to look at personality change as an intervention objective; but this formulation highlights the societal sanction for this type of activity and permits us to give a positive answer to one of the ethical questions. However, the societal sanctions for social intervention efforts directed at personality changes are far from unambiguous. And this presents the social worker with several ethical and practical dilemmas. Aside from gross deviations and those behaviors defined as criminal, societal norms are not always sufficiently clear to guide social intervention activities. What is often identified as a societal norm may reflect only the preferred behavior pattern of the middle class. But these life styles may not be functional for youngsters who grow up in the urban slums where other behavior patterns may be essential for survival.

What can or should a social worker do when society fails to provide clear guidelines? What is his role when norms are clearly class-bound? Should he try to change the personality of his clients so that they fit better the image of one segment of the society, even if the clients come from another population group? Are such change efforts indicated if the client's present behavior causes problems for him? What if they cause problems for others? For example, should a social worker try to change the speech patterns of slum children whose "native" vocabulary has become an obstacle to school achievement? (Bernstein, 1964; Whiteman and Deutsch, 1968.) Until recently, social workers and teachers did not hesitate to reshape speech patterns, thoughts, and personalities of immigrant and minority group children since they believed firmly that the English language (as it is spoken by the educated middle class), Anglo-Saxon institutions, and English-oriented cultural patterns should be dominant and standard in American life. Today there is far less certainty about the propriety of interfering in personality systems for the sake of assimilating the minority to the majority culture. And increasingly client groups speak out that they do not want to change since they are not prepared to accept the norms of some other group, even of the majority group. To put these observations in another way, some of the major participants in the social intervention process have limited the potential scope of social intervention goals by refusing to validate those societal sanctions which permitted social workers to attempt personality changes.

What about the social worker's authority to attempt changes in the social system? Some social workers claim that their sanction for this comes from such overriding professional values as the inherent worth of every individual and of every group. When the societal system frustrates the attainment of individual and group potentials, these values are presented as authority for societal change efforts. Many agree that the social structure often blocks the satisfaction of various needs of the individual and his group. But there remains the question whether this is sufficient sanction for change efforts which may have negative outcomes for others, even though they procure benefits for the clients. Here, as with the question regarding personality changes, the worker faces a dilemma to which there is no easy answer.

*Personality changes in adults.* How reasonable is it to expect personality changes in adults? Many believe that a person's characteristic personality structure is fairly set by the time he becomes an adult and that thereafter basic personality changes are not possible. Yet others suggest that changes in certain aspects of the personality system can occur even during adulthood. After reviewing the evidence, Helen Perlman (1968) raised questions about intervention activities which are designed to create entirely new life styles in adults; she thought that social workers should not expect "a major reformation of personality" but instead should aim for more modest and more realistic personality changes when working with adult clients. Those changes which do occur in adults generally take place as a result of abruptly changed circumstances or because of traumatic changes in the environment—and not as a consequence of planned intervention. Yet social work, as well as every other helping profession, is based on the proposition that there is distinct possibility for some significant changes in the adult years. The real question is not whether personality changes are possible among adults but under what circumstances are such changes possible. Before exploring the answer to this question we will consider briefly whether changes in society are possible and feasible.

*Societal changes.* The experiences of the 1960s indicate that there are definite limits to societal changes even in the American society, which is one that encourages change. The sudden and premature end of the war on poverty and of a variety of related social change efforts once again demonstrated the validity of the law which states that every society will resist those changes which it believes will threaten the established order. No society will permit its own destruction, nor will it finance efforts directed toward such a goal. Social work programs whose goals include changes in basic societal arrangements cannot expect societal sanction, cooperation, or funding. When Mobilization for Youth, the prototype of the community action antipoverty agencies, was attacked in the press and in Congress, this was generally interpreted as society's way of slowing down and even putting a stop to the system-change efforts of that innovative agency. The 1967 amendments to the Economic Opportunity Act placed greater power and control over local community action programs in the hands of the mayors; this legislative action also was intended to mute the system-change efforts of many of the antipoverty agencies. (See Fried, 1969, for an account on the attacks on Mobilization for Youth; also Marris and Rein, 1967.)

Social workers who thought that the federal government was ready to finance revolutionary (though nonviolent) changes in the social structure were mistaken. Some social workers have tried to circumvent these societal limits. Instead of working in established social agencies they have joined innovative radical service organizations. But they have learned that society can set limits to their efforts, no matter where their base of operation.

The sanctions for both personality changes and societal changes are ambiguous and problematic. Nevertheless, within broad limits, personality changes and societal changes are possible goals for social intervention. Social workers who want to do more than merely adjust a person to his problem or to the *status quo* must learn under what circumstances and to what extent such changes are possible. It may not always be feasible to find a "cure" for every problem, but adjustment to the current condition is never a first-choice intervention goal. With the resources available, problem resolution may not always be attainable, but modest and realistic changes in the person and in society should become a part of most goal statements.

*People-changes and society-changes.* The uniqueness of social work is in the fact that as a profession it does not pick one or the other change area as its sole turf but insists that in most problem situations changes in both areas are necessary. This stance derives from locating the target problems of social work at the interface of the personality system and the social system. Such problems usually require a change in both systems before they can be resolved. A "cured" drug addict generally will resume his dependency on drugs if he is returned to the environment from which he came unless changes have also taken place in that environment. Minority group children may learn all of the "desirable" personality traits, but unless there are simultaneous changes in the society, their efforts may come to naught. Without changing those societal conditions which make it so hard for a black teen-ager to find a job, it will be pointless to try to influence black children to stay in school. Nor will environmental changes suffice unless there are concomitant personality changes. Opening up job opportunities for the chronically unemployed requires a simultaneous training program which resocializes the hard-core unemployed to the labor force.

OBADIAH WILSON, age twenty-five, has never held a regular job. After the social worker finds a job for him, he must help him learn the routines necessary to retain a job (such as coming on time, coming every day, and so forth). But at the same time the social worker must help the employer learn how to accept persons like Obadiah Wilson who can become good workers but who are different from those now working in the plant. Unless there are simultaneous change efforts directed at the personality system (in this case, Obadiah Wilson) and the environment (in this case, the plant), the goal of returning Obadiah Wilson to independence will remain an empty dream.

The change objectives of social workers frequently focus on helping people (individually and in groups) cope with their problems and/or resolve them. Usually a condition for effective change in either personality or society is a concomitant change in the other area. Far from being contradictory, people-changes and society-changes are the complementary goals of social intervention practice.

## Short-term Objectives and Long-range Goals

The time dimension is an important consideration which affects goal-setting. Some goals are meant to be achieved within a relatively short period of time while others require considerably more time and are meant to be achieved only in the more distant future. The choice is usually not between one or the other type but is rather one of priorities and emphases. Many if not most problem situations require both short-term objectives and long-range intervention goals. Sometimes only one type is mentioned while the other remains implicit, but it is preferable to state both.

*Short-term objectives.* These seem to offer several advantages for the social intervention practitioner. Outcomes become evident fairly soon, and in case of failure or threatening failure it is possible to change the intervention strategy early in the process. On the other hand, short-term objectives often deal only with symptoms and not with the real causes of the problem. Quick success in achieving short-term objectives may not result in anything of lasting worth. The accomplishment of the short-term objective may be so small that the problem-carrier may become disillusioned about the efficacy of social intervention. He may fail to see the connection between the short-term objective and his problem; even though the objective has been achieved, the problem remains. Nevertheless, social workers and social agencies often favor intervention activities focusing on short-term objectives because they believe that the successful conclusion of such activities will result in greater acceptance of social work services by the beneficiaries and by the general public. Such activities give the worker an opportunity to demonstrate that social intervention can be a successful technique, and this, in turn, may make it easier to engage others in the future. Psychiatrists have also reported success in the use of short-term objectives in their initial work with lower-class patients, many of whom initially are suspicious about the effectiveness of talking therapies (Hoehn-Saric et al., 1964).

*Long-range goals.* Some of the undesirable consequences of short-term objectives can be avoided if we relate these from the very beginning to long-range goals. It will be useful to think of a means-ends paradigm where each achieved short-term objective becomes a step in achieving the long-range goal. There may be a series of short-term objectives; as each is accomplished, it becomes in turn a means toward achieving the next objective. Thus, one short-term objective for MRS. KING was to obtain accurate information about her husband's medical condition. Achieving this objective led to some reduction of uncertainty, which in turn resulted in a reduction of stress and tension (a further objective) so that MRS. KING was better able to mobilize herself to work on the key problem of securing a regular income for her family. Each short-term objective may be a small part of the long-range goal, or the relation between the two may only be indirect. In either event, it is desirable that all participants keep both short-term objectives and long-range goals in view. If the attention is only on the immediate objective, participants may withdraw as soon as initial success has been achieved, even before the basic or key problem has been resolved. But if attention focuses only on the long-range goal, participants may drop out because success seems too far away or too difficult. KEVIN MINTON's social worker was well aware that a relatively quick accomplishment was necessary to keep up Kevin's interest and motivation to work on the key goal of staying out of prison. In his meetings with Kevin the worker focused attention both on immediate, short-term objectives which promised quick success and on the long-range goal. The connection between one and the other was clear to Kevin and to the worker.

## Participants in Goal-setting

The various participants in the social intervention process have different expectations and will introduce varying goals. The members of a teen-age boys club simply wanted "to have fun" in the community center, but the staff's goal was "to resocialize the boys and prevent their becoming involved in delinquent activities." Quite likely, the parents of each of the boys had still other goals in mind when they approved their son's participation. And the leader of the club may have seen this as his opportunity to provide the boys with some sound vocational counseling. Another example is that of a parent who requests help in arranging for the institutionalization of a retarded child, but the worker feels that placement is not the best goal. In some situations a multiplicity of goals is possible, but in others, one goal precludes another. When this happens, whose goal should guide the social intervention activity?

Some have suggested that the worker with his professional expertise and knowledge should take responsibility for goal-setting. Others have assumed that the social agency has a mandate which defines the goals. Still others have indicated that only the goals of the client count. We believe that effective social intervention will occur only when client and worker agree on a set of goals which are acceptable to both. This position finds wide support in the social work literature, with writers from various approaches endorsing it. Helen Perlman (1960), for example, called for "mutual agreement on goals," while Edwin Thomas (1967) stipulated that goals be "a product of mutual assent."

*Worker's goals.* Though a social worker must be objective, he cannot pretend that he does not have any goals for a particular problem situation. The worker who claims that he has no goals either does not care or is less than honest. On the other hand, no worker may claim that only his goals are relevant and those of all other participants count for nought. The worker's frame of reference must be an open one, permitting goal inputs by clients and other participants. Such an open stance must be more than mere lip service. Joel Fischer (1971) warned against practice theories which determine the nature of goals in advance, even while claiming that clients do have an opportunity to participate in goal-setting. When a worker defines a problem in such a way that only one type of goal is possible, he virtually negates client participation in goal determination.

*Client's goals.* Perhaps the first step in client participation is the worker's willingness to listen to the client's expectations: What does the client want from the social worker? What does he expect to happen? This step is so elementary that it should be self-understood, yet the failure to listen and observe may be one of the key causes for some of social work's failures. Arthur Segal (1970), in his study of social work with mentally disabled clients, reported a wide gap between clients' own goals and those which the social workers had for them. Most of the social workers studied by Segal did not seem to be aware of their clients' expectations. Twelve out of thirty-eight clients identified education or further skill training as a goal, but none of their social workers reciprocated this expectation. On the other hand, twenty-seven social workers but only twelve clients listed recreation and peer activities as a goal for social intervention. How can a worker be effective if he is not even aware of his client's expectations?

It is vital that a worker understands what his client wants to achieve. The client, at the same time, should know and understand the worker's goals. But the client's goals rate priority consideration. He is the person who has requested service and help. He is the person who lives with the problem and who must live with the solution. His interests and his wishes, therefore, are of primary importance in developing the goals. When differences do occur between a client and his worker, they are more often the result of disagreements about strategies than about goals. Clients frequently come to the social worker to request a specific service. At times the worker may not be able to offer the service or he may feel that the service is inappropriate. One of the ways of helping a client see that there are other, perhaps even better, ways of achieving what he wants to achieve is to engage him in goal identification.

When MRS. LEFFERT asked the social worker to place her three young children in an "orphans' home," he did not argue with her nor did he tell her that he thought assigning a housekeeper to help her with the housework might be a better strategy to keep the family intact; instead, this worker asked Mrs. Leffert what she really wanted out of life. Only after he had helped her identify a set of goals did he begin to consider with her various ways which might help her attain what she wanted to achieve. By this time the original request for institutional placement for her children was no longer a point of disagreement.

The Tenth Street Gang was planning a holdup. The gang worker who had been with this gang for several months did not put up an argument or plead against the idea. He did remind the boys that they had agreed not to engage in criminal activities while he was with the group. But instead of judging the boys or preaching about their behavior, this worker asked the boys what they were after. In the subsequent discussion he helped the gang members clarify their goals and establish some priorities. There was a sharp division as to whether adventure and excitement or recognition and approval were more important, but all agreed that both sets of goals were desirable for the group. Only after this discussion did the worker move to the question of strategies which would help the boys achieve those goals that they really thought were important for them. At this point no one even mentioned the holdup as a possibility.

There will, nevertheless, be times when client and worker will not be able to agree on goals. The social worker knows that his client's goals have priority since the social intervention process was not designed to meet the worker's interests and needs. Yet the worker has a professional responsibility to assess the client's goals. He cannot accept automatically whatever the client identifies as goals since these may be harmful rather than beneficial. As long as the client's goals are feasible and do not harm anyone, the social intervention process can continue, even if the worker would have preferred some other goals. But if agreement cannot be reached, worker and client together should examine the causes of this disagreement. Perhaps they will agree that under these circumstances it is best to discontinue the intervention. But discontinuation because of goal differences is rare since more often the disagreement is about priorities or strategies.

## Summary

Goal setting is an essential component of the problem-identification phase because no problem is really defined until the problem-free condition has been described. At the same time, goal-setting is the first step in developing a social intervention strategy because an effective strategy cannot be designed until worker and client have a specific idea of what they want to accomplish or achieve. Thus, goal-setting serves as the bridge between problem definition and strategy development. Even though goal-setting occupies such a crucial position in the intervention process, it sometimes tends to get lost in the complexities and emergencies of the moment.

We discussed in this chapter three types of goals: (1) generalized goal statements which indicate the type of outcomes which social workers generally wish to achieve; (2) middle-level goal statements which focus on the activities designed to bring about the desired outcome; and (3) differential goal statements which identify the specific operational goals and objectives for every given situation. Differential goal statements usually include both short-term objectives and long-range goals.

Social intervention goals generally will specify changes in the personality system and in the societal system because in most cases one type of change without the other will not lead to effective results. The participation of clients in goal-setting, both short-term and long-range, is considered essential for successful social intervention. And these considerations apply no matter whether the participant is an individual, a group, or a community.

# chapter five

# People
# with Problems

The person (or persons) with a problem is at the core of every social intervention activity. Yet there are some social workers who are concerned only with problems and with those social conditions which make for problems; it is as if they look only at the problem and do not consider the people involved. And there are other social workers who invariably believe that their clients are the problem which needs to be corrected. Neither approach does full justice to the reality which faces the social worker—and that is a person or persons with a problem.

In the previous chapter we discussed the problem. In this chapter we will consider various aspects of the person who has a problem. This person may be the client or he may be someone for whom the client has some responsibility, such as a child, an aged or sick parent, a prisoner, and so on. Or the "person" may be a group or a community which suffers from a problem. The precise relationship of the person to the problem is not fixed and cannot be assumed by the worker since it differs from situation to situation. Every time the worker meets a new client this relationship must be explored anew. The social worker must approach every person with an open mind and without any prior assumption that he is either sick or the innocent victim of social conditions. Either or both possibilities may apply. The person may be the victim of the problem, he may carry the problem and at the same time aggravate the condition, he may be the cause of his own problem or he may even cause someone else's suffering. But above all, the person who meets with the social worker is a human being who is entitled to the respect which every human being deserves. The social intervention activity should in no way diminish the genuineness of the relationship between the various human beings who participate. In fact, the genuineness of this relationship may be one of the crucial factors in the outcome. However, to be both professional and genuine requires a high level of skill and understanding on the part of the social worker.

## Ignorance about Clients

Understanding is an essential prerequisite for effective social intervention. But complaints that social workers do not understand the people with whom they work are almost as old as social work itself. In the 1890s labor union leaders charged that Charity Organization Society workers, the first modern social workers, had little awareness of the problems faced by the poor recipient families (Pumphrey, 1973). And more than fifty years later, William Whyte (1955) noted that social workers did not have an impact on the life of Cornerville because they lacked systematic knowledge about the social backgrounds of the residents. Similarly, Herbert Gans (1962) observed that most professional caretakers, including social workers, did not have the understanding and empathy necessary to provide the services needed by the residents of the lower-class neighborhood he studied. But the ignorance of social workers is not limited to residents of slum neighborhoods and to lower-class families. One researcher who interviewed clients and workers in a marital counseling center whose clientele was mostly middle-class concluded that social workers systematically overestimated their clients' perception of the problem severity and underestimated their hopefulness and sense of personal responsibility (Ronald Bounous, cited by Briar, 1971:120). The study of social work with mentally retarded clients, cited earlier (Segal, 1970), also revealed that social workers did not have sufficient information about their clients to engage in effective social intervention. These social workers were not aware that many of their clients engaged in various desirable activities, including housekeeping, crafts, and recreation. Instead, they applied stereotypes about the inactivity of mentally disabled people to all of their clients. Our own current research on chronic welfare recipients suggests again that social workers do not know enough about their clients.

*Social distance.* Not understanding the people who have problems results in ineffective and unsuccessful intervention. Workers may fail to understand the people with whom they work because they do not realize how different they are from themselves. Social workers often assume that clients share their preconceptions about problems, but working-class clients, for example, usually view their problems in quite a different way than do middle-class social workers (Mayer and Timms, 1970). Socioeconomic class differences are not the only differences which make for misunderstandings. Color, age, and sex are cultural differences which may differentiate workers from clients and which may prevent them from truly understanding their clients. Alfred Kadushin (1972) cites a large number of studies which indicated that such differences tend to limit empathy and understanding; in chapter 10 we will report on studies which suggest that there are ways of bridging at least some of these differences.

Often social workers come from a different part of the city, geographically and culturally far removed from the neighborhood where the clients live. Many do not know about the realities of life in the urban ghetto, the rural reservation, or the exclusive suburban neighborhood because they generally spend only their working hours with clients and meet them only in the agency office. Even language may be a problem. One group of social workers who provided counseling

services to ex-prisoners became aware that they did not understand the unique communication patterns and jargon of these
men. Once they became aware of this problem, they were able
to do something about it, but too often social workers do not
realize that clients speak a "foreign" language, even when they
use the same common English vocabulary (Pew, Speer, and
Williams, 1973). Most social workers believe that the social distance between themselves and their clients should be bridged,
but there are a small number who consider this gap desirable.
Citing Goffman's observation (1959:49) about the importance
of audience segregation for professions which have not yet
achieved full public recognition, they suggest that distance between worker and client will guarantee objectivity and will result in better client service. Most social workers reject this position and attempt to narrow the gap between themselves and
their clients. There should be no contradiction between remaining objective and understanding the people with whom
we work. And reducing social distances is one of the best ways
to increase understanding.

Ignorance and misunderstanding of the client's social situation are perhaps unwittingly reinforced by the social work
norm which warns against becoming overinvolved with clients
and their problems. The effective social worker, it is suggested, must be able to shed his clients' problems at the end of
each day so that these do not interfere with his own personal
life. But this professional norm has been misinterpreted.
Overidentifying with a client's problem so that the worker can
no longer view it objectively may be harmful, but the social
worker who does not occasionally lie awake at nigh worrying
about one of his clients show a lack of heart. It is not enough
to speak of empathy during working hours only. A genuine
relationship will express itself in caring when caring really
counts. Trying to put oneself in the place of the client and attempting to view his problem as he does are recommended as
the correct stance for competent social work practice. But this

empathy cannot serve as an antidote for ignorance. It is genuine only when it comes as a result of understanding and caring.

## Understanding the Person

The average social worker sees dozens of clients every week of the year. In many ways one client resembles the next. Many bring the same kind of problems, live in identical apartments, think in similar ways, and sometimes even look alike. Many social workers find it difficult not to be bored when they have already heard the same story a hundred times. But when the worker thinks that he knows what the problem is even before he has listened to the client, routine treatment replaces individualized intervention. Social intervention is the very opposite of routine treatment. It requires that the worker understand every person with whom he comes in contact as an individual, separate and different from every other person, each group as unlike any other group, and each problem as a new problem, unique to the person or group which brings it.

Basic to an understanding of people and their problems is an ability to understand human behavior. The alert social worker must try to take into consideration all of the factors which shape this behavior, including the *biological* factors, *personality* factors, *social* factors, and *cultural* factors. If an explanation of human behavior and problems includes only one or two of these factors, the explanation will be only partial and may result in generalizations which will not provide a sufficient base for planning an effective strategy. For example, when working with the partners of a disintegrating marriage, such as the CAREYS, the social worker must not limit his probing to an understanding of the personality of the husband and wife. He must also attempt to understand the role which families are expected to fill in this society, the occurrence of family breakup in the particular subculture, as well as other social and cultural factors which are relevant to the current problem situation.

Similarly, a social worker who is designing an intervention strategy for a young adult who is about to be released from a mental hospital must understand the biological and psychological causes of mental illness, as well as the role and function of mental illness in this social and cultural system. He should recognize that in a society dominated by rationality, madness is frowned upon and suppressed while it may be tolerated and even sanctified in another society. The insane asylum of just a few decades ago, located in an out-of-the-way place behind high walls, was illustrative of one approach to mental illness, while many of the medicine men, wise men, and prophets of other eras might be classified as psychotics today (Foucoult, 1965). This social worker needs to understand that the incidence and significance of mental illness vary in different social classes. Mental illness is more prevalent in the lower than in the upper classes. And when it does occur among members of the lower class, it tends to be more severe and less likely to be treated—and if treated, the treatment tends to be custodial rather than psychotherapeutic (Hollingshead and Redlich, 1958). At the same time, deviant and abnormal behaviors are generally more tolerated by lower-class families than by middle- or upper-class families. All this the social worker must keep in mind when developing intervention strategies for his young adult client.

*Biological factors.* In the past many social workers have been reluctant to explain human behavior in terms of biological factors, preferring instead psychological or sociological explanations. Everyone recognizes that there are situations where the biological factors are so crucial that they cannot be overlooked. When a pregnant woman suffers from malnutrition, for example, the early lack of protein often results in irreversible brain damage to the fetus. Medical researchers also suggest that some psychotic disorders, including several types of schizophrenia, may be caused by genetic factors or by organic diseases (Clausen, 1966). Yet social workers who readily admit the significance of physical disabilities (such as blindness, deafness, deformed limbs) on human behavior generally have been hesitant to consider the role of genetic factors as possible causes of problem conditions. Though the impact of genetic factors is still somewhat controversial, many modern geneticists indicate that individual behavior differences may, at least in part, be due to biological and genetic factors. Occasional reference to these factors in the social work literature shows that there is at least a beginning awareness of their importance among social workers. (See, for example, Ginsburg, 1966; Pritchard, 1973; Schild, 1966 and 1972.) The interest of social workers became most evident after the publication of Arthur Jensen's controversial article (1969) in which he suggested that intelligence differences between white and black children could be attributed to genetic factors. While Jensen's thesis failed to gain wide acceptance among social workers, his article did serve to direct attention to the importance of the biological structure for behavior analysis. With the increased recognition of genetic influences on human behavior, some social workers have developed new strategies, such as genetic counseling, to use when appropriate in social intervention practice.

*Personality factors.* These include all those attributes which an individual holds as an individual, including his temperament, attitudes, instincts, and so on. Most often personality factors are equated with psychological factors, but they need not be so limited. Social workers have emphasized personality factors in their explanations of human behavior ever since they embraced Freudian theories in the early 1920s. Even though the early Freud based much of his analysis on biological factors, social workers followed a somewhat later Freud who taught that behavior was an unconscious function of a person's personality. Restricting his explanations almost entirely to the personality and biological level, Freud took social and cultural factors as given and deserving little attention. Later psychoanalytic theories, such as those of Erikson (1950), Fromm (1947), and Horney (1939), elaborated and expanded the Freudian scheme by adding explanations from other levels. Much of current social work theory is based on these neo-Freudian personality theories.[1]

*Social factors.* The identical behavior may have varying consequences for people located in different parts of the social structure. Placing one's mouth over another person's mouth is known as kissing, but when a different goal is involved we call the same behavior resuscitation! The meaning we attach to kissing and the consequences of this behavior will depend to some extent on the social structural position occupied by the kissing actors. A kiss between a mother and her son has a different meaning than the kiss of two lovers. A campaigning politician may kiss babies with impunity, but another middle-aged man may be arrested if he tries to kiss babies in the park. Not only kissing but any behavioral act depends for its meanings and consequences on the social structural status of the actors. A medical doctor will not be penalized for coming to work late, but a factory worker will. Drug addiction and narcotic abuse were generally ignored so long as this behavior was limited to residents of the netherworld of our large urban areas. But when middle- and upper-class youths became drug users, the alarm was sounded and priority attention was devoted to this problem. Another example of the difference resulting from social structural factors is that the stigma of unemployment is never applied to the millionaire playboy or to the middle-class mother who prefers to stay at home with her children.

Social structural variables not only affect the meaning and consequences of behavior, they also tend to have an impact on behavior itself. Children who live in inadequate and over-

1. For examples of other approaches to social work theory see Hearn (1968), Middleman and Goldberg (1974), Thomas (1967).

crowded conditions tend to spend more time on the street than at home—and congregating on street corners is more likely to lead to behavior patterns that are classified as deviant or delinquent. It will be difficult if not impossible to understand the behavior of these children (or of anyone else) without taking into consideration social structural factors. For example, a social worker who works with aged clients must know whether a particular person is working or is retired. Though retirement is usually culturally determined (or may be caused by poor health), a person's work or retirement status is a characteristic of the social structure. And this characteristic is central to understanding much of the aged person's behavior. Another social structural characteristic, the proportion of aged in the general population, may also have an important impact on behavior patterns. The opportunity to interact with people of all ages will be much greater in communities where the proportion of aged remains small. And a sufficiently large working population is necessary to pay (directly or indirectly) for the services which the aged require. Yet the success of many retirement villages occupied exclusively by older people may indicate that this structural variable is of little importance for those who are economically independent.

*Cultural factors.* The fourth area for behavior analysis consists of the cultural factors. Culture is an abstraction and includes the norms, beliefs, and expressive symbols which give meaning to the basic values of a society. Those shared ideas which make up a culture serve as guides for human behavior. The results of the socialization process provide one indication of the impact of culture on behavior. Socialization is more than conforming; it involves learning to like doing what one has to do anyway. For example, once children have been socialized to use toilets (we call it "toilet-trained"), they always prefer using bathrooms to the more natural way of relieving themselves. But the objectives of socialization differ in various cultures. This explains why infants raised in different societies are taught to carry out the same activity in a variety of ways. Anthropologist Clyde Kluckhohn (1962:22) notes that "it is virtually impossible to discover a single act which is carried out precisely in the same manner by members of all societies." Even such apparently basic biological activities as eating, sneezing, sleeping, and making love are performed in dissimilar ways in different societies. Yet the members of any one cultural group learn how to act, talk, and even think in pretty much the same way. This is the result of the impact of culture on behavior whenever the socialization process is effective. And socialization is not limited to infancy and childhood but occurs throughout the life cycle.

What people do in a given situation or under a given circumstance depends on the options open to them in their culture. Whom to ask for help with a problem is rarely a completely free choice; whether the first request is made of a relative, a religious leader, a social worker, or a complete stranger is more or less culturally determined. Even the ways of committing suicide are culture-bound! Americans generally do not commit hara-kiri, nor do they practice the suttee, but typically they jump off bridges or tall buildings, take an overdose of sleeping pills, or turn on the gas. These are American suicide options which are not available in many other cultures. Or when a husband and a wife have an argument, it is culture rather than the loudness of voice or the logic of the argument that is likely to determine the winner. Among the Navaho Indians, where women enjoy a high degree of independence and where husbands go to live with their wives' families, the wife is most likely to win the argument. But among the Utah Mormons where the man is the traditional head of household and reigns supreme, it is the man who usually wins, while among Texas Presbyterians, where equality is the norm, wives win just about as many arguments as their husbands (Strodtbeck, 1951).

## Behavior Analysis Grid

When observing human behavior we generally begin to interpret it even while observing it. Thus, we observe a group of tenants about to enter the project manager's office and say to ourselves, "Here comes an angry crowd." Or we see a smiling high school graduate receive his diploma and say to our neighbor, "There's a happy fellow." Actually, we do not know how the other person feels or what he thinks. Instead, we ascribe to him how we would have felt under similar circumstances or how people in our society generally would feel in this situation. But if we really want to understand human behavior we must not only view it through the eyes of the larger social system, we must understand it from the viewpoint of those who participate in that behavior. A certain teen-ager's behavior may be "deviant" or "acting out" when measured by societal standards, but for the teen-ager it may be a very useful way of adapting to the pressures and problems which face him. Before planning an intervention strategy, the social worker must attempt to understand the behavior patterns from various viewpoints, especially from that of the teen-ager. The social worker who was trying to help CARLA GUSTAMENTA return to school noted the cultural and social structural factors which *he thought* were responsible for her father's refusal to let Carla go to school. This worker used his best judgment and tried to take into account all possible factors, but without considering Mr. Gustamenta's views the analysis would be incomplete.

Use of the Behavior Analysis Grid may be helpful in the systematic analysis of the behavior of individuals, groups, and communities. The Grid provides an opportunity to analyze behavior according to the four levels along two axes: (1) as viewed by the society and (2) as viewed by the client or by his cultural group. The Behavior Analysis Grid makes it more difficult to hide behind vague generalizations because each observation challenges every other observation. The worker must review his findings and interpretations until there is a general consistency between each pair of observations. The worker assigned to work with ALICE SAMORA used the Grid early in his explorations and made the following notations:

### Behavior Analysis Grid

| Level | Behavior as Viewed by | |
| --- | --- | --- |
| | *Society* | *Client or His Group* |
| Biological | Paralyzed from waist down (result of childhood accident) | Believes she is a cripple |
| | | Unable to move around or do anything useful because of physical limitations |
| | Full mobility from waist up, including full use of hands | |
| | Mobile with crutches | |
| Personality | Withdrawn | Considers self a failure, a loser |
| | Highly submissive | |
| | | Apathy and withdrawal as defense against being hurt |
| | | Has no choice but to be dependent on parents |
| Social | No peer relationships | Wants to relate with peers but has no opportunities and does not know how |
| Cultural | "Sick," "cripple" | Ambivalent about current cripple role |
| | Lacks suitable adult models | Desires to be a more autonomous adult |

The Grid does not provide instant prescriptions, but it does offer an opportunity for better understanding the client and his problems. The above analysis of Alice Samora's behavior and problem was prepared after an early visit to the Samora home. Subsequent visits resulted in revisions and updating of the Grid.

## Stereotypes about the Poor

So much has been written about the poor that it is often difficult to distinguish between fact and myth. The alert social worker who wants to understand his poor clients is not always sure of the validity of the assumptions and propositions he uses to interpret his data. Does the "culture-of-poverty" theory help explain a client's life style? What are the consequences of this theory for social intervention practice? How helpful are other theoretical frameworks when it comes to explaining an observation about the poor?

The world of the poor has been described as brutal. Only those successfully socialized to the demands of that environment have a chance to survive. While among the nonpoor a second and a third chance are common, the poor usually do not have even a second chance. How does a poor mother feed her children when there is no money in the house until the welfare check arrives next week? Most poor people do not have credit cards, nor do they have access to a rich uncle. Where does a poor family go when the landlord evicts them for failure to pay rent and when the welfare worker says that it will take three weeks to process an emergency claim for relief? The skills necessary for survival under these conditions may not always be considered nice in middle-class society, but without them survival would not be possible. Yet it is important to try to understand why poor people, and particularly our clients, have chosen one rather than another behavior pattern. Why, for example, has OBADIAH WILSON never held a steady job and why did Josef GUSTAMENTA not want his daughter to attend school?

One explanation suggests that *inadequate superego formation* is a crucial factor in the development of lower-class behavior patterns. The frequent absence of the father and the subsequent dominance of the mother result in a negative masculine identity. Even when both father and mother are in the home, it is alleged that the quality of lower-class life presents obstacles to adequate internalization and object-cathexis. Lower-class mothers are distant, punitive, and unloving, while fathers are harsh, punitive, and forbidding. As a result, it is maintained, many lower-class children never internalize behavioral controls. But many scholars have found fault with this formulation. One large-scale research study reported that there was no lack of conscience or internalization among lower-class boys. They felt guilty about stealing and about being disobedient, just as middle-class boys did. Even though they engaged in more antisocial behavior than middle-class boys, there was no indication that these lower-class boys suffered any less from the pressures of internalized standards (Miller and Swanson, 1960).

The *culture-of-poverty theory* is of a different order. Many students of poverty have noted that the poor of every industrialized country resemble each other more than they resemble their more affluent countrymen. Propinquity to violence, alcoholism, and drug abuse, resistance to change, a high degree of individualism, present rather than future orientation—these are some of the characteristics which are in evidence among the poor of all industrialized countries. Few disagree with these observations, but there is no agreement that these characteristics constitute a culture of poverty. Instead, many hold, these characteristics represent an appropriate response to similar real-life conditions.

Sociologists and urban anthropologists argue back and forth about the validity of the culture-of-poverty hypothesis, but social workers become impatient when they read about these academic disputes. They ask other questions which are more relevant to their work. They want to know, for example, whether apathy will occur among the children of today's poor only if they experience the same sort of failure as their parents endured—or whether apathy has already become a cultural characteristic which will occur even when there are no specific experiences of failure. In the first case, a program which provides teen-agers with jobs after they have completed their schooling will prove to be an effective intervention strategy. But if the second situation reflects reality, a job program would hardly make a dent on apathy. The second situation prevails if the culture of poverty thesis is correct.

Most social intervention programs have been designed as if the culture of poverty theory is not valid. Social workers generally believe that victims of poverty and discrimination can be helped and can help themselves if they are given access to the opportunity structure and if the obstacles which block their participation in the mainstream of American life are removed. Some social intervention strategies, however, do take the culture of poverty theory into account. Sometimes an attempt is made to dissolve that culture and assimilate the culturally deprived as fast as possible into the majority culture because it is believed that the poverty culture is dysfunctional and harmful to the individual and to society. The racist tinge of this approach is hard to conceal, and it has, therefore, found little response in social work circles. A third approach, put into practice only recently, accepts the culture of poverty as a fact and identifies intervention goals that are appropriate to the culture of the victims. Those who advocate this approach suggest that social workers have no more right to change the culture of the victim population than they have to superimpose their own culture on that of a foreign people (J. Cohen, 1964; Mendes, 1974; Shannon, 1970).

## Pathways to Help

Understanding the client requires that the social worker realizes how the client came to him. Most people first attempt to obtain help from their immediate family or from someone whom they know well. One extensive study of Americans with mental health problems found that thirteen persons approach an informal helper, such as a relative or a friend, for every one who seeks professional help (Gurin, Veroff, and Feld, 1960). Though people usually request help from someone whom they know, sometimes a sense of shame or strained family relationships prompts the troubled person to seek help from another source. More often, however, an approach to a stranger, such as a social worker, occurs only after people have failed to obtain help from those in their immediate circle. By the time most persons arrive at the social worker's office, they are already extremely distressed because thus far they have not found an answer or a solution. One client, perhaps typical of many, reported that the social agency "is the last place anybody wants to go to unless they are really desperate" (Mayer and Timms, 1970:105). Nevertheless, people do turn to social agencies for help. There are a number of different access routes or pathways which people use to reach a social agency. Different pathways make for some difference in the subsequent client-worker engagement so that it is important to identify the unique features of each. Among the pathways are: (1) informal referral; (2) social circles; (3) self-referral; (4) formal referral; (5) reaching-out; and (6) mandatory referral.

1. Often people with a problem come to a social agency because a neighbor or an acquaintance has told them that they once had exactly the same problem and received help from the agency. MRS. KING is an example of such an *informal referral,* so-called because the referral occurs without the assistance of a professional worker. People who follow this pathway typically have had the problem for some time and have previously turned to one or more informal helpers. Somewhere along the line someone told them about a social agency. Though they have specific expectations of the social worker, their expectations are often based on misinformation. Their problem may not be like that of their friend, and they may not even be eligible to receive service. Nor are they aware what social intervention means and what it requires of them.

2. The road is a different one when the applicant is a member of a *social circle* which has regular access to social agencies. Members of a social circle do many things together. For some the common activities include drinking in taverns or betting on horses; for others it may be working in the same factory or doing the laundry in the same laundromat; and for still others going to the same concerts and plays may constitute the common activity (Kadushin, 1966). In some social circles

requesting help from a social agency has become a common and acceptable activity, one that is talked about openly with one's friends and one that may even confer status on the person who has become a client. Here the suggestion to see a social worker is neither casual nor covert but supported and sanctioned by the social circle. The people who follow this pathway are not desperate when they arrive at the agency and generally have a good idea what is expected of them by the social worker.

3. *Self-referral* has become an increasingly common pathway. Instead of using the social worker as a last resource after all other attempts to obtain help have failed, a growing number of people view the agency as a first-aid station for various kinds of problems. Some newspaper readers learn from the advice columns how social agencies can help people with certain problems. Couples who want to adopt a baby often read articles or books which recommend social agencies as places where prospective parents can get babies. The slick magazines and the week-end supplements describe how social workers help pregnant girls. And an increasing number of former clients return when a new problem arises. By going directly to a social worker when they have a problem, these people avoid the danger of losing face in front of their relatives and friends. They no longer need to worry who will know about their troubles since it is known that social workers respect the confidences they receive. And they have the assurance that the social worker has the required skill and ability to help them. Though the client who follows this pathway may arrive before he is desperate, there is no assurance that he knows what will happen to him at the social agency. And many self-referrals come with the unrealistic expectation that the social worker can effect a quick and painless cure.

4. In addition to the various informal referrals there is the more *formal referral* of clients from another agency or from another professional, such as a teacher, physician, or clergy-

man. The reasons for formal referrals may vary from "passing
the buck" to directing the person with the problem to the most
effective helper. Generally, clients who arrive at the social
agency as a result of a formal referral have only a vague idea
of what to expect since a professional in another setting will
not want to commit himself about services over which he has
no control. Therefore, these clients often are anxious and ambivalent when they arrive at the agency. The social worker's
first task will be to lower the tension by clarifying the procedures which will be followed and explaining what is expected
of the client.

5. At one time all pathways to the social agency were one-
way streets. The prospective client was required to advance on
one of the pathways until he arrived at the social agency. In
fact, there were often obstacles which made it difficult rather
than easy to enter the social agency network. Social intervention services were limited to people who were able to reach the
social agency. Many others, even though they were eligible for
services, never came in contact with the social worker because
they failed to reach the agency under their own power. In the
past decade some of these pathways have increasingly become
two-way streets with many social workers leaving their offices
in order to search for people who can benefit from social intervention. Characteristic of these efforts, variously known as
"reaching-out" or "aggressive case-finding," is the fact that the
prospective client often does not know that he has a problem
or that a social worker can help him with his problem; in other
words, the target of the service has not asked for help. In
these situations there is a danger that social workers who in-
tend to do good impose their service on people who really do
not want any help. In reaching-out the social worker must be
especially careful that he does not impose himself. He has a
responsibility to protect people's right *not* to engage in the
social intervention process, just as he has an obligation to
make his service available to those who do want to engage. But

the social worker must remember, as Henry Miller (1968:19) once stated, that every person has "the freedom to make shambles of his life."

6. Finally, there are clients whose arrival at the social agency is not voluntary but mandated by some authority. Here we speak of prisoners and delinquents, as well as abusive parents and other adjudicated persons, who have been directed by some judicial authority to come to the social agency. *Mandatory participation* does not make for the best beginning in the social intervention process, but it does not preclude the subsequent development of a relationship between client and worker which will make meaningful engagement possible. Allen Webb and Patrick Riley reported on a successful intervention experience with a group of young girls on probation who had no choice about their initial involvement with the social worker. The involuntary client generally arrives either hostile or passive, challenging the worker to do something to him. Yet there is now sufficient experience to "cast considerable doubt on the assumption that voluntary initiation . . . is required for successful involvement of the client" (Webb and Riley, 1970:572).

## Becoming a Client

Once a person arrives, regardless of the pathway he followed, he faces a number of requirements which he must fulfill before he can be considered a client. In many agencies he must admit that he has a problem and he must express a willingness to give up the behavior which caused the problem. He must be cooperative, not complain too much, and, above all, not do anything which might lead to a suspicion of malingering. Yet many potential clients will not or cannot admit that *they* have a problem or that *they* need to change. These demands are especially difficult for the many whose problematic behavior patterns have proved functional and who feel that they cannot afford to give them up. Those applicants who do assume the

traditional client role, or who feel that they have no real
choice in the matter, often find themselves torn between the
agency's expectations and the demands of their own environment. The agency demands punctuality in keeping appointments, but the group norm may assign little value to coming
on time and much greater importance to the rules of hospital-
ity. Whether to leave a neighbor in the middle of a cup of tea
in order to keep an appointment with the social worker may
become a real dilemma for a client.

An additional difficulty in the process of becoming a
client is the practice of requesting help from an impersonal
agency and not from a specific worker. The applicant cannot
select his own worker—the agency assigns the worker. But the
arbitrary assignment of an unknown worker may be highly
disturbing to a new client, many of whose problems arose out
of his inability to cope with bureaucratic organizations. The
social agency's bureaucratic procedures may intensify his
problems rather than reduce them. Those who suffer from
"bureaucratitis" need to identify with a real person, not with
an impersonal agent. Nor is the assignment of a worker the
only problem which faces the new client.

Many clients, as noted above, have false or partial information about the agency's function and the social worker's
role. Many expect that the worker will do everything for them
while they sit by passively, much as they do in a doctor's office.
Others expect immediate solutions for their difficulties. This
failure to understand the social intervention process and the
worker's role in it is not the result of inadequate public information or of language difficulties alone. There appears to be a
basic cultural difference between the middle-class life style
upon which most of social work practice is built and the life
styles of many of our client groups. Numerous studies have
shown that working-class people have different problem-solving modes, based on different premises, than social workers.
Lower-class clients generally follow a unicausal, moralistic, and
suppressive approach to problem-solving, while the social

worker's approach is precisely opposite (Mayer and Timms, 1970:76–78).

People with problems, once they ask others for help, want specific and practical help. When they are hungry, they want food. When they are unemployed, they desire a job. They need a doctor when they are sick. But when people come to a social agency their problems are often redefined to fit the agency's preferred modality of service. No doubt many poor people have personality problems. Years of deprivation undoubtedly have left an imprint on their life. But when hunger pains are killing is no time to analyze interfamilial relationships. People whose problems arise out of a lack of basic resources need concrete services. They are usually not ready to talk things out, at least not until their basic needs have been met. Many potential clients, especially those coming from the lower classes, find it strange that *they* could be responsible for their trouble—another person is always at fault, and the client cannot understand why the worker does not do something to limit or change "them." The worker need not accept this formulation of problem causes, but he must understand it and deal with it before he will be able to involve this client in the social intervention process.

## Summary

Social intervention, if it is to be really effective, must be based on a full understanding of the client and his problem. Intervention activities based on generalizations or stereotypes will be less than effective and may even be harmful. The behavior of people and their problems can best be understood by analyzing it in terms of biological, personality, social, and cultural factors. This analysis must include observations from the participant's view and from society's viewpoint.

Workers must learn to understand their clients' problems as well as their requests and expectations. They may or may not be able to accept them and act on them—but without understanding what it is that the clients want, they surely cannot be helpful. We noted that many clients are extremely distressed when they come for the first time to a social agency. Certainly relief from suffering and distress is one legitimate request that all clients have, whether or not they voice it in this way. Lydia Rapoport's comment (1970:309) that "motivation for relief of suffering may be a better starting point than motivation for change in behavior or feelings" remains a useful guide for beginning the social intervention process.

# chapter six

# Social Workers
# and Social Agencies

We cannot understand what social workers do unless we understand the social agencies in which they practice. While there are individual differences among workers, the policies and structure of an agency tend to determine the range of permissible and expected worker activities. One social agency expects its workers to go out of their way to assist clients, while in another the "rule" is that clients are seen only in the office during designated office hours. One agency serves only blind people, while in another eligibility is limited to persons from one religious group. In one agency applicants must wait for weeks before they can talk to a social worker, but in another agency every applicant is seen within twenty-four hours. The organizational setting, it has been said, is far more important for social workers than for physicians or lawyers. Understanding the social agency and the ways in which it influences practice is crucial for effective social intervention.

After first considering the basic characteristics of helpers, social workers as well as others, we will focus on an analysis of social agencies and their impact on practice. In the last section of this chapter we will return once more to a consideration of the role of social workers in the social intervention process and especially to an examination of the relations between workers and clients.

## Characteristics of Helpers

Earlier we noted that the effectiveness of social work and other types of interpersonal intervention has not yet been proved. Some evaluation studies have reported a modest rate of success, while others have emphasized the high rate of failure. Several of the studies reported that as many people benefited from social intervention as did not. Some researchers compared people who had received interpersonal help with others who had not received any help; generally, the rate of improvement or recovery was about the same for both groups. Evidently, as many people among those who saw a social worker or other therapist got well as among those who had no contact with any professional helper. When Edward Mullen and James Dumpson (1972) examined sixteen major studies of social work practice they found that only four gave evidence of positive outcomes, six reported that social work intervention had failed, and the remaining six studies presented mixed results. Joel Fischer (1973) analyzed all published studies of casework effectiveness which utilized an experimental research design, a total of eleven studies spanning almost twenty years. He observed that in nearly half of these studies those clients who received services from a professionally trained social worker "deteriorated to a greater degree . . . or demonstrated improved functioning at a lesser rate" than control subjects who did not see a social worker or whose only contact was with an untrained worker (Fischer, 1973:18). Donald Kiesler (1966) reviewed a large number of research studies of psychotherapeutic intervention and found that some therapists produced positive changes in their patients but that the vast majority either had no effect or produced a marked deterioration. Charles Truax and Kevin Mitchell (1971) concluded on the basis of a review of all published studies that psychotherapy "on the average" was quite ineffective. Similarly, Steven Segal (1972) concluded that social work therapeutic intervention did not produce consistent positive results.

One problem common to many evaluation studies is that successful outcomes are often confounded with unsucccessful results. When, for example, a study reports that there was no improvement in 58 percent of the cases, one may conclude that this intervention approach was not wholly effective. Nevertheless, success was evidently achieved in four out of every ten cases (42 percent). A blanket over-all assessment of effectiveness may not be particularly useful. Instead, it might be more helpful to indicate under what circumstances a particular method or approach may be effective so that workers can be guided in its utilization.

The effectiveness of any particular intervention strategy will depend on many different factors. In previous chapters we have examined several of the factors which make for effective practice, including the selection of appropriate problems (chapter 3), the identification of relevant goals (chapter 4), and the need for client participation (chapter 5). Other elements which will be examined in this and in the next chapter are appropriate service delivery systems and suitable intervention strategies. But first we must explore the characteristics of the effective helper which may contribute to successful intervention practice. It is no secret that some social workers are more successful than others, just as some teachers are more successful than other teachers. Even when everything is the same (same agency, same type of problem, same amount of experience), differences in the characteristics of the social workers themselves tend to have a significant impact on the outcome.

*Inherently helpful persons.* Variations in the social workers' or therapists' personalities, however, do not explain the reported finding that improvement seems to be as frequent among people who do not receive help as among those who do. One explanation of this seeming "spontaneous improvement" was offered by Allen Bergin (1966), who suggested that even though the people in the control group did not receive professional help, they undoubtedly received help from "inherently helpful persons" in their immediate environment. Often there is no awareness that help has been given or received since the two people are in natural contact with each other. Volunteers without special training sometimes achieve what appear to be miraculous results with children who have serious behavior problems. We can explain their success only if we assume that these volunteers are inherently helpful persons. The most unlikely places can provide the setting for the inherently helpful person. One research study reported that a college student's average could be predicted better from a knowledge of his roommate's personality than from his own aptitude tests; higher grades resulted when the roommate was understanding, warm, and genuine, even when no active help was requested or offered (Shapiro and Voog, 1969). Perhaps the characteristics of the effective roommate suggest a model of the helpful person. People who are understanding, warm, and genuine will contribute toward successful outcomes, while those who lack these characteristics will always be ineffective, no matter what their training or title. These characteristics are as important for the social worker as they are for the inherently helpful person. We can even say that being an inherently helpful person is a prerequisite for becoming an effective social worker. One client may have put her finger on these essential characteristics when she reported what her social worker lacked:

Once I got talking to the social worker, I felt at ease but then I realized that she wasn't entering into what I was saying at all. And I thought, you are not really listening to me. You are not really interested. She just wasn't giving me an answer or any advice at all . . . (Mayer and Timms,1970:73)

There are at least four obstacles which prevent a social worker from understanding another person. And these are the very obstacles which also prevent him from becoming an effective helper. These obstacles are:

1. *Fear of people.* When the worker is afraid of people in general, or of this particular client, he will focus on his own fears rather than on what the other person is trying to tell him.

2. *Lack of interest.* When the worker is not interested in the other person or is bored by him, his attention will wander.

3. *Concern with his own problem.* When the worker is concerned with his own problem, he cannot pay attention to the other person's problem.

4. *Presenting a façade.* When the worker tries to be someone other than himself, he must concentrate on maintaining the façade rather than on listening to the other person.

The opposite qualities characterize the helpful person. Truax and Mitchell (1971), on the basis of a large number of research studies, reported that an effective helper must demonstrate the following characteristics:

1. *Genuineness.* The worker must be genuine in the helping relationship: that is, he must be nonphony, nondefensive, and authentic.

2. *Warmth.* The worker must accept others in a nonthreatening and trusting way; he must radiate nonpossessive warmth.

3. *Empathy.* The worker must have a high degree of accurate, empathic understanding. He must know how to "be with" the other person and how to grasp the meaning of the other person's statements.

4. *Activity.* The worker must participate actively in the intervention process since distance and aloofness suggest that the worker is either not listening or not interested in the other person.

These basic personality characteristics are difficult to develop if they are not already present. On the other hand, persons who have these characteristics can easily learn the interpersonal skills necessary for practice application. Good results have been achieved in training workers who scored high on the basic qualities of empathy, warmth, and genuineness, even when they did not have a high school diploma.

Social workers must have these characteristics if they want to be effective. But if social workers possessed only these characteristics and no more, they would be like every other inherently helpful person. Social workers differ from such persons by virtue of their professional training, their professional, full-time commitment to social work, and their having accepted the professional ethic and values as a guide for practice. However, these additional characteristics must never become substitutes or replacements for empathy, warmth, and genuineness.

## The Social Agency—a Participant

The social agency is much more than a place where the social worker sits and practices. In a very real sense it is one of the key participants in the social intervention process. A social worker's personality and skill, of course, do play an important part in determining the social intervention strategy—but just as the client and his problem influence the choice of strategy, so does the agency. In some ways the agency is perhaps the most important participant. A small but growing number of social workers are engaged in private practice. Their unique problems arise primarily out of the fact that they do not practice in an agency. These special problems will not be discussed here. When these private practitioners engage in social intervention there is no agency participant.

A superficial examination of social agencies might suggest that they exist to enable social workers to practice. Agencies do provide the sanctions and resources which social workers need. They do provide the monies, space and auxiliary manpower without which social work practice is difficult. But the social agency is far more than a supply depot, ready to furnish whatever the social worker needs. Instead, the contemporary social agency has its own mission and objectives which may not necessarily coincide with those of the social work professionals whom it employs. Through various means the agency tries to make certain that the attainment of its objectives receives priority attention, even when these objectives run counter to social work goals. This may explain Irving Piliaven's somewhat cynical comment (1968:35) that "serving the client is not the sole, perhaps not the major, concern of social agencies." The worker's commitment to client service is derived from the profession's basic value stance, but the agency's mission reflects more directly the expectations of its sponsors. Often these objectives are spelled out in laws or ordinances; at other times the annual budget gives evidence of the agency's mission.

Agencies in the voluntary sector also reflect their community's expectations, but they have more leeway in selecting a more specialized or more limited community as their sponsor. Yet, no matter how defined, the community is the source of every agency's mission. Thus, in our society, work for its own sake and for the sake of supporting one's family is a high-priority value. And reinforcing this value is an objective assigned to many social agencies. Public welfare agencies, for example, provide emergency and long-term relief to designated groups of recipients; but they are also expected to return all employable adults to the labor market as quickly as possible. Various strategies are utilized to accomplish this objective. Sometimes relief is denied outright or the welfare check is far below the amount required to maintain a minimum standard of living. These are sanctions used to force applicants to seek work. The criterion of need often takes second place to reinforcing the work value so that even when general economic conditions deteriorate and unemployment rates climb, the number of people receiving welfare does not always increase. Political and fiscal considerations rather than human needs limit or expand the agency's services and the help that social workers can offer (Piven and Cloward, 1971). Here and in many other situations it is the agency's mission and objectives rather than the social workers' commitment which direct the pattern of work.

It may have been an historical accident that the social work profession developed at the very time when formal bureaucratic organizations became the preeminent mode of organization in the Western world. Yet this accident of timing (if it was an accident) has been significant for social work. Socialization to the social agency has emerged as a crucial prerequisite for successful practice. As a result, one of the objectives of social work education is to enable the student to adapt to the culture of the social agency; this explains why the practicum or field work has always held a central place in the social work curriculum. This socialization to the agency is necessary precisely because the agency's objectives are not identical with those of the profession. Because this is so, many social workers learn early in their career that a bureaucratic orientation may be more functional for them than a professional one. Often this adaptation to bureaucratic norms occurs unconsciously, and a worker may not even be aware that his practice has been affected. But many knowledgeable observers have confirmed that social workers do not function as free agents; instead, their activities are guided by the bureaucratic structure of the agency which employs them. (See Billingsley, 1964; Blau and Scott, 1962; Peabody, 1964; Piliaven, 1968; Toren, 1970; Wasserman, 1970 and 1971; Zimmerman, 1969; and many others.)

Since almost all social workers are employed by social agencies, it is important that we understand how practice is influenced by the organization and its structure. There are many different ways in which this occurs. Here we will discuss briefly five structural and procedural elements which shape practice: (1) eligibility rules; (2) caseloads; (3) administrative requirements; (4) budgets; and (5) supervision. This list can be expanded easily, but these five elements will suffice to indicate the overwhelming importance of the organization for social work practice.

1. *Eligibility rules.* Some people are eligible for a service which the agency offers while others are declared not eligible. Screening-in and screening-out are not always done on the basis of need or of the potential usefulness of the service but rather on the basis of a policy decision or rule which may have been formulated into law. Edward Newman and Jerry Turem (1974:11) perceptively observe that "eligibility requirements tend merely to reduce the universe of potential users rather than select among potential clients those whose utilization does most to accomplish the program's ends." The clientele of the social worker does not necessarily consist of those in greatest need of help nor of those for whom social intervention is likely to be most effective. Instead, caseloads are composed of people who have met the eligibility requirements established by legislators, policy-makers, or administrators. Eligibility requirements may be stated in terms of age (older adults, children), income or employment status (unemployed, destitute), family composition (one parent), physical handicap (blind, crippled), ethnic or religious group, occupation (armed forces), or the presenting problem (alcoholism, marital difficulties), but the attempt is always to limit service to one or another group without considering who needs the service the most. The decision that Mr. Bing is eligible to receive social services generally will not depend on a professional assessment that he will benefit from these services. Instead, he will be eligible as long as he meets certain specified criteria. If eligible, he will receive these services even if there are other people who would receive greater benefit from them but who, according to the eligibility rules, are ineligible. Policy decisions, often made by members of the legislature or of the board of directors who are not social workers, determine who can and who cannot become a client of the social worker.

One consequence of eligibility requirements is that in

many agencies social workers must use a considerable part of their time and effort to establish the eligibility of potential clients. Though the use of applicant declarations of presumptive eligibility has reduced the time that workers previously needed to devote to eligibility investigations, scarce resources must still be assigned to this effort. The worker's and client's activities concerned with eligibility determination usually are not directly related to the desired outcome of the social intervention process; at times this allocation of time and resources may even be counterproductive. Edward Schwartz (1967), for example, reported that in the Midway Project even experienced social workers required "an enormous investment of time and effort" to learn eligibility rules and other administrative procedures, leaving them less time for more direct intervention activities. Yet here, as elsewhere, the demands of the social agency took precedence over the service objectives of the social work profession.

But eligibility requirements are not entirely dysfunctional. If there were no such rules, or if eligibility requirements were ambiguous, each application would require an individual and personal decision by the worker and his supervisor before services or benefits could be given. The absence of formalized administrative criteria would permit but not guarantee the utilization of professional criteria. But when eligibility rules are unclear, protracted negotiations and bargaining between applicant and worker might occur, and this would do little to enhance the effectiveness of the social worker.

2. *Caseloads.* Clients generally do not chose their workers nor do workers select their clients. Instead, in most social agencies applicants and clients are assigned to workers on the basis of some more or less formalized routine, designed to ensure the most efficient utilization of staff. But the number and type of clients assigned exert an influence on the worker's pattern and style of work. Agencies make various demands of workers, such as periodic home visits and periodic reports, which must be completed regardless of the number of cases

carried. Clients request specific services which often are not related to the immediate problem but which nevertheless must be handled. Emergencies requiring priority attention occur, more frequently with some cases and less so with others. Social workers speak of "managing" their caseload when they talk about all of these additional activities to which they must give time. The number of cases assigned to a worker is one factor which complicates the management of a caseload. A worker with a large caseload will be so tied up in paper work and in responding to emergencies that little time will remain for planful social intervention. Almost everybody agrees that most caseloads in public welfare agencies are too large, but there is not yet any agreement on the optimum size of the caseload. While social workers have always pleaded for smaller case-loads, they have not yet convincingly demonstrated that better results can be achieved with twenty cases than with forty (Brown, 1968; Sample, 1967).

The type of cases assigned to a worker affects his style and pattern of work as much as the number of cases. Clients whose problems are not suitable for social intervention require a different type of worker activity than those with suitable problems. One situation prevails when applicants are willing and able to participate in the social intervention process, an-other when they are not willing or not able. The street-corner worker who is assigned to an antagonistic, resisting gang of teen-agers faces an entirely different challenge than does his colleague who is working with a gang that has requested a worker.

A worker is not free to select the type of cases for which he feels he can achieve best results nor can he determine the number of cases that he should carry. These are generally agency decisions. There are, however, some agencies whose clients do have an opportunity to select their worker. Thus, in some children's institutions, the children are free to select a caseworker from among those available. In some group work agencies, groups can request the services of a certain club leader, and, all other considerations being equal, the request will be honored. But despite the appearance of free choice, the final decision remains with the agency which employs the worker and which dispenses the services.

3. *Administrative requirements.* The managers and directors of every bureaucratic organization must keep themselves informed about the activities which occur throughout the organization. This may be a simpler problem for a production organization than for a service organization. It becomes particularly critical for organizations where the activities of workers are not observable and where direct results cannot be ascertained clearly and quickly. Securing correct and meaningful information about worker activities and outcomes is a major problem for social agency administrators. Since outcome information is generally not available, social agencies have always required specific outputs and have demanded detailed output reports in lieu of outcome assessments.[1] One agency requires home visits every six months, another insists that every eligibility investigation be completed within thirty days, and a third directs that every client be seen for one hour a week. The details differ, but the focus always is on worker activity, that is, outputs, rather than on outcomes or changes in the client's situation or problem. Written and statistical reports are almost always demanded. Both the requirements and the reports may serve valid purposes as far as the agency is concerned, but they do not necessarily contribute toward reaching the intervention goals. Instead, such requirements often take on a life of their own and persist long after the reasons for their initiation have ceased to exist. Workers may resent the time they must devote to administrative details and statistical reports, believing that this time would be better spent in providing direct services to clients. This claim may not be valid,

1. Outputs are the quantitative products (service units, interviews, home visits, and so forth) which the worker is expected to provide. Outcomes refer to the impact of these activities on the client or others in terms of the previously specified goals. See Rosenberg and Brody (1974:13).

yet the workers have no choice but to follow agency instructions. In this way, as in many other ways, the agency directs the activities of the social worker, sets priorities, and governs the pace and pattern of his work.

4. *Budgets.* The budget is one of the most direct ways through which the agency controls and directs its workers. In agencies which provide direct financial aid, assistance grants are usually set according to prescribed budgetary categories and not on the basis of individual need. In other agencies, specific intervention strategies can be implemented only if the budget provides the necessary resources. One of the more effective strategies with teen-age prostitutes, for example, utilizes a temporary shelter to give these girls a chance to escape from the environment which pressures for their continued prostitution; but when budgets do not provide the funds for a shelter, the worker must develop other, less effective intervention strategies. Of course, even under the most liberal budgets there is never enough money for everything. The question is, who decides how the available monies are allocated? Frequently, agency funds are earmarked for specific purposes; many agencies operate on a line-by-line budget where monies can be spent only for the purpose for which the sponsoring organization or funding source intended them to be spent. If, for example, all staff positions were not filled at the beginning of the year, money may still be available on the personnel line, but this money cannot be used to buy urgently needed equipment. Or the budget line for direct relief may be underspent while the special fund for winter clothing may already be exhausted, yet no matter how severe the winter it will not be possible to utilize the unspent funds for buying needed winter coats. Through the process of budgetary control someone other than the social worker decides how the money is to be used or which intervention strategies may be employed. An additional consideration is that budgets are often developed many months (and sometimes years) before the expenditures

occur. Such budgets rarely reflect current or new needs accurately. They therefore tend to be conservative.[2]

5. *Supervision.* Here we will not examine social work supervision in detail but merely note the ways in which the agency uses supervision to influence the worker and his practice. Although social workers practice without being observed by their supervisors, they do receive close supervision over an extended period, sometimes forever. Even though the professional organization of social workers has been encouraging steps toward more autonomous practice, the general pattern of individual, growth-oriented supervision continues to prevail. The social work supervisor tries to be both a teacher and a hierarchical superior, combining educational and assessment functions. In this way the social worker can be guided to utilize the agency's preferred intervention strategies. Supervisors have developed a number of effective ways to educate, train, and socialize workers, but they cannot accurately assess the skill and performance of their workers. Instead, many evaluate their workers on the basis of their "attitude conformity" (Toren, 1970). Given these circumstances workers learn quickly to follow their supervisor's suggestions and to utilize the supervisor as a model. As a result, a worker's commitment to professional objectives is often deflected by his desire to obtain his supervisor's approval. Robert Peabody (1964) reported that 87 percent of the public welfare workers he sampled received conflict-producing instructions from their supervisors and that in such situations eight out of every ten complied with their supervisor rather than with their professional commitment. Andrew Billingsley also noted that the

2. The budgetary process described here is known as budgeting by expenditures. There is also another process, known as budgeting by objectives. This latter process was designed to overcome many of the problems raised here. The federal government's Program Planning and Budgeting System (PPBS) is one example of this newer type of budgeting by objectives. (See Elkin [1969]; Gross [1969].)

professional staff members in the two social agencies he studied were generally oriented toward carrying out agency policies even if these were in conflict with professional commitments. He concludes: "Because social work is tied to the agency, a bureaucratic orientation seems functional" (1964:404). More recently Laura Epstein (1973) confirmed these findings, observing that the institutional framework of social work is not yet ready to support a larger degree of autonomous practice, even though many social workers demand relief from close supervision.

## Bureaucratic and Professional Organizations

In one sense all social agencies are bureaucratic organizations. All follow, more or less, the formal organization pattern associated with the name of Max Weber (1946). Specialization, hierarchy, universal standards, impersonal detachment of the worker, employment on the basis of technical qualifications, promotion on the basis of merit—these are some of the characteristics of the Weberian model of bureaucracy which can be found, to a greater or smaller degree, in every social agency. The relative importance of these bureaucratic features depends on the source of authority in any particular agency.

How does it happen that social workers accept the authority of their supervisor? Weber once suggested two possible sources for organizational authority: *discipline* and *expertise.* In social work, the supervisor's authority generally is derived from both sources. He is both the representative of management and the expert professional. However, whether the emphasis is on one or the other does not depend on the particular supervisor so much as it does on the agency structure and climate. In some agencies discipline-authority is emphasized; in others, expertise-authority. In the former, bureaucratic rules and procedures play a much greater role than in the latter. Generally, expertise-authority is emphasized in organizations which are staffed exclusively or largely by professionally trained workers, while fewer such workers will be found in agencies which place emphasis on discipline-authority.[3] Some writers have designated organizations with an expertise-emphasis as *professional organizations* and those with an emphasis on discipline as *bureaucratic organizations*. Though this dichotomy oversimplifies the actual situation, it does point to certain unique features which characterize professional organizations:

1. *Qualifications of workers.* Only those qualified in terms of training and commitment are employed. If qualified personnel is not available, the organization will limit its services or even close its doors. This may be the reason that professional organizations tend to have waiting lists while bureaucratic organizations usually do not.

2. *Evaluation and error.* The work is evaluated and error is judged only by professional colleagues. Even where recognition and rewards (for example, promotions) come from other sources, such as a board of directors or a city council, the recognition is based on professional evaluations and recommendations.

3. *Debureaucratization.* Collegial relationships are emphasized while little importance is attached to hierarchical relations.

4. *Decision-making.* The organization's mission and goals are determined by professionals on the basis of the profession's commitments and values.

Few social agencies will meet all of these criteria because the ideal type professional organization does not exist, yet some of these features will be encountered in many social agencies.

What difference does it make whether the director of a

3. In social work the terms "professional" and "professionally trained" used to refer to social workers who had earned the MSW degree, but since 1969 graduates of accredited undergraduate programs in social work have been admitted to the National Association of Social Workers (NASW), the professional organization, and are considered professional workers.

social agency is a social worker or a schoolteacher, whether the immediate supervisor is a professional social worker or a veteran employee who, though not a college graduate, was promoted because of his seniority? And if there are differences, will these be reflected in the worker's practice? While it is difficult to generalize, some conclusions can be stated with considerable confidence on the basis of a large number of studies of formal and informal organizations, both within and outside social work.

In the more "professional" agencies social workers usually have more autonomy and greater responsibility for autonomous decisions because there tends to be more delegation of authority to the worker who is in direct contact with the clientele. In the more "bureaucratic" agencies, on the other hand, workers must obtain the supervisor's approval more often and, even when approval is not specifically required, they check more often with their supervisors in order to make sure that they are doing the correct thing. In bureaucratic agencies, routines tend to take on a life of their own and often continue to be followed long after the original reason for their observance has lapsed. In the more professional agencies, on the other hand, routines are viewed as means rather than ends so that procedural changes occur more frequently. Efficiency plays a different role in the two types of agencies. In the bureaucratic organization, efficiency is generally viewed as the ultimate criterion or the highest value in making any decision, while in the professional organization it is only one of several criteria used in evaluating or predicting outcome.

It is generally believed that bureaucracy interferes with the achievement of social work goals. Professional workers tend to be attracted to professional rather than to bureaucratic agencies because they believe that it is difficult to practice social intervention in the latter. However, the findings of at least one major social work experiment, the Midway Project (Anderson and Carlsen, 1971), "appear to be in opposition to the notion that working through bureaucratic procedures is a major obstacle to client service." But the director of this experimental project was quoted earlier in this chapter to the effect that bureaucratic rules and eligibility requirements demanded entirely too much of the time of his experienced workers. Evidently, bureaucratic elements have both functional and dysfunctional consequences, even in social work.

## Social Workers

As noted, almost all social workers are employed by social agencies or by other formal organizations, such as hospitals, schools, and so on.[4] Their status as employees has far-reaching consequences for client-worker relations. Social workers are formal rather than informal helpers. Their help or intervention is not spontaneous and, therefore, may seem to lack authenticity. The informal helper helps only those whom he wants to help. Usually he helps only people whom he knows, people who are like himself and who come from his own social circle. The formal helper is different; he is expected to help all those who qualify. His clients come from different social circles and are not at all like the people whom he would pick as friends. Jesse Jackson (1968), one of the leaders of the civil rights movement, saw one side of this problem when he observed succinctly: "The basic problem here as we

---

4. A new phenomenon is the solo social worker who is instrumental in starting an innovative service outside the established agency network. Such a service might be a store-front information bureau, a drug detoxification center in an apartment, a crash pad for runaway teens, and so on. At times these services are subsidized by a federal grant, by a special grant from the central voluntary funding agency, or by a church. Often other professionals are involved as volunteer workers or sponsors. Whenever these innovative services are successful, they tend to take on the characteristics of the more established social agencies.

Social workers are not the only professionals who are employed. Almost all nurses, librarians, and teachers are employees of large bureaucratic organizations, as are most engineers and many architects. The proportion of employed physicians and lawyers is constantly increasing. The problems facing social workers today may face these professionals before long.

look around [is that] the people [requiring help] are basically young, poor, and colored. Those that are administering the aid are basically old, rich, and white, which is an interesting dilemma."

In a racially divided society, skin-color differences make for social distance while in a more integrated community this would not be a significant distinction. Socioeconomic differences or educational differences may be of great importance in some societies while occupational differences or age variations matter more somewhere else. Social distance refers to those differences which are subjectively important to people. And social distance can become an obstacle to effective social intervention. The wider the social distance between client and worker, the greater the resistance to intervention efforts. This is especially true when the intervention seems imposed and is not desired by the target of the change efforts.

As the social distance increases it also becomes increasingly difficult to involve clients in the social intervention process. A greater social distance usually means that the worker has a higher status than the client, but this higher status level does not increase his credibility as it did in a more traditional society. Instead, in today's world the effectiveness of a worker seems to be related inversely to the social distance gap. The narrower the social distance between client and worker, the greater the worker's influence on the client. For example, in institutions the cottage attendant who typically has little education may be a more effective intervention agent than the highly educated social worker. In mental hospitals, ward attendants often have a greater impact on patients than psychiatrists (Goffman, 1961; Polsky, 1962). Some have suggested that a worker's effectiveness may be more related to frequency of contact than to social distance. Cottage parents spend many hours daily with the children while the social worker may see each child only one or two hours every week. It may be that less social distance and more frequent contact are causally related. Any significant social distance gap may become an obstacle to genuine informal relations, whereas social proximity may facilitate meaningful contacts. Indigenous workers who work and live in the same neighborhood as their clients often find it difficult to separate work time and personal time. When shopping they meet people who are both neighbors and clients; neither they nor their friends seem to know or care whether the meeting takes place on work time or leisure time. The question is whether this type of informal contact facilitates the achievement of social intervention goals. The very informality of the indigenous worker may explain in part the somewhat limited success experienced by these workers in many areas (Loewenberg, 1968).

The social worker's status as an employee tends to limit his autonomy. Agency regulations restrict the worker's options and prohibit certain worker activities altogether. For many decisions he will need his supervisor's approval, and some plans will require authorization by the supervisor's superiors. Clients soon understand that there are ways in which the worker would like to help but cannot because agency rules prescribe otherwise. The worker's need to consult with the supervisor suggests to the alert client that the worker is far less powerful than the client had thought he would be. Clients also learn before too long that the worker-client relationship is not entirely confidential and that many people within the agency (and perhaps even outside it) have knowledge of what was to be a secret between worker and client. And once clients realize that the agency can change workers at will, the development of a secure and trusting relationship becomes even more difficult. These examples of bureaucracy are especially counterproductive if the client's problem resulted from his having difficulties in relating with formal organizations. Instead of receiving the help he needs, the client is made to face yet another bureaucracy.

The social worker employed by a formal organization is accountable to his supervisor, who represents that organization. But the social worker also has a professional commitment to his clients. Most of the time the worker can meet the expectations of both the agency and his clients, but there are instances when this becomes impossible. This was the dilemma faced by Mark Ortego, the community worker assigned to the KENNEDY HOUSES TENANTS COUNCIL. His commitment to the tenants' council was to implement the action strategy, but his supervisor reminded him that the agency would not sanction a militant action strategy of any kind, even if it was developed by the clients. How many workers will disobey an agency regulation which forbids a worker from joining a client picket line even if picketing seems to be the most effective strategy? How many social workers are ready to resign their jobs rather than participate in such obnoxious activities as "midnight raids" designed to check on clients' continued eligibility? Sometimes, of course, agency demands are in such gross violation of professional ethics and human rights that resistance or resignation is the only honorable course to follow. But more often it becomes a question of priorities or emphases. At times it almost seems as if the worker can do more for his client by "playing the game" according to the agency rules than by standing on professional principles. Here the worker faces a real dilemma: should he assign priority to giving service to the particular client (or group) or should he devote his efforts to changing agency rules and regulations so that ultimately all clients will receive more effective service?[5] There are no easy answers to this dilemma.

## Summary

Inherently helpful persons must be understanding, warm, and genuine. These characteristics are as important for social workers as for other helpers. Fear of people, lack of interest, concern with one's own problems, and presenting a façade—

5. This dilemma is quite distinct from another strategy dilemma—whether to concentrate intervention efforts on changing the client or on changing the environment. This latter dilemma was discussed in chapter 4.

these are obstacles which interfere with establishing and maintaining the interpersonal relationships necessary for social intervention. However, these personal characteristics, important as they are, are not the only determinants of the social worker's practice pattern. The organizational structure of the social agency which employs the worker is another factor which greatly affects his practice.

The agency's interests do not always coincide with the profession's goals or the worker's objectives. A recognition of the sources of the agency's sanctions will help in understanding this discrepancy. Within each social agency there are forces which emphasize bureaucratic elements and others which stress professional elements. These different forces are related to discipline-authority and expertise-authority and find expression in various ways in the practice of social workers. Specific differences can be found in the commitment of staff, judging of error, decision-making, and delegation of authority. The interplay of the environmental characteristics of the social agency and the personality characteristics of the social worker set the pattern for social intervention practice.

# chapter seven

# Developing
# a Social Intervention
# Strategy

The social worker who wants to be effective must understand his clients and their problems—but understanding alone is not enough. Understanding is only the first step toward doing something about the problem. And this "doing something" must involve more than well-intentioned but aimless activities. The purpose of the social intervention activity is to achieve the specific goal or goals, identified by the client and the worker, in the most effective and most efficient manner possible. Random activities and routine interventions at times may be helpful but generally are haphazard. To increase the chances for successful goal achievement, worker and client must develop a plan which will guide them throughout the implementation phase of the social intervention process. This plan is called the strategy.

If the strategy is to be helpful, it must identify: (1) the person(s) or element(s) which must be changed; (2) the short-term objectives; (3) the specific intervention activities which are necessary to achieve the desired outcome; and (4) the specific tasks which each participant must accomplish in order to effect goal achievement. The strategy should never be a generalized statement which can be applied to any number of problems but must be a specific plan developed in response to a particular problem situation. Though the strategy may be based on generalized procedures and past experience with similar problems, the exact details of the strategy are derived from, and must be congruent with, the specific problem and a particular set of goals.

*Social work methods.* Casework, group work, community organization do not represent strategies since they "hint neither at the purpose of the intervention nor the operational procedure" (Bisno, 1969). Instead, the traditional methods reveal only the number of people in the target population. When a social worker reports that he is utilizing "group work," we understand that there is more than one person in the unit which receives service but we do not know anything about the problem, the goals, or his intervention activities.

The strategy must fit the particular problem. It must not be predetermined by the agency's routine service or by the worker's preferred modality of intervention. When a person presents a problem to a group worker, it should not be assumed that the strategy must include participation in a group. Even though group participation is socially desirable, it should not be included in the strategy unless this type of intervention relates specifically to the problem and the goals. Sometimes a worker who knows only one method feels that, rather than send an applicant away empty-handed, he should suggest a strategy based on this method, even if this approach does not exactly fit the problem. Or some social workers will define problems and identify goals in a way which requires the use of the very strategy with which they have the most experience. Even though this strategy is compatible with the problem and the goal (as defined by the worker), the social intervention is likely to be ineffective because it fails to deal with the client's real problem. For example, at one time many social workers urged unmarried mothers to give up their babies for adoption. This strategy seemed to "fit" because the problem was defined only in terms of the baby's immediate well-being; this strategy also happened to coincide with a service that was readily available and with which these workers had a great deal of experience. Had the problem been defined in other terms, such as the needs of the young mother, additional goals might have emerged and other strategies might have taken priority. We are not suggesting that adoption is necessarily a wrong strategy but merely pointing out that it should not become a standard solution for unwed mothers. In some public child welfare agencies, to cite another example, foster home placement is relied upon almost exclusively for older children and adolescents who cannot live with their own parents, yet another strategy (perhaps institutional placement or radical intervention in the home environment) might be more effective for a particular youngster (Wasserman, 1970).

Strategy development is the last step in the assessment process and is followed by contract negotiations and implementation activities. The strategy, in other words, serves as the bridge between assessment and implementation. Assessment is incomplete and meaningful implementation all but impossible without the development of a strategy. In actual practice, certain steps of assessment may occur simultaneously with strategy development and contract negotiations.

Strategy development is based on the assumption that rational planning is desirable for social intervention. Even though social workers must be flexible and ready to change, success in goal achievement depends in no small measure on effective planning. Understanding the distinction between strategy and tactics may be helpful in this connection. In the military use of these terms, strategy refers to the planning and maneuvering prior to the battle with an enemy, while tactics denote the rearrangement and reordering of resources during the battle for the purpose of taking advantage of developing opportunities. Similarly, the social worker and the client, after developing a strategy, always make tactical changes to take advantage of new opportunities. Let us say that the strategy developed with MRS. KING called for her going to work after completing a secretarial training course. One short-term objective was to find a solution to the child-care problem: what to do with her children while she was at school and, later, at work.

The specific intervention activity relative to this short-term objective called for Mrs. King to explore a number of different child-care arrangements to find the one that seemed best to her. When Mrs. King's sister unexpectedly moved into town and offered to have the two youngest children live with her for the next two months, client and worker agreed that this was a far better temporary solution than any they had thought of until then. Accepting the sister's offer involved a change in tactics but not in strategy. Tactical changes occur relatively often; strategy changes do occur but less frequently. If there is need for constant strategy changes, the worker must consider this as an indicator that something is amiss.

## Target Selection

Selecting the most effective target (or targets) is one of the key tasks in strategy development. We define the *target* as the element(s) in the environment and/or in the client which need(s) to be changed in order to make goal achievement possible. There is no prior assumption that the best target is the client, another person, or an element in the social system. The choice of the most suitable target is not arbitrary but is derived from the assessment.

*Multiple targets.* Since most problems which come to the attention of social workers have more than one cause, it happens often that a strategy will indicate more than one target. Sometimes there is a different target for each of the sequential short-term objectives, while at other times several targets are present throughout the social intervention process. The idea that there is only one correct target (or one group of targets) for every goal is an oversimplification and most probably a mistaken notion. For most problems which come to the attention of social workers there will be a variety of potential targets, each offering some opportunity for goal achievement. With limited resources, client and worker may have to decide which target(s) offer the best opportunity. MRS. KING, it will be recalled, was unable to obtain information from the hospital about her husband's medical condition. If the objective is to obtain this information, there are at least two potential targets: (1) Mrs. King and/or (2) the hospital staff.

The first target, the client herself, suggests intervention activities which focus on helping Mrs. King become a more effective and more forceful person, perhaps teaching her certain skills necessary for dealing with bureaucratic officials. Other types of activities are indicated if the target is the hospital staff. In this instance, client and worker agreed that learning how to deal with a bureaucratic organization was not the immediate problem. They needed to know Mr. King's medical condition and prognosis before they could proceed with other plans for the King family. They agreed, therefore, that it would be best in terms of the over-all problem that the worker get in touch with the hospital. He immediately called the hospital social worker and had the desired information within twenty minuters. Note that the immediate objective was achieved without making any permanent changes in either the client or in the environment. But scarce resources were now available for working on other parts of this problem.

In another example, a worker received complaints from the relatives of several older adults who were patients in a nursing home. Each of the complainants alleged abusive treatment by the nursing and caretaker staff. It was obvious that the goal of the social intervention should be the elimination of abusive treatment. One "logical" target was the director and the staff of the nursing home. With this group as a target, the social worker could attempt to change staff behavior patterns in order to ensure a more humane treatment of the patients. But at an agency staff meeting the worker learned that other workers had received similar complaints about other nursing homes. The staff discussed the situation and wondered whether a strategy which called for intervention with each individual nursing home staff would not be too time-consuming and require more resources than were available.

Perhaps another strategy with a more central target could result in changes in patient-care practices in all nursing homes. One worker noted that most nursing homes receive a large part of their income from Medicaid payments. He wondered whether the Medicaid staff in Washington and in the regional offices could be designated as the target. In this case, the intervention activity would focus on helping the Medicaid staff enforce regulations (or issue new ones) designed to prevent abusive care in nursing homes. Another worker thought that the low reimbursement rates made more adequate care unlikely. He thought that Congress might be a more effective target since the congressmen and senators would have to pass any legislation which raised the reimbursement rates. The staff decided on a two-level strategy. In terms of the specific problem identified by the clients, it was decided to continue efforts to effect changes in the particular nursing homes about which complaints had been received. The director of each home was designated as the initial target since his cooperation was a prerequisite for other work with staff. Once his agreement had been secured, the next target might be the head nurse. While these efforts took place, another social worker was assigned to explore the feasibility of effecting system changes with the Medicaid staff.

It was no oversight that the individual patients were not identified as the targets. They are the victims of the abusive treatment and will benefit from any successful intervention, but they are not the target since any changes must occur in the nursing homes and their staffs, not among the patients. This example also illustrates how target identification and intervention activity selection are intertwined and not always sequential stages of strategy development. Sometimes the target is selected first; at other times, short-term objectives come first; and at still other times, the target is selected only after the intervention activity has already been identified.

*Indirect targets.* The intervention activity is not always aimed directly at the identified target. At times changes in the target can be secured more efficiently by directing the intervention activity at another element, an indirect target, which in turn will influence the primary target. In this case, desired changes in the target may occur without any direct intervention contacts. One example of an indirect intervention strategy comes from the field of early child development. Many researchers have become convinced that once a child enters elementary school, cultural deprivation is almost irreversible. They believe that the crucial time to reverse the consequences of deprivation is during the first three years of life, the earlier the better. As a result, a number of intervention programs have been designed to give children from deprived backgrounds a better chance later on.

One immediate objective of many of these programs is to provide young children with genuine emotional relationships with significant adults, particularly with their mother. One program used successfully in a number of poverty neighborhoods is a games workshop where mothers learn how to play with their young children. Mothers who participate in these workshops can borrow games from a game library. Even though the goal is healthy personality development in the children, not in the mothers, the mothers and not the children are designated as direct targets. This is done because it is believed that changes in young children will occur only in response to behavioral changes in the mother and in other persons who regularly associate with them (Blank and Solomon, 1969; Caldwell, 1969; Dittman, 1968; Kedem, 1974).

We noted earlier that the target(s) is deduced from the assessment. One of the factors examined during assessment is the cultural setting in which the problem has developed and in which the social intervention will occur. The cultural setting often limits or directs the choice of target. In the matrilineal Navaho culture, for example, child support cannot be sought from a father who no longer lives with the child's mother, as would be the case in most other American communities. In the traditional Chicano family the central position of the father cannot be ignored; when working with such a family it would be an error not to include the father in the first approach. One social worker in a home for delinquent boys was concerned that some of the boys were never visited by their families. By learning something about the communities from which these boys came, the worker was able to determine the most promising intervention targets—in one case it was a mother; in another, an older sister; and in a third, the local politician was identified as the person who could best convince the boy's family of the importance of visiting.

## Developing Intervention Activities

The choice of an appropriate target is one step in strategy development. The selection of specific intervention activities is another. The objective here is to identify a set of activities which will permit the most effective and most efficient achievement of the desired goals. Though this statement may appear elementary, even redundant, research findings suggest that social workers do not always select intervention activities in this manner. Instead there appears to be a tendency to emphasize intervention activities which are highly valued, regardless of their effectiveness. Activities may be selected because they are believed to encourage client involvement and self-determination or because they permit the utilization of "professional" techniques. Some social workers seem to select intervention activities without giving sufficient thought to the outcome. Aaron Rosen and Ronda Connaway (1969) say that "it is unfortunate, indeed, that in the past social workers have tended to choose their methods primarily on the basis of value consistency, disregarding the criteria of method efficacy and purpose-method correspondence." Rosen and Connaway agree that intervention activities must be consistent with societal and professional values, but they warn against overemphasizing this one criterion at the expense of other criteria, particularly at the expense of effectiveness of outcome. Other investigators have reported that many workers do not consciously select intervention activities but depend instead on their intuition, experience, and feelings (Macarov and Golan, 1973).

*Alternative activities.* A number of different intervention activities may be possible for any one problem or goal. We should be suspicious when someone claims that there is only one way to handle a given problem. Chances are that insufficient thought has been given to defining the problem, to setting the goal, or to developing strategy options. Skill in developing different intervention options and in selecting the most appropriate and relevant one is a characteristic of the effective social worker. Unless a worker has developed several alternative intervention activities, he has no choice and no way of knowing whether what he is doing is better than something else. But even when he has developed several options, he must learn to assess these—and this can be problematic. How can a worker know in advance which intervention activity will be most effective? Rosen and Connaway (1969) suggest that the social worker select the activity which *"has been found* to be most effective in accomplishing the objectives of the service" (their italics). Past experience with similar problems is a helpful but not always a sufficient guide since the details of every situation vary.

Many social workers contend that outcomes cannot be estimated in advance with any degree of accuracy. They therefore attempt to select intervention activities which are more or less logically related to the desired outcomes. The assumption is that intervention activities cannot be effective when they bear no relation to the goals. In line with this assumption Alfred Kahn (1973) points to the lack of success reported for many of the major social work studies that used intervention activities which were hardly appropriate for the clients served or for the objectives to be achieved. How are therapeutic interventions related to the goal of securing adequate income? Or group activities, to preventing pregnancies? Social workers evidently find it difficult to select activities that are logically related to the identified goals. In one study more than half of all worker activities were congruent with neither long-range goals nor short-term objectives. Yet the reported congruence rate was about twice as high as would have resulted from chance alone. In other words, some of the workers in this study did select intervention activities which were logically related to objectives, but many made practice decisions on some other basis (Macarov and Golan, 1973).

Our discussion so far has dealt only with worker activities, but according to our practice model, the strategy must specify both worker and client activities. Joint participation of client and worker in strategy decisions must lead to tasks for both of them. To be sure, worker and client do not participate in the same fashion. Each partipates in a way appropriate to his role and his experience. But complementary participation, with each contributing according to his best abilities, should be the rule in all phases of the social intervention process.

## Strategy Selection

There are no prescriptions or formulas which will help a social worker become an instant expert in strategy development. But there are a number of hints that will ease the way. Perhaps the most important is to consider various alternative strategies before selecting *the* strategy. There is a danger that a worker has a standard strategy for each major type of problem that he will encounter. To avoid this danger it may help to practice "thinking big," supplementing the traditional with the new, the customary with the creative, and the habitual with the innovative. A modified brainstorming technique has been found useful by some; here a group of workers (or even a single worker by himself) develops strategy options for a problem but suspends critical judgment until after a large number of options have been listed. Alternate approaches are too often overlooked or prematurely dismissed because at first glance they seem impossible or unattainable. However, no strategy should be selected merely because "it feels good" or "sounds right." Nor should a strategy be accepted because it is novel. After alternate options have been developed, they should be subjected to rigorous analysis and assessment. In order to select the best option possible at least the following three criteria must be examined: (1) effectiveness; (2) efficiency; (3) motivation, capacity, and readiness.

1. *Effectiveness.* How effective will the proposed strategy be in achieving the desired goal? Can a change in the target produce the desired outcome? Or is another target more suitable? Goal achievement is the crucial (but not the only) criterion for strategy selection. A strategy may be elegant or popular, but unless it contributes toward reaching the desired outcome it is not suitable and should be revised or discarded in favor of one that promises better results. When comparing two alternative options, the one that promises to be more effective is the more desirable one, all other factors being the same. Sometimes a given strategy appears effective because it solves an immediate problem, but the social worker must also consider the long-term impact. Placing a child in an institution may solve an immediate problem, but may not be consistent with the eventual outcome desired for the child or for his family. A food order may help an unemployed father feed his family, but this approach may not be the most effective way of helping him regain his economic independence. Assistance with immediate problems must, of course, be provided; yet concern with the immediate must not divert the social worker from assessing the effectiveness of the strategy (and other options) in terms of the long-range goals. The social workers' effective way of dealing with small and big emergencies may have boomeranged by contributing toward the fostering of long-term, chronic dependency among some welfare recipients. Social workers must develop new and more creative intervention strategies which are congruent with short-term objectives as well as with long-range goals. When working with

populations in economic need, for example, ways must be found that will provide resources for daily living and at the same time will restore and strengthen the independence and autonomy of those receiving such emergency aid.

The major problem facing social workers in applying the criterion of effectiveness is their lack of experience in utilizing outcome measures. The illogical division between practice and research has contributed to a state of affairs where too many social workers pay attention only to practice concerns, leaving outcome evaluations to others. But responsible practice requires that every practitioner constantly monitors his practice, before, during, and after the actual intervention. Estimating the effectiveness of any proposed strategy should become a standard procedure in strategy development. A practitioner's skill in estimation will increase if he consistently compares pre-intervention estimates of effectiveness with post-intervention evaluations of outcome.

2. *Efficiency*. After estimating the effectiveness of an intervention activity, the worker must examine whether there are better ways to achieve the same outcome. When comparing two strategies with the same degree of effectiveness, the worker must determine which is the least costly in terms of money, time, manpower, client efforts, and other resources. When two strategies are comparable in effectiveness, the less costly will be the more desirable, all other factors being equal. With limited resources (and the available resources are always less than those needed), it is difficult to justify a strategy that is not efficient if a more efficient and equally effective one is available. But this does not mean that a social worker will always select the "cheapest" strategy. The strategy which appears to be least expensive often turns out to be a very expensive one. Thus, housing an unemployed family in a run-down slum tenement may require a smaller cash outlay from the current year's departmental budget than continuing the mortgage payments on the family's home—but the "cheaper" strategy may create many more problems than it will solve,

and, in the long run, may be much more expensive. Often social workers will respond to requests for help by providing their standard service without considering whether there might not be a more efficient way of helping. An office interview with a client may be "efficient"—but another intervention activity may be more efficient. A street demonstration may be an efficient method to achieve the specified objective—but not always. The efficiency of each proposed strategy cannot be assumed but must be assessed on the basis of the facts of each specific situation.

The efficiency of a proposed strategy is evaluated not only in terms of its monetary cost; the efforts necessary to overcome resistance also are a cost which must be considered. If the resistance to a particular strategy is too strong, an otherwise effective strategy may have to be abandoned for another, less effective one. Family planning, for example, is a strategy which, when employed together with other programs, has been found effective in helping young families gain economic security and independence. However, among groups where there is strong religious or cultural opposition to family planning, this strategy may be less efficient than others. Generally, it is more difficult to modify human behavior than to alter the environment or to introduce technological changes. Strategies that depend on the latter kind of changes may, therefore, be more efficient than those that call for behavioral changes. If the objective is to provide relatives with more information about hospitalized patients, it may be more efficient to install a computerized information system than to attempt to change staff attitudes and behaviors.

But whenever efficiency is stressed as an exclusive criterion, there is danger of a value-strategy conflict. If the strategy is selected merely because it promises to be efficient, it may violate the very values for which social work stands. It may be "efficient" to crowd a nursing home to twice its capaicty, but such a strategy is hardly consistent with basic social work values. In this example "efficient" may refer either to the nursing

home operator who will profit from the larger number of patients or to the social worker who must somehow or other find
housing for his many older adult clients. In the same manner,
it may be more efficient to convince a victim of discrimination
and exploitation to accept his fate quietly, but such a strategy
does violence to the basic social work concept of the dignity of
every human being.

Whenever an easy goal is pursued instead of a more difficult one, greater efficiency may result—but the service provided may be only partial or superficial. With most people
there are a number of different objectives which must be met.
MRS. KING, for example, had several problems for which she
needed help; each called for one or more objectives. Some of
these objectives were met more easily than others; obtaining
information about her husband's condition was one of the
easy objectives. Yet a strategy which was designed to secure
only the easy objectives would be inadequate since it would not
come to grips with the more important of Mrs. King's problems. A stroke victim, to take another example, needs medical
and rehabilitative services, while his family may require financial support and perhaps counseling to accept the changed
family conditions. It will be much easier to make the financial
arrangements than to restore the patient to autonomous functioning, but financial aid is only one step in the social intervention; without other strategies money alone will be insufficient.
Similarly, a street worker may find it easier (and therefore
more efficient) to involve his gang members in a basketball
tournament than to have them resume their interrupted education. Again, the first-named activity is desirable and a step in
the right direction—but only a step.

Overemphasizing the efficiency criterion can result in
problems because there is a tendency to avoid those intervention activities which are difficult to achieve. On the other
hand, the danger of ignoring the efficiency criterion is that,
despite the worker's best intentions, his efforts will bear little
success—or greater success could have been achieved if a

more efficient strategy had been selected. But the worker who does not consider the efficiency criterion will never know that there could have been a more efficient strategy.

3. *Motivation, capacity, and readiness.* Even when a strategy is believed to be effective and efficient, it is important to assess the motivation, capacities, and state of readiness of the major participants in the social intervention process. If client participation is desired, then client readiness or potential readiness to participate in the proposed strategy is of critical importance. If the client cannot be motivated sufficiently to become involved in a certain activity, it may be best not to pursue that strategy even if it is thought to be the most effective and most efficient one.[1]

One social worker reported that a foster home placement for a seven-year-old girl appeared to be the best temporary solution after the sudden death of her mother; but when her father categorically rejected this plan, another perhaps less efficient strategy was devised. In a similar situation some months earlier this same social worker had not paid sufficient attention to another client's lack of readiness; in that instance the child became so obstreperous after being placed in a foster home that she had to be returned to her father within forty-eight hours. While a person's motivation and readiness are not fixed, this type of change often takes a long time to effect so that alternate interim arrangements must be made.

A person's lack of capacity may also counterindicate a proposed strategy. The parents of Karen, a seventeen-year-old cerebral palsy victim, wanted her to study bookkeeping at a local business college. Karen was agreeable, and the rehabilitation worker also thought that some sort of training program would be desirable because it would help Karen in many dif-

---

1. The strategy is not selected for the sake of making client participation possible. Instead, we are suggesting that an efficient and effective strategy may not be suitable if the client is not ready to participate appropriately. Some strategies may not require client participation during particular phases; for such phases, client motivation is not relevant.

ferent ways. The worker checked out the physical arrangements at the school to make sure that Karen's physical handicap would not interfere with her school attendance. He also
arranged for Karen to take a number of intelligence and aptitude tests. When these indicated that Karen would not be able
to meet the intellectual demands of the program, the worker
realized that another strategy was necessary even though this
client was highly motivated. Her capacity simply was not sufficient for this particular program.

Sometimes the readiness or capacity or motivation of the
client is crucial, but at other times that of other participants is
even more important. A strategy designed to return a school
dropout to the town's only high school will be in vain if the
board of education is unwilling to alter the readmission policy.
While legal action may be used to force the members of the
board to change the rules, past experience has shown that the
use of the courts is a time-consuming strategy. Any revision of
the readmission rules will not come in time to help this particular boy. In this case it will be necessary to devise another
strategy even though the client's motivation, capacity, and
readiness to return to high school are extremely high. A job-
training program may seem to be an effective and efficient
way to help a released convict acquire a useful and employable
skill, but if at the end of the training period no job can be
found or created for this person, another strategy may be indicated. There are a number of effective and efficient ways to
reduce the incidence of unplanned teen-age pregnancies, but
is any community ready to adopt a strategy which calls for the
free distribution of birth-control pills in high school cafeterias?

At times the techniques and knowledge necessary to implement a proposed strategy have not yet been developed sufficiently. At other times there may be a question whether the
means or resources required to implement a proposed strategy are available. If monies or manpower or worker skills are
lacking and cannot be found, a different strategy must be

devised. But here we face another dilemma, the danger that community and worker readiness will become a priority criterion. If we select only those strategy options for which resources are readily available or for which the community is most ready, regardless of their effectiveness and efficiency, we run the risk of engaging in what Marris and Rein (1967) call "piecemeal pragmatism" where problems and goals become less important than the availability of funds. If funds for a new program are available, we will use the monies for whatever problem comes along. Thus, Daniel Moynihan (1969) ascribes the final collapse of the war on poverty to the fact that strategies were selected on the basis of what was available for speedy implementation rather than on the basis of what was effective and efficient. Community and agency readiness are important, but they should not become the sole criterion for assessing a social intervention strategy—and this caution is equally valid for intervention strategies on the individual, group, and community level.

## Summary

Strategy development calls for skilled and purposeful analysis of problems, goals, and proposed solutions. The elements of a complete social intervention strategy include: (1) the change target; (2) short-term objectives; (3) specific intervention activities; and (4) specific tasks for each of the participants. Before selecting a strategy, the social worker and the client should develop a number of appropriate alternatives and evaluate these in terms of: (1) effectiveness; (2) efficiency; and (3) motivation, capacity, and readiness of the various participants. Sometimes a proposed strategy rates high on all three criteria; at other times, an effective strategy may be so expensive or so difficult that it is virtually impossible to implement it, while a seemingly efficient strategy may be quite ineffective.

Strategy development is not the search for the perfect solution but for the best possible way of dealing with a problem in order to achieve the desired objectives. The social worker's task is to select, together with the client and other participants, the optimum strategy; that is, the strategy that is best under the existing circumstances.

# Part Two
# Core Skills

# Introduction

Skills are an important ingredient in social intervention, yet the learning of specific skills may be limiting and constraining for the student who must prepare himself for a lifetime of professional service. Those who hold this position, as we do, face a dilemma in deciding which skills are appropriate for inclusion in a university social work course. Teaching too few skills or the wrong kind of skills may not adequately prepare the student for social work practice, while teaching too many skills may produce a technician rather than a professional worker.

The usual answer to this dilemma is that generic or basic skills are suitable for teaching at the undergraduate level. This answer may be correct, but it is not sufficiently precise to serve the teacher as a guide. Sidney A. Fine's work on task analysis (1967) offers some further clues. We have freely adapted Fine's ideas for the present purpose.

On every assignment a social worker must be proficient in two general types of skill—adaptive and functional skills. For a social worker the adaptive skills are those which he will need in order to adjust to the organizational and interpersonal environment of the bureaucratic social agency. Functional skills are the skills necessary to relate to, and cope with, things, data, and people as the social worker goes about discharging his primary professional responsibilities. They include such tasks as problem-solving, decision-making, analysis, assessment, and so on. Both adaptive skills and functional skills can be further subdivided into specific-content skills (which are necessary to perform a specific job or task) and general or generic skills (which are applicable to all kinds of jobs and, once learned, are freely transferable).

The primary learning of generic-adaptive skills occurs early in life when a youngster learns how to adapt to his environment. Specific-content skills, both of the adaptive and the functional variety, are most efficiently taught in in-service training programs or in technical education programs; they are most effectively learned on the job or in preparation for a specific job. Generic functional skills appear most appropriate for inclusion in a college curriculum—and some of these will form the subject matter of this part of the book. The skills selected for emphasis here are those used most often by social workers. Other professionals use the same or similar skills, but the focus here will be on these skills as they are used by social workers.

A textbook can provide only an introduction to skills. It can raise questions and offer cues but, strictly speaking, it cannot teach skills. Learning of skills occurs in the field when the student applies the concepts and theories he has learned to real-life situations. But the first step in skill learning, as Eileen Younghusband (1967:366) points out, "is a reasonably accurate perception by the learner of the skills to be mastered." And this will be our objective in the following chapters.

# chapter eight

# Interviewing, Observing, and Writing

Interviewing, observing, and writing are skills that play an important role in every phase of the social intervention process. The social worker who is not a skillful interviewer, a proficient observer, and an adequate writer will be less than effective. Admittedly, these skills are not unique to social work. Newspaper reporters use these same skills, and so do lawyers, clergymen, and many other professionals. Yet when social workers employ these skills, there are differences arising out of the unique value structure and the specific objectives of social work. In this chapter, therefore, our focus will be primarily on how these skills are used in the social intervention process.

## Interviewing

"A conversation with a purpose" reads one classic definition of the interview (Bingham and Moore, 1924). And it is the *purpose* which differentiates the interview from a conversation. Two friends will chat because they enjoy each other's company or because they want to share their experiences. Two strangers, sitting on a park bench or waiting at a bus stop, will talk about the weather or the deteriorating bus service. Or they may be curious about each other: "Where are you going?" "Do you know Barbara Jones?" "What do you do?" In the social work interview it is also necessary to share past experiences and to talk about current events. The social worker asks questions to find out certain things about the other person, just as the client or applicant will ask questions to obtain information about the agency and the worker. But the purpose of the social work interview is not to strengthen friendship bonds nor is its purpose to satisfy the worker's idle curiosity. Instead, the social work interview is an instrument for helping worker and client achieve the social intervention objectives and goals. In addition to this generalized purpose, there are also more specific purposes for each particular interview session. These specific objectives include exploration, clarification, advice, and so on.

Purpose is one difference between a conversation and a social work interview. *Preparation* is another. A conversation usually does not require any specific preparation. It moves along more or less freely without a charted course. The social worker, on the other hand, prepares himself to make sure that each interview is a step forward toward achieving the intervention objectives. Sometimes there is little or no time for advance preparation because a client arrives unexpectedly or because an entirely new and unplanned development is presented in the midst of an interview. But planning and preparation are desirable whenever possible. If the worker is prepared, he can select the most appropriate techniques and methods. He will be clear about what is possible in today's interview with this particular client and what is better delayed until some other time.

The first step in preparing for an interview is a review and an assessment of all the information already available about the person coming for the interview. On the basis of this material the worker will select a suitable interview strategy. With some clients a nondirective technique may not be suitable for exploration but quite effective for clarification, while for other clients a nondirective technique will always be inappropriate, no matter what the objective. The worker must decide, on the basis of the available information, where the interview shall take place, whether in his office, in the client's home, or in some other place. Since the interview's purpose is to facilitate effective and efficient goal achievement, the decision about the place of the interview should never be a routine one.

Preparing for an interview means to learn as much as possible about the other person before the interview. For all but the very first interview, the preparation starts immediately after the conclusion of the previous interview. When the worker reviews his notes or writes up the record, he begins to plan for the next encounter. What went especially well today? What did not succeed? Why did the client respond to certain questions the way he did? The answers to these and similar questions should be more than mere guesses. A skillful review of past encounters will reveal much valuable information which can be useful in preparing for the next interview.

Some preparation is desirable even before the first interview. Unless the service is rendered on a drop-in basis where people can come without a prior appointment or application, the worker should learn the client's name before he enters the room. The name can be obtained from the application form or from the appointment roster. Greeting a person by name, and pronouncing his name correctly, is more than a nice gesture. It tells the other person that the worker thinks of him as a real person, not just another case or number. If the worker does not know how to pronounce the name correctly, he should ask rather than guess since few people enjoy hearing their name mispronounced. Using the correct name with the correct title is always important but especially with persons who come from disadvantaged groups. Mr. Wilson, who has been called "hey , boy" for most of his life, will respond more positively when addressed as Mr. Wilson. And Mrs. Brown will be relieved that she is not called "Sally" by a worker who is younger than her youngest child.

In the beginning phase of the interview the worker must attempt to reduce tensions and decrease hostilities so that mutual engagement will be possible. Only when the client feels comfortable and is at ease with the worker will he be able to participate fully in the interview. The worker should encourage the client to take off his topcoat. In rainy or snowy weather the client may be more comfortable if he can take off his boots. Needless to say, the worker must give his full attention to the client. If the worker is talking on the phone when the client enters, he must at least acknowledge his presence by greeting him and then terminate the telephone conversation as quickly as possible. If it is not possible to stop telephone calls during the interview, the worker should make the incoming calls brief, offering to call back later. When it is necessary to keep a client waiting, either at the beginning or during the interview, the worker must apologize and show his regret for inconveniencing him.

Mutual engagement is at the core of the interview. Both the social worker and the client must participate if the interview is to be fruitful. But until mutual engagement has been achieved, the worker has a special responsibility to reach out and help the client become an active participant. Setting the tone is one way in which the worker can help. Asking the right questions at the right time is another way. Many people do not know how to express themselves or state their problem. They may not have much experience in formal communications or they may be too embarrassed to talk about their problem to a stranger. A few strategic questions followed by sympathetic listening may provide sufficient encouragement. Timing is of great significance. Asking a question too early may be perceived as criticism or unwarranted probing, but raising the same question twenty minutes later may be the signal to start talking. "What happened last night?" might be the key to unlocking the problem, or it can result in a spell of tears and monosyllabic groans.

When Mark Ortego, the community worker assigned to the KENNEDY HOUSES TENANTS COUNCIL, first arrived in the project he visited with Mr. Scott, the council's chairman.

Though he was warmly welcomed, Mark soon noticed a certain reluctance, and before long the conversation came to a halt. At first Mark thought that Mr. Scott might have had unpleasant experiences when talking with strangers in the past. But before long he realized that Mr. Scott really did not know how to express himself. When asked a direct question he would respond willingly but only briefly. Mark followed this clue and asked many, many questions in order to help Mr. Scott participate in the interview. Normally, he would have asked fewer questions but here, he felt, this was the best way to proceed.

**Interviewing Techniques.** The social worker must play an active role in the interview, but must not dominate. Encouraging the client to talk will not only ensure his participation in the interview but will also provide the worker with feedback data which will keep him alert to what he is doing. The skill in interviewing lies in developing effective techniques which at one and the same time give direction and focus to the interview but avoid domination and control of the client's responses.

The way questions are asked, the type of questions used, and the language employed by the social worker are important elements of the effective interviewing technique. In asking the questions, the social worker should project the warm and accepting tone of voice of a helpful person rather than the sarcastic and accusing tone typical of many prosecuting attorneys. Even when the worker knows that the client is distorting the truth or withholding facts, he should reach out to make it easy for him to change his report without losing face.

*Open* and *closed questions* are the two general types of questions used by social workers. Most of the time it is possible to use questions of either type; the social worker must therefore know the advantages and disadvantages of each. "Mrs. Dore, what happeded when you and your husband quarreled last week?" is an open question since it permits the client to define and answer the question in his own way. In answering this question, Mrs. Dore can focus on those events which she feels are most important. She can talk about the circumstances which led to the quarrel, she can describe how her husband abused her, she may relate how their children reacted to seeing their parents fight, or she can discuss her plans for escaping from her predicament. The answer to the open question will reveal what bothers her, even though the social worker may not learn much about the specific events which led to the quarrel. On the other hand, a social worker might ask, "Does your husband beat you often?" This is a closed question because it forces an answer along the specific dimensions which are of current interest to the worker. Of course, "beating" and "often" may have different meanings for Mrs. Dore and the worker so that in fact the answer may not be along the dimension desired by the worker.

The closed question is particularly effective for obtaining or verifying specific factual information ("Did you receive your check yesterday?" "Mrs. Green, do you want to move into the housing project?"), but it does not permit a person to reveal how he really feels nor does it always give him an opportunity to express his doubts and hesitations. It might be better to ask Mrs. Green, "What do you think about your moving into an apartment in the project?" since the response to the open question is often nonspecific, though revealing, it may be necessary to follow up this type of question with additional closed or open questions. After Mrs. Green has told the worker that she sees both the good and the bad points of living in the project, the worker still needs to know whether she really wants to move there. At this point a specific closed question might be appropriate. It is possible, of course, to start with a closed question and follow this with a "Why?" but in Mrs. Green's case (and in many other cases) the "why" would only lead to a defense or explanation of the answer to the original question. When the primary objective of the question is to facilitate the engagement of the other person, closed questions are usually more effective. Mr. Scott remained almost silent when Mark Ortego asked him to tell him what happened when the KENNEDY HOUSES TENANTS COUNCIL made contact with the City Housing Commission last year, but when Mark asked specific closed questions ("Did they answer your letter? Did they give you an appointment?"), Mr. Scott became more verbal and started to participate.

Every worker must be sure that his questions have been correctly understood, no matter whether they are open or closed questions. This is especially important when worker and client come from different cultural or socioeconomic backgrounds because the very same word or phrase may have different meanings in different groups. When the worker asked Mrs. Dore whether her husband beat her, he wanted to know if her husband hit her in anger. But in Mrs. Dore's neighborhood "beating" was used only as a synonym for whipping with a belt. Even though she had black-and-blue marks all over her body, Mrs. Dore told the worker that her husband did not beat her since he only used his fists! The answer to an open question usually will indicate whether the worker's question has been understood correctly, but this is not always apparent when a closed question is used. Clients may nod their head and say "yes" to indicate that they are listening or because they think that some reply is expected, but not necessarily because they understood what has been asked. A worker cannot assume that a client will understand him merely because both speak English.

The importance of using a language style which the client can understand is obvious but not always easy to implement. Technical language and social work vocabulary always should be avoided but dialect or slang expressions may at times be appropriate, especially to make sure that a question is really understood. One client, for example, was unable to provide the name of the "putative father" but had no difficulty in naming the "fellow who got you pregnant." However, social workers should avoid the regular use of dialect or slang because it will be viewed as condescending.

Misunderstanding is a two-way street. Sometimes the client misunderstands the social worker and at other times the social worker misunderstands what the client has said. The reasons are often the same. The worker attaches a meaning different from that intended because he does not understand the words used by the client or because he interprets the message in terms of his own perspective rather than in terms of that of the client. If the worker does not understand the client and is aware of this, he should not hesitate to ask for clarification. But more frequently he thinks that he understands when he really does not.

Interpretive summaries may help avoid this type of misunderstanding. In this feedback technique the social worker summarizes in his own words what he has learned from the client. Used at appropriate intervals during the interview, the interpretive summary serves to verify the worker's understanding of the situation and gives the client an opportunity to correct anything which the worker has misunderstood. At the same time, the interpretive summary can point the way to the next objective and thus can serve as a bridge between the present and the future. But the interpretive summary should not be used in situations where the client feels that he cannot disagree with what the worker says or in situations where the client believes that whatever the worker says is more correct than his own version. Only when a mutual give-and-take is possible will the interpretive summary be a useful tool. If this is not the case, other techniques are required for structuring the situation to permit assessment of the correctness of the worker's understanding.

Listening is more important than talking, yet there are times during most interviews when the social worker will have to do most of the talking. The worker must be more active when he explains the agency's services and policies or when it is time to give an interpretive summary. Yet it is vital that even at these times the client has an opportunity to ask questions and make comments. Talking merely to fill silent periods is of questionable value. Silence is not something which must be avoided at all costs. Silence can serve some useful purposes in the social work interview. At times a client may want to say something but will hesitate because he cannot find the right words or because he is embarrassed to talk about the problem. This client may need a period of silence to prepare and strengthen himself. A worker's question, no matter how well-intentioned, would only make it more difficult for this client.

There are certain nondirective therapies (such as Rogers, 1951) which instruct the worker to remain silent almost all of the time, leaving it entirely up to the client to decide what he wants to discuss. Stories of social workers and clients greeting each other and then sitting in complete silence until it is time to say good-by may be apocryphal, but they do stress the value placed on worker inactivity by those who follow the nondirective approaches. Most social workers do not support such methods. Though recognizing the value of silence and worker inactivity at the right time, they feel that leading or strategic questions are necessary, even desirable, in many situations in order to encourage the client to participate. While every client has the right to remain silent, the worker must help those clients who want to become engaged in the interview but do not know how.

Complete silence is infrequent, but occasional periods of silence are not uncommon. However, most clients, most of the time, do participate in the interview. The social worker must listen to what they are saying. Sometimes the social worker is so "busy" that he literally does not hear what they are saying. In one neighborhood center a group of residents approached the social worker one evening with a complaint. The social worker, who had had a very busy day, knew exactly what to do as soon as he heard the word "apartments." Without listening further, he suggested organizing a picket line outside the landlord's home and sending a delegation to see the building inspector. It was only days later that he realized that these residents had no problem with their landlord; their complaint was about the noisy city buses which kept them awake late at night. The social worker had been too busy and too tired to listen to them. And they went along with his suggestion because they did not want to disappoint him. As one of the residents said later, "John is such a nice fellow and he knows best. So we did what he said even though it made no sense to us."

Listening may become especially taxing when the interview is with more than one person or when meeting with a group. Trying to listen to what one person says often makes it difficult to hear the others. Great concentration is required to take in as much of the interchange as possible. Only practice will improve worker skill in this area. A particularly good technique for improving listening skills is to tape an interview (of course, only with the client's permission) and then listening to the tape several times afterward to pick up things missed at the first (and second) time of listening. See also chapter 12 for a further discussion of listening as a communication skill.

The worker's role during the interview and the specific interviewing techniques he will use will depend to a great extent on the specific objectives of the interview. If the primary purpose is to obtain information, the worker will play a more direct role than if the objective were another. If the purpose is to involve an outsider in the social intervention process, techniques of persuasion and influencing will be particularly important. Some guides, however, apply to all types of interviews. A social worker must never argue with a client unless the argument is planned to test his reactions or to move him to consider other possibilities. Correcting factual errors may be appropriate in some situations but not in others. The social worker must know with whom he is interacting and how such factual corrections will be perceived by the client. Interrupting a client is usually not a good idea, except when asking for clarification about something just mentioned. But even then the worker must weigh the risk of interrupting the client against the risk of misunderstanding.

Keeping a person from talking about nonrelevant topics

can be a problem. Interrupting or reprimanding him is not the answer. Leading questions may often result in more relevant answers. It is helpful, of course, if the client is aware of the interview's purpose; otherwise, he cannot be expected to stay on target and remain relevant. At least one study found that welfare clients generally did not understand the purpose of the interview with the social worker. In this study clients reported that they considered the worker's home visit as "little more than a relatively infrequent, pleasant chat" (Handler and Hollingsworth, 1969). Although this perception is not entirely negative, it does not provide the basis for a meaningful interview or for effective social intervention.

**Distortions and Errors.** The story the client tells, the answers he gives, and the recollections he shares are not always entirely accurate. In the interview the social worker does not deal with overt behavior which he can observe directly but instead receives data which are once or twice or even more often removed from actual events. Each removal increases the chance for errors and distortions. Though there is value in understanding how the client views his own situation, even if this perception is in error, effective social intervention must be based on accurate and objective assessment of the actual situation.

The worker must understand how distortion and error come about if he wants to be able to detect and correct inaccurate information. Error and misinformation may be purposeful or may come about unconsciously, without the knowledge of the client or other informant. Purposeful misinformation involves deliberate distortion or error in order to mislead the worker. The following are examples illustrative of purposeful distortions:

1. *Influencing the worker.* Mr. Miller fails to tell the worker about a part-time job in order to qualify for a larger welfare check.

2. *Avoiding police and court action.* Mrs. Witherspoon does

not tell the worker about her husband's incestuous relations with their teen-age daughter because she wants him at home rather than in jail.

3. *Not trusting the social worker.* Johnnie Barth does not tell the school social worker about the constant fighting between his parents because he thinks what happens at home is none of the worker's business.

4. *Denial.* Mrs. Glaser knows that her husband has an affair with his secretary but refuses to talk about it, hoping that by denying it, it will pass away.

5. *Obtaining the social worker's approval by responding in accordance with societal values or by giving what is believed to be the desired response.* Mr. Mullins, a retired police officer, tells his worker that he is feeling fine when in fact he can hardly walk, but he believes that the worker does not want to hear his complaints. This type of error is not always conscious (see also no. 9).

No one knows how prevalent purposeful errors and distortions are in social work, though some suspect that they occur more frequently than most social workers believe. On the other hand, there is no question that unconscious errors and distortions occur very often. The following are some examples of this type:

6. *False perception.* Mrs. Jones reports that Mary, her foster daughter, is making good progress in school. Mrs. Jones actually believes that this is so, but the fact is that Mary is doing poorly and there is some question whether she will be promoted at the end of the year.

7. *Lack of knowledge or partial knowledge.* Mrs. Quine reports that her husband earns $200 a week when in fact he earns nearly twice that amount; unknown to her, he is a gambler and uses the monies he retains for gambling.

8. *Faulty recollection.* Mrs. Wallace had forgotten that fifteen years ago she and her husband had come to the agency to obtain help with the same kind of problem which faces them now.

9. *Internalization of societal values.* Mr. Land told his worker that he had been very busy getting in contact with potential
employers because he is aware that in our society healthy men
are expected to work. Even when their behavior is not in ac-
cord with value prescriptions, many people unconsciously distort descriptions of their behavior so as to report a more conforming behavior. Of course, this type of distortion may be
conscious (see no. 5).

10. *Misunderstanding the question.* To the question, "How
old is your car?" Mr. Allerton answered, "Two years," when
actually he had bought a ten-year-old car two years ago.

11. *Inaccurate listening.* To the question, "What is your
family income?" Mr. Dembey reported only his own take-
home pay, forgetting his wife's and his son's salaries. Sometimes the "forgetting" is conscious (see no. 1), but often it is
unconscious. Mr. Dembey may have been too preoccupied to
listen accurately or noise may have made listening difficult. Or
he may consider only his salary as family income, since the
other salaries belong to the individual earners, not the family.

12. *Cultural differences.* When asking Mr. Alfonso about
problems in his family, the worker was inquiring about the
nuclear family, but Mr. Alfonso answered in terms of the extended family since for him, as for many Spanish Americans,
"family" means spouse, children, parents, in-laws, aunts, un-
cles, cousins, and godparents.

It is not always possible to know whether a distortion or
an error is conscious or unconscious. Mrs. Jones may not have
been aware of what was happening to Mary (no. 6) or she may
have wanted to make the worker believe that she was a good
foster mother (no. 1 or no. 5). Mrs. Glaser's denial (no. 1) may
have been conscious but also could have been unconscious.
Whether conscious or unconscious, distortions and errors interfere with obtaining the information necessary for assessment and for planning an effective strategy. Though the
source of the distortion or error does make for some difference, the worker's first concern must be with spotting the

misinformation and, once having identified it, with correcting it.

There are various ways in which errors and distortions can be detected. Comparison of the client's responses with information provided by others or with information from official records is one way. The worker learned that Mrs. Wallace had a prior contact with the agency by checking the agency's master file. Mrs. Quine's lack of knowledge about her husband's income became apparent when Mr. Quine showed the worker a pay stub. An interview with Mary's teacher revealed Mrs. Jones's misconception. When there is a discrepancy between two sources, it must not always be assumed that the client's information is incorrect. Wallace is a common surname, and the client fifteen years ago may not have been the same person as the current applicant. A neighbor who wanted to settle a grudge may have given the worker deliberate misinformation about Mr. Land's job-hunting activities. Yet when there is a discrepancy, the worker is duty-bound to learn the facts.

Others ways to discover errors may be a bit more difficult. Sometimes error becomes apparent when the same information is asked for in different ways. For example, when the social worker reviewed the Allerton family budget he asked why the repair costs for an almost new car were so high. Only then did he learn that the car was not two years old but twelve years old. Sometimes information just does not sound right or does not fit what is alreeady known about a situation. The worker would not have found Mr. Land at home whenever he called if he had really been trying to find a job. Looking at Mr. Mullins and seeing all the medicine bottles on the kitchen table made it quite clear that he was not as healthy as he claimed. But there are no simple, foolproof ways to detect and correct all errors and distortions. The best advice is to develop the type of worker-client relationship which is based on trust and mutual respect. While this relationship will not guarantee the avoidance of errors, it will reduce them. There is a greater likelihood that a client will share things as they really are when he feels that he can trust his worker.

**Ending the Interview.** The end of an interview is as important as its beginning, if not more so. The last few minutes of an interview and the final impression left with the client will make the difference in what will happen during the next few days and weeks. Whether the client will do the things he agreed to do, whether he will take seriously the suggestions made by the worker, and whether he will return for the next interview, will depend in no small measure on the way in which the interview ends. The client who leaves the worker with a sense of satisfaction and accomplishment is more likely to continue along the paths explored during the interview than one who leaves with a sense of frustration and disappointment. If the interview itself has gone badly it will be difficult for a worker to retrieve it in the last few minutes—but even earlier successes can be lost in this final stage of the interview if the meeting does not end on a positive and purposeful note.

A perennial question facing social workers is how and when to end an interview. The simplest way, though not always the most satisfactory, is to mention from three to five minutes before the end that the scheduled time is almost up. Client and worker can then use the remaining minutes for summarizing the interview and for preparing for the next session. Using the last few minutes in this way is a good idea because it provides an effective bridge to the future. But letting the clock determine the length of the interview or meeting may not always be the best plan. True, a social worker has obligations to more than one client. If he does not end an interview on time, the additional minutes must be taken from the time scheduled for another client. Yet the "hour" may end just a few minutes before the objectives of the interview have been reached. Stopping at this point merely because the clock says so may be an inefficient use of time when so much time has already been invested in this interview. A little extra time now may have a far-reaching effect on what the client will be able to do himself in the coming days and weeks. In social intervention, time should be used flexibly and purposefully, not rigidly and mechanically. Just as there is no point in continuing the interview if its purpose has been achieved before the end of the scheduled time, so the worker should terminate the interview at the end of the appointed time if the interview is not making any progress and has reached a dead end. But if things are moving along well and it seems probable that the worker and the client can accomplish what they had set out to do with an extra ten or fifteen minutes, then the worker should not hesitate to go over the appointed time.

The *ending summary* is the worker's way of summarizing the current interview and of preparing for the next one. It will be remembered that there are two types of objectives for every interview. The immediate or short-range objectives may include securing information necessary for accurate assessment or exploring and weighing alternative intervention strategies or some other specific purpose. But whatever the short-range objectives, neither worker nor client should leave the interview without understanding how the accomplishment of these objectives has contributed toward attainment of the long-range goals. The success of the interview will depend in no small measure on the fact that both worker and client realize that this interview was a step in the direction of achieving the social intervention goals. The specific task of the ending summary is to connect the present interview with the long-range objectives. Here is an example of how one social worker used an ending summary:

You have been very helpful, Mrs. Stowe. Before leaving let's review what we accomplished today. . . . The information you presented today helped both of us gain a better understanding of your problem. And as you know, understanding the problem is the first step in solving it. Now that you and I understand the problem, there appear to be several ways which we can follow. Next time we will want to examine these in order to pick the one which you think is best for you. In the meantime you and your husband might want to think about. . . .

The ending summary should be positive, stressing the progress made in today's interview. At the same time, it should be honest and challenging, pointing out the areas where additional work is needed.

What meaning does the end of an interview have for a client? What meaning does the end of a meeting have for group members? If the relationship between worker and client is routine, it probably matters little that the interview is over. Some clients may even feel a sense of relief that they will be left alone for another week or another month. When the interview is aimless and the worker-client relationship routine, clients show little concern about the end of the interview, according to the findings of one study (Handler and Hollingsworth, 1969). But when the relationship is meaningful, the end of an interview can take on a special significance. For clients who are very lonely or who have recently experienced abandonment or desertion, ending the interview can be especially stressful. Once such people have established positive relationships with a worker they may fear that they will once again be deserted. The worker must recognize these feelings. It may even help if the worker discusses them with the client. But the worker must not make promises which he may not be able to keep. He must not tell a lonely oldster that he will visit him every Thursday; he may not be able to do so indefinitely because he may be transferred to another district or he may change his job. Yet he can assure such people in other ways. His regular on-time arrival every week is a far better demonstration of his interest and concern than any verbal promise. He can arrange for ways in which a housebound client will have more contact with the outside world: a telephone near his bed, frequent volunteer visitors, meals-on-wheels, and similar services which connect the client with the outside world. The way to deal with separation anxiety (the technical name for what we have discussed in this paragraph) is to face it openly and to demonstrate through concrete activities that the worker has a continuing interest in the client even though a physical separation is necessary at the end of every interview.

The client may not be the only one who experiences separation anxiety. Many social work supervisors can recall workers who have found it difficult to end an interview or terminate a case. Some social workers continue to work with groups long beyond the period contracted for because they have become so involved with the group that they need to continue this relationship. Most often the inability to terminate an interview or end contact is masked by a deep concern for the welfare of the client. How can they get along without me? What will happen to the children while I am away? Who will help Mr. Dean once I leave? There is some reality to these concerns, but they also tend to hide the social worker's feelings about becoming separated from a person (or a group) who has come to mean much to him. Separation from a friend is always painful, but social workers must remember the difference between clients and friends. Whenever a social worker suffers from separation anxiety he is not performing at the highest level of practice.[1]

## Observing

We constantly observe and note what is going on around us. Yet professional observation is more than merely seeing things or idly watching what people do. It is a purposeful and planned activity designed to assist the social worker in acquiring the information necessary for planning relevant intervention activities. Observation can provide the kind of information that the social worker cannot obtain in other ways. It can also support or contradict data obtained in other ways and thus provide the worker with a more complete picture of the problem and the client.

Observation is a purposeful and planned activity which involves the deliberate choice of what the social work observer

1. Further and more extensive information about interviewing can be found in Kadushin (1972) and Schubert (1972), two books which deal especially with the social work interview.

wishes to see since it is never possible to observe everything. Anyone doubting this should try a simple experiment: ask two friends to walk through a slum neighborhood or through a busy bus station and to observe everything they see. Have them report to you separately after their observation, and you can be sure that their findings will not coincide since each will see only what interests him or what he thinks is relevant or important. One may note the decrepit housing while the second may see the children covered with running sores. It is the same when two social workers are asked to observe the same client. One worker will notice his apprehensive behavior during the interview while the other will be struck by the expensive suit he wears. Such random observations are interesting but not always conducive to skillful practice since the data noted in this way are not necessarily relevant. One way to improve observation skills is to plan carefully, deliberately selecting for observation those items which may be useful for assessment.

The importance of client involvement has been noted in earlier chapters. But clients cannot always provide the desired information, and at times the information they provide is not entirely accurate. Observation is often a preferred information-gathering method because it is independent of the client's knowledge and will. The social worker can learn much during the interview or group meeting by observing the client's appearance, behavior, and tone of voice. Are these appropriate to the present situation? Are they consistent with the problem presented and compatible with the services requested? Did the client become more excited during some parts of the problem presentation than during others? When, for example, one client claimed great concern for the welfare of her children but always spoke of them in an emotionless and controlled tone of voice, the social worker realized that further study was necessary before her information could be accepted as completely accurate. A school principal told the community worker that he had no ethnic problems in his school. But when the worker observed that all the new members of the school's honorary society were white even though 60 percent of the student population were black, he realized that this school faced a serious intergroup relations problem.

Observing a client in the office is one type of observation, perhaps the most common. But often it is desirable to have other observations, particularly since the social worker is interested in information about the client's interactions with others. It is all but impossible to assess the problem of an adolescent school dropout without having information on how he relates with his parents, his friends, and his teachers. Though some of these data may be obtained through interviews, real-life observations often provide more accurate and more useful information. One experienced social worker characterized a certain boy as "completely asocial" on the basis of information collected in office interviews, yet later observation of this same boy in his peer group revealed that there he functioned as a peer leader (Sherif and Sherif, 1964:117). The social worker's first assessment may not have been entirely wrong, but it certainly was premature and partial since he did not know how this boy behaved outside the office. Similarly, when working with a family problem, the worker should try to observe the total family, preferably outside the office. In this way he can discover how different family members interact with each other: who is a leader and who, a follower; how various members react to stress and conflict; and in what ways different family members respond to the problem initially presented to the worker.

**Getting Ready.** Careful preparation is necessary if an observation is to be more than happenstance. The preparation starts as soon as the social worker establishes or defines the specific purpose of the observation. The purpose of the initial observation may be to identify and assess the problem brought by the client. Later observations may focus on defining the strengths and limitations of the client in relation to the problem. And still later, observations may be useful for specifying potential targets or for clearing up contradictions in the assembled information. If the client is a community, the initial observation may provide the data necessary for defining the community's problems or information on the services available to cope with these problems.

Before the observation takes place the social worker must learn as much as possible about the person(s) and the situation which he will observe. Information about the person's cultural and ethnic background is especially important. Without this knowledge it is too easy for the observer to mistake the trivial for the important and in this way interpret the observation incorrectly. Thus, a social worker who is not aware that different cultural groups respond to pain and illness in various ways is likely to describe some hospitalized patients as "overemotional" or even as "mental cases" when these persons merely respond to pain as do most people in their circle (Zborowski, 1969).

Despite the need for careful preparation, observation should never become a routine activity. Many of the problems which require social intervention may seem routine and obvious—a family lacks money, a husband and wife quarrel, a neighborhood needs a new school, a teen-ager is in trouble. It will not take long before even a new social worker will find that his latest client is "just like" earlier ones who had the "same" problem. It is not always easy to approach every new situation as a unique event. Yet social workers must remember that the current problem situation, though it may appear similar to many others, is quite different if only because the people involved are different. And if it is a different situation, then it will require study and observation. The strategy which was successful on Sixth Street may not work on 60th Street. Even though a social worker must bring what he learned from other situations to the current one, he must approach his present assignment with fresh eyes so that he can see things that he may not have noted before.

**Obstacles to Accurate Observation.** No observer will be able to avoid all of the obstacles to accurate observation, even when he plans carefully and prepares adequately. The principal obstacles which affect the accuracy of observations are: (1) cultural bias; (2) incorrect inferences; (3) impact of observer's presence; and (4) use of language. We will explore each of these obstacles because social workers can overcome or reduce them only when they are aware of them.

1. *Cultural bias.* All observations are culture-bound and value-laden. Abraham Kaplan (1964) once noted that there is no such thing as "immaculate perception" since every observer approaches his observations with tools and concepts which are grounded in his own culture. Thus we were not surprised to read Bertrand Russell's finding (1927) that experimental animals generally display the national characteristics of the scientists observing them. Animals observed by American scientists rush about frantically while those in the laboratory of German scientists nearly always sit still and think! Social workers are likely to focus on those client characteristics which are important in the social worker's culture but which may have little significance for the client. And they will inevitably interpret these observations in terms of the value system with which they are most familiar; that is, their own value system. The social worker assigned to the JOHANSEN FAMILY was struck by the fact that the television set seemed to be turned on all the time. The social worker's own home was a quiet, relaxing place, and the constant noise in the Johansens' small apartment offended his sense of propriety. But the Johansens were accustomed to a different noise level so that the added noise from the television did not bother them at all.

Social workers, just as other professional workers, are prone to various types of cultural bias which can mar their observations. There is little need to mention prejudice and racial bias, two characteristics which will cast serious doubt on any observation data. But cultural differences between worker and client may make for problems even when there is no overt prejudice. A social worker who has been assigned to work with a Japanese-American family cannot make meaningful observations if all Orientals look alike to him. The worker who is unfamiliar with his client's cultural background may misinterpret what he observes. He may assign great importance to a routine event and overlook what is really important. The worker who is ignorant of French culture is likely to jump to the wrong conclusion when he observes his male client embrace and kiss another man. A worker who comes from a background where fists are raised only in anger may find it difficult to make much sense out of a meeting where fist fights break out every few minutes but subside almost as quickly as they start.

Another type of bias arises out of the need of each profession to look for the kind of data which will facilitate its work. Medical doctors focus on health data and often overlook social information, even though it may be significant for discovering the cause of the illness. Many social workers concentrate on personality pathology or the social problems of their clients and may fail to observe their strengths and potentials for change. Social workers who favor a psychological or psychoanalytical interpretation of human behavior may ignore observation data which might indicate that the problem is really located in the client's environment. Since social workers require a broad range of information from both the internal and the external environment, they should not narrow the scope of their observations prematurely. A decision about the cause of the problem is best left open, especially in the beginning phase. Before deciding whether OBADIAH WILSON's chronic unemployment is due to a personality pathology or a societal malfunction (or perhaps a combination of both), the social worker should make a series of observations which might support or refute either hypothesis. He must find out how Obadiah Wilson interacts with others and how be copes with various problem situations. And he must also obtain information about the home and community in which Mr. Wilson was raised and where he now lives. Observation will be a primary method for gathering much of this data.

2. *Incorrect inferences.* Jumping to a wrong conclusion or drawing an incorrect inference is another obstacle often encountered in the observation process. One social worker observed that OBADIAH WILSON stuttered. Since the purpose of an observation is more than collecting mere descriptions of unrelated events, the social worker could have attached some significance to this stuttering behavior and drawn an inference from this observation. But it would have been entirely unwarranted to conclude from a single observation of stuttering that Obadiah suffered from an unresolved Oedipus complex. "Instant Diagnosis" may be a popular parlor game, but it is not the hallmark of responsible social work.

However, the social worker does face a dilemma. How does he go about attaching meanings to observations yet not jump to unwarranted and incorrect conclusions? The best advice is never to draw inferences from a single observation. Hearing a person stutter repeatedly is still one type of observation. Several different hypotheses should be tested until sufficient evidence has been accumulated to make the acceptance of one hypothesis and the rejection of the others persuasive. In the case of OBADIAH WILSON, for example, the social worker hypothesized that the unhealthy relationship between husband and wife contributed to his apathy and chronic unemployment. A second hypothesis stated that the lack of employable skills was the primary cause for his present condition. In attempting to "prove" one or the other of these hypotheses, the observation on stuttering was only one of many items. Other observations made in the Wilson home and in the employment skills testing center proved to be important. Observing Mr. Wilson in contact with his friends and acquaintances also was helpful. On the basis of many different types of data this worker concluded that there was sufficient evidence to suggest that the poor marital relation was one of the crucial causes of Obadiah Wilson's inability to work steadily. An intervention strategy which would not take this cause into consideration could not be effective.

At times incorrect inferences occur when workers jump to wrong conclusions before they have sufficient facts upon which to base their interpretations. At other times, insufficient knowledge about the clients' life style leads to incorrect inferences. One social worker observed repeatedly that his teen-age client refused to go to the movies or attend parties. Since he knew that this boy's father died during the summer, he diagnosed his behavior as excessive and pathological mourning. Had this worker been aware that Orthodox Jews do not participate in any type of entertainment during the entire first year after a parent's death, he would have understood that this boy's behavior was not unusual for someone from his background.

3. *Impact of observer's presence.* People tend to behave differently when they know that someone observes them. Generally, they want to please or impress the observer or they try to act in culturally approved ways. Doc, the principal informant for William Whyte (1955:301), was able to verbalize this feeling; he said, "Now when I do something, I have to think what Bill Whyte would want to know about it and how I can explain it. Before I used to do things by instinct." Most parents will make every effort when outsiders are present to appear as good homemakers who love their children even when at other times their behavior is quite different.

When a chemist mixes two chemicals and observes the result of this mixture, his presence makes no difference since he does not interact with the chemicals. But the person being observed and the social worker observer do interact with one another. This person-to-person interaction affects the observation process in various ways. Interaction between the social worker and the person being observed is quite general in social work because there are only a few situations where the observation occurs without the knowledge of the person being observed. From my own experience I can recall only one time where interaction was not necessary; this occurred when I observed a nursery school class from behind a one-way screen. But it is rare when the person or group a social worker wishes to observe happens to be in front of a one-way screen. Usually, the social worker must interact with the person whom he wishes to observe. He must allow time for overcoming the client's initial curiosity, suspicion, and mistrust since these will affect the very items he may wish to observe. Even when the social worker's presence can be explained rationally (judge in a competition, monitor in a classroom, videotape technician, and so on), time must be allowed for him to blend into the scenery and become accepted before the behavior patterns will return to what they were before he entered the room.

Social workers who make home visits have commented on the differences between the first visit and subsequent visits when they are no longer strangers. Nevertheless, one of the limitations of home visits remains even after the first visit. People do not act naturally when a stranger or an outsider is present. The change in interaction patterns may not be conscious, and the client may not try to put "something over" on the worker, but the social worker's presence does change things. Noting this limitation is not an argument against the desirability and usefulness of home visits, but it does suggest that observations obtained in this manner may not give an entirely accurate picture of the real family situation.

Client behavior also will be different when the gap between the observer and the observed is great. Many social workers complain that they are not able to understand their lower-class clients. Part of their problem may result from a change in client behavior in the presence of a stranger. People often behave in ways they think are expected by the observer. If the observer is like themselves, their behavior will depart little from their regular behavior, but if the observer comes from a different social class or status group, behavioral responses may change significantly. One of the most effective uses of indigenous personnel in the antipoverty programs was as observers. Coming from the same background and talking the same language as the recipients of service, indigenous workers were able to report experiences and behaviors which most middle-class social workers were not able to observe.

Some social scientists have argued that those being observed should never be aware of the observation lest this knowledge affect their behavior (Sherif and Sherif, 1964). However, in most situations in which social workers are involved observations without the observed's awareness are not feasible or desirable. Concealed observation is not desirable since the entire emphasis in social intervention is on the client's participation and involvement in decision-making. Participant observation where the observer becomes a participant in order to blend more naturally into the setting being observed also is used rarely in social work practice because it places the worker in an untenable position where he cannot meet the role expectations demanded of him. Once the worker becomes part of the client system, he takes on obligations which may contradict those of the social worker. Some social workers, when first coming in contact with a teen-age group, mistakenly believe that they must become "one of the boys" in order to be accepted, but they forget that their role is quite different from that of a group member. When the worker is a group member he may overidentify with the group's purposes and lose the very objectivity necessary for functioning as an effective social intervention worker.

In summary, the social work observer almost always remains visible, almost always must identify himself as an observer, and whenever possible should explain what he is doing. At the same time, the observer must recognize that his presence does affect the behavior of those whom he observes.

4. *Use of language.* The language used to describe the observation makes for one further obstacle. Since all language uses value-based concepts, any statement describing an observation always implies more than was observed. For example, an incident observed outside my window can be described in

different ways, such as: (1) two men are wrestling; (2) a black man is wrestling with a white man; (3) a white man is wrestling with a black man; (4) a white policeman is wrestling with a black man; or (5) a black man is wrestling with a white policeman. Each of these statements is accurate since it describes the scene observed, yet each carries a slightly different message and will lead to different action consequences. This is a problem which arises out of the structure of our language. There are no value-free words or completely neutral concepts, so that this problem cannot be overcome entirely. It is, therefore, vital that social workers choose their words and concepts with care when they report their observations, always keeping in mind the purpose of the observation and what it is that they want to record.

**Observation as Feedback.** Observations serve various other purposes in addition to gathering information. One common use in social work practice is to utilize observations as a feedback mechanism. At times the social worker can obtain a more accurate response to his question by watching the client than by listening to his words. Using sight and sound together will result in an even more accurate response pattern. Sometimes a client may not agree with the strategy proposed by his worker but is not willing to risk disagreement.

One social worker had worked for several months with a group of AFDC mothers. During this time it had become clear to the group members that they were not receiving all the special grants to which their families were entitled. Various strategies were tried—each recipient talked with her own welfare worker; they sent letters to the commissioner of public welfare, as well as letters to the newspapers—but none of these strategies produced any positive results. The worker therefore suggested that a picket line around the welfare center might publicize the group's struggle and result in some public support. There was quick agreement to the worker's suggestion. But during the remainder of the meeting all kinds of strange things began to happen. Group members who had been the best of friends suddenly started to fight and shout at each other, coffee was spilled and dishes were dropped, and the closing ritual at the end of the meeting was "forgotten." When, after the meeting, the worker reviewed these observations, he understood the message. At a special meeting of the group's executive committe on the next day, the worker reopened the question of the picket line and helped the group's officers say that they were really afraid to picket the welfare center.

Feedback is not limited to group meetings. When working with individual clients, the social worker can also receive valuable feedback by keeping his eyes open. Even while asking a question or making a statement, it is possible to observe the client's reaction. Facial expressions often convey a fuller and less disguised response in less time than do verbal responses.

**Observation is Only One Method.** A social worker can obtain much valuable information through observation. But observation is only one of the methods useful in social intervention. When utilized together with other methods, such as interviewing, searching documents, using questionnaires, and so on, observing can be a powerful tool in the social worker's armatorium. Though somewhat different skills are used in observation and in interviewing, in practice it is neither possible nor desirable to separate the two methods arbitrarily. The social worker observes during every interview, and he often finds it necessary to ask questions during an observation. In social intervention practice these two methods usually go together.

## Writing

Written communications play an important role in modern life, yet lack of skill in this area is all too common. According to one study (National Assessment of Writing, 1970) one out of every five seventeen-year-olds is unable to record pertinent facts from a telephone conversation, while 47 percent are unable to prepare an accurate accident report. College professors lament that today's undergraduates do not know how to write term papers, while social work supervisors complain that some workers cannot write even a simple letter. Poor writing skills may be a common problem, but it is particularly serious for social intervention practice because there is no problem situation for which the intervention strategy will not involve a variety of written communications. Letters, memos, reports, and records are much more than bureaucratic requirements. When correctly used they can become useful tools in achieving the intervention goals.

Many social workers regard writing as an unpleasant interruption, tacked on to their primary assignment of working with people. Rare is the social worker who recognizes that writing is a basic intervention skill. When a worker writes a letter to request information or to plead on behalf of his client, he is not engaged in a peripheral activity. The worker who records a summary of his contacts is not (or should not be) following a routine ritual. He is making a permanent record which, among other functions, will inform others of the progress he has made in achieving the intervention goals. The problem, goals, strategy, client and worker activities, and other relevant information are recorded so that these data are available should another worker suddenly be assigned to the case. This information will also be crucial for evaluating progress toward goal achievement. And if this client should later return with the same or another problem, the ready availability of these data will be useful for assessment and planning at that time. Preparing a report for the agency executive or board of directors is not merely an exercise in bureaucratic management but an opportunity to influence the decision-makers. The point to keep in mind when writing is that the purpose of every document is to communicate with others.

This is true whether the communication is in the form of a letter, a case record, a memo, or a budget presentation.

A written message will not be effective if the receiver cannot or does not want to understand it. The writer must take into consideration the characteristics of the person(s) for whom the communication is intended. Before sitting down to write, he must know who will be the recipient, what that person needs to know, and what he is supposed to do with the information. On the basis of these data the worker can decide how best to communicate the material that he wants to transmit. In chapter 12 we discuss in greater detail the characteristics of an effective message. The discussion there also is relevant for written communications.

The written word is not always the best way to transmit material. It should be used only when appropriate. When requesting information about a client from another agency, for example, the worker must attempt to learn whether the request is better made by letter or through a telephone call or perhaps both ways. When the decision is for a letter, the language, style, and manner of presentation must be appropriate to the occasion. It would hardly do to use the identical letter when requesting information from a police clerk and a psychiatrist. A short two-line memo may be sufficient to request a document form one's own agency files, but if the request is sent to another agency the worker may have to explain in a bit more detail why he needs the document and what he intends to do with the information.

The content of each written communication varies according to the purposes it serves. Some agency manuals prescribe the specific content needed for each communication. But generally the social worker himself must decide what is appropriate and what is necessary for any given written communication. Though there are differences in emphasis, every communication will contain the following:

1. Statement of the problem or of the purpose of the communication

2. Reason for requesting the information or the manner in which the information has been secured

3. Presentation of the information or of the findings or of the type of information requested

4. Analysis of data, implications, follow-up plans, or how the requested information will be used.

The style of every communication must be simple, clear, and grammatically correct. Brevity is a virtue which is always desirable. When a social worker reviews what he wrote, he should ask himself: Does this say what I want it to say? Will the reader understand it? Could this be expressed more simply? Is it clear?

Even though the primary purpose of a written communication is to inform others, the process of organizing the material and putting it into writing also may help the worker. The writing may provide the opportunity to analyze the information collected, but this useful by-product is not the primary objective of the written communication. This consideration has resulted in many agencies in the abandonment of routine recording of every interview. There was a time when social workers were urged to write detailed process records on every case or group with which they worked. This requirement was based on the assumption that practice skills could be sharpened and improved through writing and the analysis which precedes the writing. With the recognition that the primary purpose of written communications is to communicate with others, alternate methods for staff development have been initiated. Some have suggested that workers, especially new workers, continue to write process records on one or two of their cases or groups so that their supervisors will be in a better position to help them grow. For their other cases or groups, workers are asked to keep summary records with sufficient details so that the necessary information will be available to those who may have need for it. Students, like new workers, are generally asked to prepare process records on several cases or groups so that their field instructors can help them learn effective social work practice. The particular style of the record, summary, or process is not important. What counts is that the worker communicates clearly and without ambiguity so that the reader can understand what occurred.

## Summary

Interviewing and observing are primary worker activities in every phase of the social intervention process. The purpose and the preparation, as well as the underlying value structure, characterize the social worker's use of these skills and set these apart from the use of the same skills by others.

Whether to interview or observe (or interview *and* observe) depends on the nature of the problem, the characteristics of the people involved, and the type of information desired. Similarly, the choice of the specific interview or observation technique flows from the worker's assessment of the client and his problem.

Misunderstanding and misinterpretation, both by the worker and by the client, are not infrequent occurrences. Distortions and errors, sometimes unconscious and at other times deliberate, are also evident in many client-worker contacts. Cultural bias is a source of error which occurs frequently when worker and client come from different ethnic or socioeconomic groups. Social workers must learn to detect and correct all of these obstacles.

Writing is another primary worker activity. It should never become a routine, but its purpsse should always be to inform others. The recipient's need for information and his ability to use it should determine the content of the written communication.

# chapter nine

# Intervention Activities

What skills does a social worker use after the strategy has been selected? No one answer can be given to this question, but there is broad agreement on a number of basic skills which social workers generally utilize. Several different studies have arrived at remarkably similar profiles of worker activities (Geismar, 1972; Reid, 1967). Some of these basic skills will be examined in this chapter.

An analysis of social intervention skills must avoid the risk of confusing the desired outcome with the worker behavior necessary to achieve this outcome. This is what Scott Briar and Henry Miller (1971:184) may have had in mind when they observed: " 'Support' and 'clarification' describe effects, not the action taken to produce them. Such prescriptions amount to telling the practitioner to 'make the client feel better,' or 'improve the client's social function.' " This criticism is well-taken, but divorcing skills from outcomes may be even more problematic. When this occurs there is danger of engaging in activities in which the worker is particularly skilled, no matter whether these are relevant to the problem and the goals. Goals-oriented skills force the worker to focus on goals, while task-oriented skills may lead in false directions. Therefore we will continue to anayyze goal-oriented skills but will attempt to avoid the confusion pointed out by Briar and Miller.[1]

1. "Task-oriented" and "goal-oriented" in this discussion refer to worker activity and not, as is sometimes the case, to group processes.

The classification of social intervention skills into distinct areas is arbitrary, as is any classification scheme. Aid, information, and direction (AID) are presented here as one skill area but could have been discussed with equal validity in two or even three separate sections. "Referral" appears as a separate skill area in this chapter but could have been subsumed under "practical help." The absence of rigid boundaries between skill areas reflects the real-life situation where social workers do not use isolated skills. On the contrary, within any one episode of contact a worker utilizes two, three, or even more different skills. Thus, in the first interview with MRS. KING, the social worker used many different skills, including engagement, assessment, practical help, AID, clarification, and support. While no social worker will be equally competent in every intervention skill, a reasonable competence in all of the basic skills is necessary, if only to know that a particular service or intervention strategy is required and that someone more skilled must be involved.

## Practical Help

Many social workers spend a great deal of time providing practical help for their clients. They authorize checks, provide food, locate housing, arrange for a meeting place, secure a bed in a nursing home, make sure that a mailing is sent out to all residents in a housing project, make arrangements for a psychological test—these are only a few of the ways in which social workers provide practical help. These services are called practical because clients perceive them as real and actual, in contrast to other services which are not tangible. Some social workers seem to do little else, while there are a few workers who almost never provide this type of service. But most social workers utilize a combination of practical help and other services to help their clients achieve the desired goals. This is true even in public agencies where income maintenance has been separated from social services. The question facing most social workers is not *whether* to provide practical help but *what, when, where,* and *how* to provide these services most effectively.

Practical help includes a wide variety of social intervention activities whose primary purpose is to effect changes in the environment rather than within the person who receives the service. Job placement is a form of practical help, while counseling designed to help this same person gain a better understanding of his problem is not classified as practical help, important as it may be. Three types of practical help are utilized by social workers: (1) concrete but nonmaterial services; (2) nonconvertible things; and (3) convertible things.

*Concrete but nonmaterial services* include all those services which are real but which cannot be touched, such as the various kinds of job-training programs, medical services, job placement, and so on. *Nonconvertible things* are goods received in kind which must be used as received; food packages or furniture are examples of nonconvertible things. When a worker offers concrete but nonmaterial services or nonconvertible things, the client's choice is limited to accepting or not accepting what is offered. *Convertible things,* on the other hand, leave a wider area of choice to the recipient because he can change what he has received into almost anything he needs or desires. Money is the most convertible of things since it can be exchanged without any restrictions. Food stamps or clothing orders are more limited because the type of goods is specified, but these still leave an area of choice to the recipient. He can decide what kinds of foods or what style of clothing he prefers. Which type of practical help to provide in any given situation should never be a routine decision.

The decision on the type of practical help to be offered must be made on the basis of a full assessment of the problem and of the request made by the client. It must not be made on the basis of agency tradition ("we always have done it this way") or agency policy ("this is a family agency and we only provide therapy!"). If agency regulations make it impossible for the worker to offer the service needed, he should not offer another, less relevant service; instead, he must arrange for the client to receive the needed help elsewhere. The school social worker assigned to work with Lynn Wilson, OBADIAH WILSON's oldest daughter, became aware that the principal problem which affected all members of this family, including Lynn, was her father's chronic unemployment and the consequent lack of regular income. Even without a complete assessment, he realized that neither counseling nor therapy with Lynn would come to grips with her problems at school unless the basic problem of this family was first resolved. If the school social worker himself cannot provide the necessary practical help, he must help Mr. Wilson obtain these services elsewhere in the community. And this referral of Mr. Wilson will be in direct response to the worker's assignment of working with Lynn.

*Client's request.* The nature of the problem is one guide to the use of practical help. The request made by the client should be another criterion. While a social worker is not obligated to do everything the client asks of him, he is accountable to the client, as well as to his agency, for what he does and for what he does not do. A worker may not arbitrarily substitute one service for another. People who seek practical help from a social worker will generally not be satisfied with a substitute unless they were actively involved in making that decision. A mother who requests a foster home placement for her infant son will usually not be willing to accept counseling instead of a placement. A group of ex-prisoners who believe that discrimination against them prevents them from finding jobs demand emergency action to solve their problem; arranging for their participation in the community center's baseball league may make for good recreation but will not satisfy their request nor will it solve their problem. If the requested service appears inappropriate or if it is not available (there are no foster homes at the present time; there are no job openings for unskilled labor in this town), the worker must explain this and together with the client explore other alternatives—but he should not ignore the original request by offering a service that the client does not want.

Practical help will not solve every problem brought to the social worker. Even when the client does not request any other type of service, the problem analysis may indicate that other or additional services are necessary. A hard-core unemployed person, for example, needs a job. Locating a job and helping him learn or relearn long-forgotten job skills may be only the first step in solving his problem. The problem analysis also indicates that in the past this client had difficulties in keeping jobs because of his extremely aggressive behavior, especially in situations where there was potential or actual conflict. Since there is every indication that the same chain of events will occur again, worker and client must also face this problem and attempt to resolve it. The tenants of the KENNEDY HOUSES need many concrete services including building repairs, more regular garbage removal, rat control, better police protection—but they also need to improve their self-image and reverse the pervasive sense of apathy which characterized the project's residents. In both instances practical help will be important, but if the worker's activities are limited to providing practical help, the real problem will remain. However, in neither instance would the social worker be justified in ignoring the presenting request for the sake of working on the underlying problem. The best approach would be to provide both types of service at the same time.

*Appropriateness and accessibility.* A decision to provide practical help requires as much thought as the selection of any other type of intervention strategy. Unless the resources or services selected are appropriate, they will not contribute to problem solution. Only when the help is usable and accessible will it assist in reaching the intervention goals. It would be inappropriate to send meat products to a hungry family of strict vegetarians. And a gift parcel of tobacco and instant coffee will be of little use when three little children are close to starvation. If surplus food is made available in an out-of-the-way distribution center, only those who have an automobile have access to this service. And when food stamps require a relatively large outlay of cash, they really are not available to the very families they were intended to benefit.

These principles—*appropriateness* and *accessibility*—apply not only to food but also to other types of practical help. When a rehabilitation worker sought to secure homework for ALICE SAMORO, the thirty-two-year-old paralyzed woman who had not left her parents' home for the past five years, his supervisor questioned whether homework was an appropriate service. Admittedly, it was far simpler to bring work to Alice than to arrange for her to go to work. And Alice had requested help in doing something useful with her time. But both worker and supervisor agreed that Alice's dependence on her domineering parents and her lack of contact with age peers were two priority problems. These would have to be kept in mind in any service rendered. Homework would reinforce rather than reduce these problems. The more appropriate help, it was agreed, was to find suitable work outside the home and to arrange for transportation for Alice.

When new services are planned or when clients are referred to existing services, social workers must be sure that these are accessible. It is not sufficient to tell parents about special services for their mentally retarded child without making sure that they have a way of getting to them. But accessibility means more than a convenient location and easy transportation. It also means that people know how to use the service. An integral part of providing practical help, therefore, is to make sure that clients receive simple and clear instructions in a language that they can understand. The worker who tells Bill, a prisoner about to be released, that he should feel free to call him whenever he feels that he wants to talk with someone, must make sure that Bill knows how to use a dial phone. And securing the right to vote for a previously disenfranchised group of migrant workers will be meaningful only if the social worker provides specific instructions on how and where to register and how and where to vote. Unless people know how to find the services and how to use available resources, these are of little or no use to them.

A degree of rigidity is sometimes associated with the provision of practical help and concrete services. This may be due to the fact that budgetary requests must be finalized months and sometimes years in advance of needs. Once a budget has been approved, there is a tendency to utilize earmarked funds even when other strategies or other services might be more relevant. When runaway children are placed in an institution because it has empty beds (and not because this is best for the children), we may be utilizing available resources but will not be providing the most effective service for these children.

Practical help is provided generally only in response to requests, whether specific or nonspecific. For a long time social workers believed that there was little purpose in offering help to persons who had not asked for it. But in recent years many have become aware that often those most in need do not know how or where to ask for help. Many social workers no longer sit and wait for clients to come to them. Instead, they go into the community and attempt to identify those who can most benefit from social intervention. This practice is frequently called *outreach* or *aggressive casefinding*. In outreach the focus may be on helping people become aware of their problems and of the available services so that they can ask for help. This is a far cry from the days when Lady Bountiful distributed her goodies whether or not they were wanted. The contemporary outreach programs are more in the tradition of the early settlement house workers who lived in the community-at-risk in order to locate those who needed their help.

*Stigma*. Accepting practical help can become a degrading experience if social workers do not take certain steps to maintain the dignity of the recipients. Doing things *for* people may result in a paternalism which is not only humiliating for them but which will also interfere with effective social intervention. When working with essentially healthy people this danger is relatively small, but when the recipient of the services already has social-functioning problems, the danger of creating or reinforcing dysfunctional dependency patterns is serious. To avoid this, the worker, even while offering practical help, must not take the problem away from the client. This is easier when the practical help is offered in the form of convertible things and more difficult when it is a nonmaterial service. But whatever the type of help, the worker must remember that practical help is a strategy and not an end.

Recently we had occasion to examine dozens of cases of second-generation dependents; that is, adult welfare recipients who grew up in families that were dependent on public welfare throughout their childhood and adolescence. Characteristic of intervention efforts in the parental generation was the focus on providing practical help, as if this alone would solve the problems of these families. Hardly ever did the strategy call for returning these families to independence or for changing their negative self-image to a more positive one. Providing money and other forms of practical help for a destitute family is a service but must not be viewed as a social intervention goal. Even where it is likely that financial assistance will always be required, this must not become the goal of the social intervention. MR. RIOS, the invalid oldster, will never again be financially independent and will require financial aid from the welfare department as long as he lives. But the social worker must not view receipt of money as the goal of the social intervention, necessary as these monies are. Mr. Rios faces a number of medical and social problems for which he requires help. The social worker who limits his activities to authorizing checks has not defined Mr. Rios's problems adequately.

## Advice, Information, and Direction (AID)

One problem facing many people today is the lack of accurate information about available services and resources. This is not an issue which is limited to the social service sector. There is need for information about all kinds of governmental and voluntary services which have an impact on people's lives. Some people need information and advice on how to use services which are already available in the community. Others need help in deciding which particular service is most appropriate for them. And still others need direction on the next steps they must take. The difference between information, advice, and direction may not be great but it can be crucial. The worker who provides *information* offers another person the tools with which that person can make his own decisions; he provides the information without attempting to influence the outcome of the decisions. When giving *advice,* on the other hand, the worker attempts to influence the decision along certain lines, even though the actual decision is still made by the other person. *Direction* implies that a decision has already been made by the worker, perhaps because he assumes that the other person is incapable of making the right decision. The other person is expected to implement the worker's decision even though he always has the option not to accept direction.

Various possible ways of working with MRS. KING illustrate the differences between information, advice, and direction. The social worker can give Mrs. King the addresses of several day care centers and suggest that she may want to visit them to see if any are suitable for her children; in this instance the worker only provides information and leaves the decision entirely to Mrs. King. Or he may tell Mrs. King that on the basis of his experience he would recommend that she utilize a certain day care center for her children while she is at work; this is advice because the worker leaves no doubt as to what he considers the preferred decision, but he still leaves the actual decision to Mrs. King. Finally, the worker can tell Mrs. King that he has arranged for her enrollment in a secretarial course, starting next Monday morning, and that he has reserved space for her children in the Walnut Avenue Day Care Center; this worker, having already made all of the decisions, gives directions and expects Mrs. King to follow them. In

practice, the differences between these three worker activities
are not so clear because value judgments are always involved.
Even information is not value-free since the worker's decision
to provide or withhold information involves a value choice.
And the nonverbal message which accompanies the information will usually indicate, more or less clearly, the worker's attitude about the information he has given. Another reason that
sometimes makes it difficult to differentiate between these
three activities is that information is needed both for advice
and for direction. Without accurate information, advice cannot be followed and directions cannot be implemented. Information may not be a sufficient cause for client activity, but lack
of accurate information is a necessary cause for failure.

The importance of information and advice in social intervention is sometimes underestimated, especially by social
workers. Many clients complain about the lack of sufficient information and advice. Mayer and Timms (1970) found that
clients who receive more advice and more guidance are generally more satisfied with their social worker than those who receive less AID. Yet many social workers hesitate to give AID.
They recall that Florence Hollis (1970:37) wrote, "advice and
guidance, although sometimes used, on the whole play a
minor role." Earlier she had written, "only the beginner or the
clumsy worker makes major use of advice" (Hollis, 1964:94).
Perhaps this hesitancy of social workers is a reaction to the
friendly visitors of an earlier period who dispensed advice
along with their food baskets; then it was believed that those
who were successful in life, and especially those who engaged
in charitable activities, had earned the right to tell others what
to do. When social workers became professionals they repu-
diated this form of *noblesse oblige*. They argued that AID encouraged rather than reversed dependency and they questioned the effectiveness of AID since most people do only
what they want to do, no matter what information or advice
they receive from a social worker.

Yet providing AID continues to be an important social intervention activity. Several studies report that social workers spend up to 5 percent of their time in this type of activity (Mullen, 1968; Reid and Epstein, 1972). Lydia Rapoport (1970) observed that problems are often based on, or aggravated by, a lack of information and knowledge. She argued that advice-giving is "an important and useful technique" whenever this is the case. And, as already noted, most clients do not resent AID but complain that they receive less than they want from their social worker. Clients often interpret this lack of advice as a lack of interest in their problems. Many social workers have begun to respond to this feeling by utilizing AID more frequently. But there remains a basic difference between the advice once given by the friendly visitor and the advice given by today's social worker. The former gave advice to satisfy her own needs, while the latter's advice is based on the needs and interests of the client.

The question today is not *whether* to give AID but *when* AID is an appropriate intervention technique and *how* it is most effectively delivered. The appropriateness of giving AID, as of every social intervention activity, depends on the nature of the problem, on the goals to be achieved, on the characteristics of the client, and on the way AID is offered. When giving advice the worker must be careful to protect and preserve the client's basic right to make his own decision. He should not imply (and certainly not threaten) that financial assistance will be cut off if he does not follow the worker's "advice." This is direction, not advice, and inappropriate for social intervention, no matter what it is called. But even when the worker wants to avoid imposing his will and only wishes to give advice, he must consider the implications of the uneven power distribution between himself and the client. When the client feels weak and dependent on the worker he may feel obliged to accept as commands statements which were never intended as such. Given this reality, social workers must take positive steps to ensure that clients are free to make their own decisions. A worker, for example, can advise his client that he should discuss the several alternatives they talked about with someone whose opinion the client values. Or he might direct the client's attention to the possible consequences if the worker's advice were followed, even if this might result in rejecting the worker's advice.

*Deciding for others.* There are several situations where it may be appropriate for a social worker to make decisions for another person. One of these involves decisions about illegal or unlawful acts. A street corner worker need not sit by quietly when "his" gang plans a holdup; a parole officer must not countenance a parole violation for the sake of giving his client an experience in making his own decisions. Limiting a client's decision-making opportunities is also indicated when the client, because of his age or his physical or mental condition, cannot make his own decisions. However, a worker must be extremely cautious before he concludes that a person is not competent to make decisions. And even when he does reach this conclusion, the worker must not take over and attempt to manage all of the client's life. Instead, the worker must make decisions only in those areas where the client cannot function adequately, making sure that there remain other opportunities for choices and decisions. A very young child cannot decide which of two families will make better adoptive parents, but he can and should be given an opportunity to decide whether he prefers to eat with his right or with his left hand, whether he wants to wear the red or the blue shirt, and so on. Self-determination is important, even in situations where the social worker must give direction. However, social workers usually do not err on the side of giving too much direction; instead, many tend to withhold advice for fear of violating the precept of self-determination.

AID should never take the place of client activity, but it should be used as a strategy to strengthen social functioning and decision-making. Positive comments, reinforcing current behavior patterns or future plans, are generally more effective than negative and disapproving comments. Suggestions and questions which raise doubt in the client's mind may be more successful forms of advice than very specific and detailed instructions. Only in the case of information which requires early follow-up are details desirable. Information must always be accurate and phrased so that the client can understand it. For example, when discussing various options open to the parents of a brain-damaged child, the worker must be sure of his facts. Are there vacancies in the institutions under consideration? If not, how long is the waiting period? What are the costs? Is there a time limit on the care offered? When can parents visit? What alternate facilities are available in the community? If the worker does not have accurate and up-to-date answers to these and othe questions, he should not manufacture fictitious answers but help the parents obtain correct information so that they can make a valid decision.

*Appropriateness of direction.* Social workers generally try to avoid giving directions, but there are situations when this is a useful strategy. For example, lack of knowledge and skill in child-rearing and homemaking is common among many problem-prone families. This shortcoming can be so basic and so pervasive that mere information will not provide a sufficient antidote, even though such information might be entirely adequate for families which are functioning on a more adequate level. An intensive educational program where women from the same socioeconomic background are assigned as homemakers for a month at a time to a problem family is one strategy that has achieved some positive results. A ten-week course in conjunction with a game and toy library has been used successfully to teach parents how to play with their very young children. In both experimental projects direction was combined with advice and information in order to help parents relate more effectively to their children; in neither situation did workers hesitate to give directions and clearly express normative expectations regarding desirable parent-child behaviors.

The same information or the identical advice will be re-

ceived in different ways by different clients, depending on
their situation, their life experiences, and their *zone of indifference* (Barnard 1938:168). Every client, before going to the
agency, has already made up his mind about certain things.
The subjects about which he holds firm opinions may be few
or many, but advice about these will be less readily accepted
and acted upon than advice about subjects about which he has
not yet made up his mind. He is still indifferent about these
latter subjects and may (or may not) accept suggestions. For
example, a woman who firmly believes that a mother's place is
at home with her children will dismiss out of hand any suggestion that she look for work to supplement her husband's
meager earnings, but another woman who has not yet made
up her mind on this question may consider the same suggestion an excellent bit of advice. Zones of indifference, though
relatively stable, are subject to change over time, but this type
of change involves value modifications which are not easily
achieved in short-term intervention.

*Effectiveness of AID.* Some have maintained that AID generally is an ineffective intervention technique because people
continue to do what they want to do, regardless of any information or advice they receive. Neither correct information nor
firsthand experience, it is claimed, is sufficient to correct false
perceptions, as Kurt Lewin (1948) noted decades ago. A person who is prejudiced against one ethnic group will remain
prejudiced even after he has been given information about the
positive points of that group, even after he has been shown
data which prove that his perception is false, and even after he
has made the personal acquaintance of some members of that
group. Various planned change attempts, including experiments in changing food habits, work production, ethnic prejudice, and leadership abilities, seem to bear out that information and advice, as well as firsthand experience, have only
limited effectiveness.

Nevertheless, AID does serve a crucial function. Even
when it seems to be ignored, AID will provide the client with

some thoughts that later may lead to the desired changes or may have some other equally significant impact on his behavior. For one thing, AID indicates more or less clearly what the normative expectations are. It tells the client what society expects of him in the present situation. Thus, a mother may refuse to accept the worker's advice that she dress her child more warmly but may understand from his comments that she is not doing too well as a mother; as a result she may begin to take a greater interest in how her son is doing at school. Even though the specific advice was rejected, it was far from ineffective because the generalized message was received.

Some have argued that AID is an intervention technique which is best used with groups. Here, it is suggested, the effectiveness of AID is greatest. For example, a hospital social worker who attempted to provide information about diets to the parents of diabetic children reported greater success when he met with groups of parents than when the advice was provided in one-to-one sessions. A probation worker found that his advice and direction were more readily accepted and followed when he met with a group of probationers than when he met with each client individually. Utilizing a group does not guarantee the effectiveness of AID but often it increases the likelihood that the AID will be accepted.

## Clarification

We assume that most people, most of the time, are capable of coping with their problems, but there are times when even the most able seem incapable of doing anything about their situation. Sometimes the problem is too big for one person. More often the person does not understand his situation accurately because he is a part of it. Helping such a person gain a more correct understanding of his situation and of himself is essential for problem-solving. In clarification the social worker does not add any new information to what the other person presents. Instead, he mirrors what has been presented, per-

haps using other words or a different order, so that this same
information becomes more understandable to him.

Once a person understands his problem, he may be able
to do something about it without further help from the social
worker. The following example illustrates how one person was
able to cope with his problem after clarification:

Manuel Gamio had been picked up by the police for beating his
wife. Since she did not want to press charges, the police referred
him to the local family agency. Mr. Gamio came for his first appointment on time. Almost before sitting down he apologized to the
worker for bothering him with this inconsequential matter. He said
that he knew he had done wrong by beating his wife but it was just
one of those things that could not be helped. The worker neither
agreed nor disagreed. Instead, he asked Mr. Gamio to tell him everything that happened to him on the day of the beating incident.
Mr. Gamio talked about the tremendous pressures he had been
under at work. The social worker wondered whether there might be
a connection between the job pressures and the wife-beating. In
response to this question he remembered other days when he also
beat his wife. Each time this seemed to occur after a particularly difficult day at work. When Mr. Gamio began to see the connection between his job and his behavior at home, the social worker asked him
what he thought he could do to prevent the recurrence of unpleasant incidents like being picked up by the police. Mr. Gamio answered without hesitation that a job change might solve his problem.
And so it did.

Note that in this example clarification did not lead to any
basic personality changes. Instead, once Mr. Gamio understood his behavior better, he himself was ready to modify his
environment. The social worker's role in this example was to
help clarify the real world by asking questions. The client
achieved all other changes by himself. Clarification often
requires more than one interview. And in many situations
clarification alone is not sufficient for problem-solving. Often
clarification is a prelude to other types of social intervention
activities.

Asking questions, the correct questions at the right time,
is one clarification skill. Listening to a person tell his story is

another. Giving a person an opportunity to talk about his problem may be a helpful act because talking to another can enhance a person's ability to understand himself and his situation. Telling the story requires at least a minimum of organization, and this by itself may be helpful. But ventilation alone often does not result in sufficient clarification. Purposeful feedback so that the other person can organize his material and understand it is desirable. Mr. Gamio hardly needed the worker's help to make the connection between what happened at work and at home, but with another client the worker might have had to be more direct, perhaps saying, "You told me that you had a fight with your boss before you finished work on Tuesday—and two hours later you beat up your wife. Last week on Thursday you also had a fight with your boss and also beat up your wife. When did you beat your wife before that?" These questions and further feedback statements may be pursued until the client understands his situation better.

Clarification can provide effective help when used at the right time with the right problem, but it can become dangerous when used inappropriately. While many troubled people find it helpful to unburden themselves to a social worker, others become more and more upset when they talk about their problems. Instead of finding relief, they become more confused by their own confusion. Social workers must learn when clarification is a useful intervention technique and when another technique is to be preferred. Most beginning social workers are not equipped to deal with unconscious and repressed material and should leave problems involving this level of data to psychiatrists or to social workers with specialized advanced training.

*Defense mechanisms.* Understanding past events can be helpful for clarifying a current problem, but the focus always should be on the present and the future. It may be appropriate to help a client understand how his own childhood problems have influenced his current relationships with his children. But the social worker's focus in social intervention must be on current problems and on trying to do something about them now, not on what happened in the distant past. Obstacles may be encountered when exploring that part of the past which relates to the current problem. Defense mechanisms such as denial, repression, displacement, and projection are not uncommon since people generally do not want to be reminded of what was unpleasant, uncomfortable, or distressful. It is important to remember, however, that the same defense mechanisms which can keep people from understanding themselves also enable them to continue coping with daily life.

MR. GUSTAMENTA could not find a better job and blamed this on discrimination against Chicanos when, in fact, there were no good jobs for people who did not know how to read and write. MRS. CAREY blamed her husband's secretary for the strained family relationships without understanding how her own behavior had contributed to the near breakup of their marriage. The members of the Black Jets, a teen-age dance band, claimed after their application to participate in the Cancer Marathon had been rejected, that they really had not wanted to play on that night.

In these and similar situations the defense mechanism must be overcome before the person can understand his situation and do something about it. When defense mechanisms prevent a person from functioning at his full capacity they are dysfunctional. However, before helping a person overcome and abandon such defense mechanisms, the social worker must make sure that the person is sufficiently strong to continue functioning without them. Can Mr. Gustamenta continue to function as the head of the family if his self-confidence is destroyed? Will Mrs. Carey be able to mobilize herself and continue to function as mother and homemaker once she realizes her share of responsibility for her present predicament? What will happen to the Black Jets if they realize that despite long hours of practice they are a poor band? The point is that clarification is not an isolated intervention activity. Usually it occurs as part of a set of intervention activities. It requires skill and experience to determine when and under what conditions clarification is appropriate and effective—and when it is best not to attempt this technique.

## Referral and Linkage

Years ago wandering beggars were given a one-way railroad ticket to the next town. In this way local charity costs were kept to a minimum. Though there may be some social workers today who utilize referral techniques in a similar vein to transfer difficult and complex cases to another agency, referral and linkage are legitimate intervention techniques because they permit the extension of services beyond those available at any one agency. Far from dumping unwanted cases, referral and linkage assure implementation of the strategy most appropriate for any given problem.

Linking the person with available resources has always been an important social work activity. A social worker in a welfare department may refer one client to the legal aid service and another to a mental health clinic. A hospital social worker refers a patient's family to the county welfare department. One neighborhood worker is popularly known as "Mr. Information Please" because he knows where to send people with their problems and where to secure services. And a community social worker does not attempt to solve every community problem singlehandedly but instead knows the resources available for most problems that come up. Social workers, no matter where they work, spend considerable time in referral and linkage activities. Bertha Reynolds (1964), veteran casework teacher, wrote that "we are ever and always a go-between profession." This characteristic can be applied to all social workers. And according to Werner Boehm (1968), this linkage function of social workers will become even more important in the future.

Referral and linkage take on a primary significance in social agencies specifically designed to facilitate better utilization of existing services. These agencies, sometimes known as Community Information Service, Neighborhood Information Center, or Citizens Advice Bureau, have been established to make established social agencies more accessible to citizens who need their services. In the past, referral services were generally available only to clients of social agencies. But these new agencies are ready to serve all citizens; generally, inquiry can be made anonymously by telephone. One of their objectives is to help people help themselves so that they need not become social agency clients (Kahn, 1966).

*Preparation for referral.* Effective referral requires that the social worker possesses a thorough knowledge of the community and its resources. A quick look through the yellow pages of the telephone book does not provide this kind of information. In many communities there are directories or handbooks of social agencies which list all available social services. But these directories are outdated on publication; further inquiry will be necessary for current information. A visit to the receiving agency, or at least a phone call, is desirable before referral if the worker is not familiar with that agency. The social worker must make sure that the agency to which he is making the referral is the correct resource for this problem and that no other agency is more appropriate for this client. He must have accurate information about the kind of cases the agency accepts, the way it operates, its intake procedures and fee scales, and other basic information which the client should have. But referral involves much more than giving the client information about the new agency. Preparation of the client, as well as preparation of the receiving agency, is part of the referral process. The staff of the receiving agency will need information about the client, his problem, his special needs, as well as the reason for the referral. Generally, a referral letter which specifies all of this information is sufficient, but there are times when a supplementary phone call or even a preliminary conference is indicated.

Preparation of the client for referral is not something that can be started ten minutes before he is sent to another agency. If the client has been involved in all of the earlier phases of the social intervention process, he will have been a partner to the referral decision. The worker may have contributed his expert knowledge of community resources and identified the specific agency which offers the required service, but the client himself was involved in the strategy decision. However, if the client was not involved in this decision, he may not understand the reason for the referral. He may interpret the referral as the worker's way of rejecting him. This danger exists especially with clients who have repeatedly experienced rejection. And unless a client is sufficiently motivated, he will not take full advantage of the services which the second agency offers. The worker must recognize that referral to another agency may be felt as a threat, just as every new and unknown experience may be threatening. The worker's acceptance of these fears and his readiness to continue work with the client even after the referral has been made tend to reduce the threat of the new and the fear of rejection.

Telling a person about another service, even sending a referral letter, does not end the referral activity. No referral should be considered completed until the referring social worker has followed up to make sure that the client did not get lost on the way but did arrive at the second agency and is using its services.

## Emotional Support

In our complex society man finds it increasinly difficult to cope with the problems facing him. The reasons for this are many and include the increased pace of change, the breakdown of traditional institutions (family, school, church, government), changes in basic societal values, multiplication of acceptable life styles, and increased social and geographic mobility. Today many of the traditional helpers are no longer available when people need help with their problems. New procedures are needed to provide the kind of help that was once proffered naturally. Offering emotional support, for example, was once a function of the family. Every family provided emotional support to its members, even when the family was not aware that it did so. Today many find that their family still provides this basic support, but others have discovered that their family is no longer effective in this area. These are the people who turn for emotional support to professional helpers, such as social workers.

Emotional support appears in two varieties: *active* support and *inactive* support. *Active emotional support* requires positive activity by the social worker. After KEVIN MINTON, the unemployed ex-convict, started working as a janitor, his social worker told him how proud he was of him for taking the first job that became available. By offering such approval the social worker provided positive reinforcement. Whenever people change their behavior markedly, they need the support of others. For Kevin Minton, accepting a low-level job was a radical change. At this particular time the worker's approval and support were most important.

*Inactive emotional support* can be even more powerful than active support because, unlike the latter, it is ongoing and not limited to the time when the worker is present. By offering his presence and his ready availability, the social worker enables the other person to feel that, if necessary, the worker would take over or do something to support him. But, in fact, he does not take over since the very purpose of providing emotional support is to strengthen the other person so that he can carry on autonomously with his life tasks.

When emotional support is offered inappropriately there is a danger that the client will feel weaker and in time become dependent upon the worker. In one demonstration project, indigenous workers were highly successful in modifying unacceptable behavior patterns of selected public housing tenants by offering emotional support together with several concrete services; the results of the demonstration were gratifying, at least in the beginning. Positive behavior changes were noted among many of the participants, but before long it became evident that they were no longer able to make even simple decisions without asking the worker what they should do. Here was a situation where the secondary consequences of emotional support were dysfunctional, even though emotional support was helpful in achieving the original objectives. A reduction of active emotional support, together with a greater emphasis on inactive emotional support, might have achieved more desirable results.

The social worker who provides emotional support, active or inactive, needs to have a high tolerance for passivity and frustration. Even though he may be more capable than his client and can get things done more quickly and perhaps even more effectively, he must learn to be passive and to remain in the background. He must also master the skill of offering support without domineering the client and without making him feel powerless or cheap. The social worker must attempt to eliminate his own punitive and judgmental attitudes, feelings which are common but which present obstacles to effective social intervention. Viewing people as either "good" or "bad," their behavior as either "right" or "wrong," or their problem as either "normal" or "deviant," interferes with providing helpful emotional support. Instead, the worker must learn to accept people as they are. When giving emotional support, he must show an interest in the other person and his problem. And the worker must demonstrate that he knows how to help and that he is ready to do so.

Empathy is a basic quality in the worker's response, yet empathy must occur within the professional relationship lest it turn into overidentification with the client's problem. While empathy is desirable, overidentification inhibits effective social intervention. Workers must learn where showing an interest ends and overinvolvement starts. In most situations when the worker is more concerned about a problem than the client or victim, overinvolvement has already occurred. If the client is unable to show concern, a worker's greater concern may be appropriate. Thus, a social worker will be more concerned about an abandoned infant than is that child. But when an adult does not care what is happening to himself, the worker must reduce his involvement without abandoning his efforts to be helpful. An interest and a readiness to help are always appropriate, but overinvolvement and overidentification must be avoided.

## Negotiating and Bargaining

Negotiating and bargaining are concepts which originated in the business world. Two businessmen will negotiate a contract to sell a certain piece of property and they may bargain over the price. The parties who participate in negotiating and bargaining assume that an agreement is both possible and desirable. Social workers have borrowed this terminology because it aptly describes a set of activities in which they and their clients engage. The target problems of social work, it will be recalled, include people-to-people relationships (interpersonal relations) and people-to-organization relationships (formal relations). In both types of relationships one party desires something that the other party has or can supply; this something may be a concrete object (such as money or clothing), a service (such as a bed in a nursing home), or a sentiment (such as love, acceptance, recognition). Usually, negotiating and bargaining are more or less natural processes which involve the exchange of resources. But natural exchanges require parity, or at least the appearance of equality, between the two parties. When this condition does not exist, the natural exchange mechanisms do not function adequately, and the assistance of a third party, such as a social worker, may be needed.

Mr. Smith had little difficulty in finding a private nursing home for his invalid mother since he can easily afford to pay the high monthly fee. Mr. Doby, who barely manages to feed his four children, cannot afford a private nursing home for his invalid father; he must rely on the social worker's help in negotiating for a place in a public institution. When Crestwood Heights, an exclusive suburban development, was hit by a series of burglaries, the residents decided to engage a private protection service. The residents of the KENNEDY HOUSES also need protection against burglars but do not know how to go about obtaining better police services. They, in the end, asked the neighborhood worker to negotiate for them with the police department.

Negotiations often are possible even in the face of obvious inequality between the parties. There are several reasons for the paradox of a powerful person or organization negotiating with a weak person. These reasons include:

1. Our culture in most instances encourages, even demands, negotiated agreements instead of conflicts.

2. The party without power may still be in a position to cause injury or harm (riots, strikes, rumors, and so forth) if it fails to receive some of the desired things.

3. Even the powerless can lend or withhold some significant support, such as the vote.

4. There sometimes is legal compulsion to render or accept services, the terms of which may be negotiable (the city must provide education for every child of school age but the location of the school and the hours of schooling may be negotiable).

Nevertheless, though there are pressures toward negotiating, the objective gap between powerful bureaucrats and the powerless masses often precludes meaningful negotiations. Some organizations offer their services on a take-it-or-leave-it basis. Others attempt to hide their services from the general public, reserving them for those who have sufficient power or skill to demand them. Given this situation, the social worker can assist large sections of the public by intervening so as to eliminate or overcome the obstacles which preclude meaningful and natural negotiations. Social workers do this in one or more of the following ways:

1. *Bringing the parties together.* Here the worker's activity is similar to linkage, but in the latter, when clients are referred to another agency, the terms of service are already established while here the parties are brought together for the specific purpose of negotiating.

2. *Defining the situation so that bargaining can take place.* Often the successful outcome of negotiations is based on a strategic definition rather than on the merits of the case or on the negotiator's skills or power.

3. *Acting as trainer or consultant to the client.* This is done so that he can be more skillful and more knowledgeable in the negotiations process.

4. *Negotiating on behalf of the client.* This worker activity is close to advocacy but differs in that here the worker remains autonomous.

Mark Ortego's work with the KENNEDY HOUSES TENANTS COUNCIL illustrates several of these strategies. Conditions in this housing project were deteriorating almost daily. No repairs had been made in over a year. A defective elevator door which had resulted in one fatal accident was only one of several death traps. But the project manager continued to ignore all complaints. When the tenants turned to Mark for help, he suggested that the Tenants Council invite the project manager to a meeting. In the past the tenants had always gone to the manager's office; shifting the scene was one way of redefining the situation. Mark himself called on the manager on the morning prior to the scheduled meeting to add his weight to the Council's invitation. He told the manager that the president of his agency would attend the meeting as an observer, thus lending the power and support of the agency to the Council when negotiating with the manager. Despite these preparations the meeting proved unsuccessful because the manager was unwilling to listen to the tenants. Mark thereupon made an appointment with the executive director of the city housing authority to see what could be done to improve conditions in the project. It is generally more effective if the

group or the individual client rather than the worker negoti-
ates, but this is not an ironclad rule. Here Mark attempted to
bring together the tenants and the officials responsible for the
housing projects, but before doing so he wanted to become
acquainted with these officials. At most other times Mark
played a more passive role, insisting that the tenants do their
own negotiating while he acted as catalyst, trainer, convener,
and consultant. However, when the occasion demanded it, he
took a more active role in the negotiations.[2]

## Advocacy

Ernesto Gonzales has been trying to find out if he is eligible
for veterans' benefits but has been unable to get an answer
from anybody. Flo Cadmus knows that she needs psychiatric
treatment but has been unable to obtain an appointment at
the neighborhood mental health clinic. The tenants of the
KENNEDY HOUSES are at their wit's end. The last garbage truck
had come by three weeks ago, and they were about to be
drowned by man-sized piles of smelly garbage. A group of
welfare mothers read in the newspaper that they are to receive
a special winter clothing allowance for their school-age children, but their workers told them that there was no such allowance.

These are typical of the problems brought to the social
worker which require advocacy services. Because they are
powerless, many people can obtain the things or services to
which they are entitled only through the intervention of an
advocate. This advocate uses himself exclusively to meet his
client's interests. He serves as a "partisan in social conflict" in
order to advance their interests (Grosser, 1965). Social workers have been urged by their professional organization to give
first priority to the rights and needs of their clients (NASW,
1969). When a social worker acts as an advocate, he places his

2. Client-worker negotiations about the contract will be discussed in
chapter 11.

professional power and skill at the disposal of his clients so that they become more powerful in their contacts with the various institutions and people with whom they must deal.

The social work advocate must identify fully and completely with his client's interests. When representing a group of tenants in their dealing with the housing authority, he becomes thoroughly involved in the conflict, much as a union organizer takes the employees' side in their dealing with management. Their fight becomes his fight. He argues their cause and maneuvers on their behalf so that they can achieve what they set out to obtain. The advocate permits, even encourages, his clients to use him in any way that will help their cause. Unlike the more traditional social worker, who attempts to connect people with institutions by giving information or by referral, the advocate social worker supplies power, his power, to those who lack it.

There are several reasons that today's clients need advocacy services and why social workers are well-suited to offer them. The changing needs and interests of clients and communities often are not fully recognized by many of the existing institutions. This may be due to the bureaucratic tendency of doing things as they were always done or it may be the result of a prior concern with maintaining the organization. Hostility to, and rejection of, those unwilling or unable to assume traditional client roles is another reason that advocacy has become a necessity. Mr. Gonzales might have been able to receive the information he wanted had he not insisted on speaking Spanish to the receptionist. Mrs. Cadmus might have received an appointment at the mental health clinic had she been willing to wait patiently for four hours. Clients and groups of clients who refuse to be submissive or who fail to follow accepted norms find it increasingly difficult to obtain services. Often clients are at a disadvantage because they lack knowledge and information about their rights and how to obtain these.

As with other professional roles, but perhaps even more

so, the social worker who is engaged in advocacy must be aware of his own behavior and the role position he occupies. He must have full knowledge of the various options available and he must be comfortable in using himself differentially, as appropriate for the problem, the goals, and the target. His activities as an advocate will cover the full range of skills, from passive to active, including exploration, negotiation, appeal, bargaining, demanding, and so on. Advocacy does not necessarily mean hostile confrontation. Though angry words may be used at times, the advocacy strategy basically depends on the use of the worker's power (and not his anger) on behalf of his clients. And power depends in no small measure on a knowledge of the resources, whom to call, what to say, how to say it.

Advocacy will hardly be effective if a single worker engages in it. Only when advocacy characterizes the approach of an entire agency will it become an effective technique (Rosenberg and Brody, 1974:8). The inevitable conflict between client interests and agency loyalties can be reduced or avoided only when the agency supports the worker's advocacy activities. But problems will arise even then. The advocacy agency which is too successful in gaining resources or benefits for its clients may be viewed as a threat to the society. No agency will be permitted for long to engage in activities to which the larger society objects. When New York's Mobilization for Youth, one of the pioneer social work advocacy agencies, was perceived as a threat to the established community, that community applied breaks to its programs. So long as social work is dependent on community support, its ability to provide advocacy services will be somewhat limited. The legal-advocate model is not applicable to social work since the lawyer-advocate is engaged and paid by his clients, while the social worker is generally hired and paid by the community. In order to avoid this dilemma and still provide advocacy services, some social agencies have attempted to redefine the function of the social work advocate. They suggest that he be a person who is sensitive to oppressed people but one whose primary commitment is to the agency. This may be "practical" social work, but it is not advocacy! The essence of advocacy is the worker's complete identification with the client's interests.

## Setting Limits

Every day social workers face situations where they must set limits, say "no," withhold permission, or in some other way exercise control functions. KEVIN MINTON asked for permission to work as a bartender, but his parole officer said "no" because the law prohibits parolees from working in bars. When ten-year-old Steve Ellis told his social worker that he was planning to run away from his foster home once again, the worker had to intervene quickly and set limits. Eve McDowell was spending too much time with her boyfriend and was not taking care of her six-months-old baby; she discovered that her social worker was ready to help her in various ways but at the same time demanded that she take proper care of her baby. At one time the family, the church, and the community itself were able to socialize and control people in natural, unobtrusive ways so that there was little need for outsiders to set limits. But these traditional control agencies have become less effective and no longer provide dynamic guidelines for behavior. Weakened internal controls, the increasing prevalence of deviant and delinquent behavior patterns, and the continued decline of traditional control agencies have brought about the need for social workers to become active in this area.

In many ways social workers have been involved in setting limits since the earliest days of the profession. One of the major assignments of early social workers was the control of the behavior of the lower classes so that they did not become too great a threat to the establishment. The vocabulary has changed, but to this day social workers are engaged in "cooling off," "socialization," and similar activities. They are still expected to modify their clients' behavior so that it will conform more closely to the community's norms. This responsibility is assumed explicitly in some agencies, such as the parole and probation service; in other agencies this control function is met in less recognizable ways, but it is always present.

Setting limits should be of benefit not only to the community, but also to the individual with whom the social worker comes in contact. The point here is not *noblesse oblige;* that is, what is good for the community must also be good for the individual. Instead, the social control activity should benefit the individual quite apart from any benefit that society derives from it. Incarceration benefits the community because it physically removes the criminal for a stated period of time; but unless incarceration also benefits the criminal, it will fail to contribute to effecting any socially desirable changes in the person.

Failure to set limits when these are indicated does not help anybody. The immature mother who mistreats her child must be stopped. The distraught adolescent who wants to commit suicide because her boyfriend has run off with her best girlfriend must be prevented from doing so. Setting limits may not be sufficient when people need help, but unless limits are set first, they will not be around later to receive help. Of course, how limits are set and in what ways people are stopped are almost as important as the act of stopping them itself. When setting limits the social worker has already set in motion forces which will either impede or facilitate the success of further intervention activities. There may be more to setting limits than "saying 'no' with a smile," but the smile and the warmth are important. When exercising controls, the social worker must be sure that the other person understands his intentions: he is setting limits to specific activities or behaviors which are harmful to the person himself or to another person but he is not rejecting the person whom he is stopping.

*Short-term and long-term objectives.* When setting limits, the social worker must be clear about his objectives since the specific mode of intervention will depend on what he hopes to achieve. The control activity may be designed to have an immediate or a long-range impact. Putting a stop to present behavior may be essential but may not have any long-range effect. The worker may use physical force to stop a teen-ager from jumping out of the window, but unless there is a more basic change in the total situation, subsequent suicide attempts are likely to occur. If the objective is a basic change in behavior patterns, ways other than physical force must be found and used. Changing the environment, though usually not considered a control activity, is one method which can be used for this purpose. The environment can be changed by modifying the physical situation in which the person is located or by moving him to another environment. When a worker places a battered child with a foster family, he has modified the parents' environment and limited their further capacity to mistreat their child. At the same time, he has provided a new and more friendly environment for the child. No direct limits were placed on the parents, but the worker has set effective limits to their destructive behavior by removing the child. In a family where there is more than the usual amount of parent-teen conflict, one way to limit the conflict behavior is to arrange for the teen-ager to attend a boarding school. Again, no direct limits are placed on the combatants, but opportunity for further conflict is reduced by the teen's removal.

Moving the person to a new environment achieves more than geographic removal. One direct consequence is that the new environment can provide more positive models who also will serve as indirect control agents. The adolescent who associates with a predelinquent gang may change his behavior if he can be helped to participate in another peer group where more positive role models are available. The effectiveness of models as control mechanisms and change agents depends in large part on the intensity and endurance of the relationship between the person providing the model and the person who is to be limited or changed: the more intense and the more enduring the relationship, the greater the chances for success.

Praising or rewarding desirable behavior and contrasting it with the behavior to be limited may increase the frequency of the desired behavior and may decrease that of the censured behavior. If the substitute behavior patterns result in greater gratification than the original, the likelihood for continued change in the desired direction is great. The child who is praised by his parents for bringing home a good report card but scolded for poor marks will try hard to improve his schoolwork, particularly if he is fond of his parents. If the rewards for completing high school could be made greater than the immediate gratification received from dropping out early, it would be far easier to solve the problem of early school-leaving. What complicates the solution of this problem, as of so many others, is the invisibility of delayed gratification. While the disapproved activity, such as early school-leaving, results in some immediate rewards (freedom from studies, a job with a cash income), the gratification from the approved activity may be years away. A greater life-time income for the high school graduate may mean little today to the poor high school student who sees his dropout friend driving his own car.

*Punishment and physical force.* Disapproval and punishment are two common control methods. While they may not be so effective as positive reinforcements, negative reinforcers also serve a purpose, particularly when it is not possible to offer immediate gratification for behaving correctly. Negative reinforcements become stronger and are more effective when they occur within a meaningful and ongoing relationship. Thus, the mild disapproval of a well-liked teacher is generally more effective than a serve punishment meted out by a remote principal. Friends, especially a group of friends, can be effective in setting limits. The peer group demands acceptance of a common set of behavioral norms and attempts to control the behavior of those who violate these norms. But a peer group is an effective social control agent only when its value system is in consonance with society's value system. However, often the very people whose behavior must be limited belong to a peer group which condones or even encourages deviant behavior patterns. Prostitutes rarely belong to a peer group which condemns prostitution. More often they find companionship among colleagues or friends who tolerate a large variety of disapproved behavior patterns. In such cases the group complicates rather than facilitates the social worker's social control efforts.

Physical force, as we noted earlier, is an effective control technique when the objective is to limit overt behavior at once. However, physical force requires physical power on the part of the person who attempts to apply the limits. Unless the social worker is stronger than the client, the use of physical force will not be feasible. Furthermore, once the worker discontinues the force, the behavior is likely to return to its former pattern unless other changes have occurred in the meantime. For example, when a teen-ager is beating a younger boy, the social worker, if he is sufficiently strong, can restrain the teen by pinning his arms behind his back. When he relaxes his hold two or three minutes later, the teen may have cooled down or the younger boy may have been spirited away—or the beating may resume. The time-limited effect of physical force as a control mechanism is one problem. The fact that it usually generates strong antagonistic feelings toward the controller may be even more serious a problem for the social worker who must establish a positive relationship if there is to be an effective social intervention. For all of these reasons physical force is not a preferred intervention technique, but it does have its place in the social worker's repertoire of control techniques.

*Worker's values and biases.* When setting limits, the social worker acts as the agent of society. Societal goals and norms become his reference point and his sanction. The worker whose own value system differs from that of the larger society must make sure that his professional activities reflect societal interests and not his own biases. Whether or not to set limits should never depend on how a particular worker feels. If society permits homosexual relations between consenting adults, a worker must not attempt to limit such behavior even if his own code proscribes it. But when limits are indicated, they should be applied even if a worker does not enjoy setting limits. And those workers who do enjoy being in authority must restrain themselves lest they set limits when these are not indicated. The style of applying limits also should reflect societal preferences rather than individual idiosyncracies. In contemporary America there is a preference for positive rather than negative limits, for informal rather than formal restraints, and for personal rather than impersonal controls. Thus, we prefer counseling to police enforcement, and voluntary family planning to compulsory sterilization.

## Summary

In this chapter we considered a variety of basic intervention activities, the kind which even beginning workers will have occasion to utilize. The specific choice of which activity to use when must be made on the basis of a full assessment of the problem indentified, the persons involved, and the goals to be achieved. A certain intervention activity might be very effective with one family and not at all with another, even though the problem and the goal appear to be the same.

The social worker must always keep in mind the client's request when selecting the intervention activity, even though he may not always be able to meet it. In most instances the client will be an active participant in developing the intervention activity. This will insure that the activity selected will be appropriate to the person and the problem. The potential effectiveness of the activity should be a major criterion. An intervention activity should never be chosen merely because it is the agency's or the worker's standard response to a given problem.

# chapter ten

# Engagement Skills

Person-to-person contact is at the heart of every social intervention activity regardless whether the client is a single person, a family, a group, a neighborhood, or a community. No matter what the nature of the problem or the type of the strategy, engagement between people is a requisite for successful social intervention. True, relationships alone often are not enough to resolve a problem situation, yet a social intervention strategy which fails to involve the various participants usually will not succeed.

Engagement between the client (or other participants) and the social worker does not just happen. If these two people were to meet on a street corner or at a social party, they might or might not strike up a conversation. Whether they will, depends on many factors, such as mutual attraction, alternative opportunities, current psychological needs, societal norms, and so on. But in the professional engagement between a social worker and a client the engagement cannot be left to chance. These factors must not determine whether the worker will become involved in the social intervention process. On the contrary, a social worker is expected to work with all people who are eligible to receive the agency's services and who want help, even if he would avoid these same people under other circumstances. A worker might not befriend a person who last took a shower two months ago, but when this person requests help from a social agency, the worker has a professional obligation to respond—and if the request is appropriate for social intervention, his first response must be the development of a professional relationship. This relationship resembles but is not the same as the interaction between friends and acquaintances, a relationship with which the client is already familiar. It is also different from the relationships which the client may have had with other professionals and with bureaucratic officials. The strangeness of this new relationship will confuse many new clients; because it is strange, they may misinterpret the worker's activities and intentions and feel that he does not care.

The worker's purposeful use of himself on behalf of his client is perhaps the key difference between a professional and a personal engagement. Developing this professional relationship requires more than merely offering concrete services, important as these are. Listening with a sympathetic ear is a crucial skill in many helping situations, but this and more are required for a professional relationship. Effective engagement in the social intervention process will occur only when there is a degree of trust and acceptance between worker and client, when the worker accepts the client as someone who is *able* and *interested* in solving his own problems and when the client accepts the worker as a person who is *competent* and *ready* to help him learn how to cope with his problems. While we cannot require that a worker like every client who is assigned to him, we must be sure that he will accept each one as a human being who has the potential to participate in the social intervention process. An involuntary client, such as a prisoner or a very young child, may not be sufficiently motivated to participate in problem-solving, especially in the beginning stage, but unless the worker can recognize that person's potentials for participation and then purposefully develop them, the engagement will remain at a most minimal level.

The social intervention process can be divided into a number of sequential phases, each with its unique tasks and requirements. The *beginning phase* starts even before the first contact between client and worker and continues until agreement has been reached on the intervention strategy and on the tasks which each of the participants will undertake. Typically, during the beginning phase the participants are anxious about becoming involved; they may express their anxiety in many different ways. The special worker tasks during this phase include making contact with the client, assisting the applicant in becoming a client, reducing anxiety, developing engagement, clarifying the problem, determining the goals, planning a strategy, and negotiating the contract.

The unique tasks of the *middle phase*, which begins once the contract has been agreed to, include implementing the strategy, maintaining the involvement of all participants, strengthening client autonomy or preventing an increase in client dependency, providing for feedback of ongoing assessment, and renegotiating the contract when necessary to assure further progress toward goal achievement. A typical problem during the middle phase is the "plateau"; suddenly, after a period of progress, progress seems to cease; it is as though everything has come to a full stop. This problem is not unique to social work but has been noticed by professionals in many different learning situations. "Rocking the boat" may be indicated to overcome the problem; the worker may need to do something unexpected, even drastic, to shake the participants out of their seeming lethargy.

The major task of the *termination phase* is to ensure that the disengagement from the social intervention process does not result in the renewal or re-creation of the problem situation. During this phase there is often a reappearance of behavior patterns which were first noticed in the beginning phase: the client who was anxious then may again become anxious; acting-out behavior may reappear, and so on. The worker must deal with this but should not be deflected from the termination tasks.

Engagement skills must be used differentially because of the varying tasks which face the worker and the client in each phase. But the ability to engage the client and to maintain this engagement is basic throughout the social intervention process. There are relatively few research findings to indicate which specific skills are most useful in creating and maintaining engagement. Nevertheless, there is general agreement that the following are essential elements for successful engagement: (1) warmth and humor; (2) accepting the client as he is; (3) starting where the client is; (4) lowering the client's anxiety and (5) fear; and (6) worker insight and self-awareness.

These elements not only represent the "practice wisdom" of several generations of practicing social workers, but they can also be deduced from the theories and propositions presented in earlier chapters. The first element can be deduced from the propositions on the characteristics of effective helpers (chapter 6). The second and third elements are corollaries of the basic social work value concerning respect for the uniqueness and inherent dignity of every human being (chapter 2). These elements are also corollaries of the basic social work value which calls for accepting and valuing differences in people (chapter 5). The fourth element can be deduced from the propositions about client participation in all phases of the social intervention process (chapters 3 and 4).[1] The fifth element is a corollary of the proposition that the purposeful use of self is a key characteristic of the professional relationship.

Social workers need a large variety of skills to effect successful engagement. In this chapter we will examine some of

1. There is contradictory evidence on the influence of anxiety and fear in the social intervention process. Janis and Feshback (1953) report that anxiety and fear immobilized people and limited their constructive participation. But Levenger (1960) and Ripple (1955) cite other studies which suggest that clients will continue in the casework relationship only as long as they are anxious. Perhaps the contradiction can be resolved by suggesting that there is a "zone of anxiety" which is functional for participation. An anxiety which exceeds this zone or which falls short of it will counterindicate active participation in the social intervention process. Overanxious people and indifferent people are among the most difficult people to involve in social intervention.

the skills needed to cope with problems encountered in the engagement process.

## Client Problems and Worker Skills During Engagement Process

| *Client Problems* | *Worker Skills* |
|---|---|
| 1. Client is unaware of role expectations. | 1. Structuring |
| 2. Client fears depersonalization and imposition of nonrelevant goals. | 2. Focusing |
| 3. Differences between client and worker interfere with communication. | 3. Bridging the gap |
| 4. Time has different meanings. | 4. Timing |
| 5. Client fears being judged. | 5. Judge not |
| 6. Client wonders whether worker is interested. | 6. Activity |
| 7. Client must perceive worker as competent and ready to help. | 7. Setting the tone |

## Structuring

Interactions in the social intervention process are similar to other relationships with which the client is already familiar but which differ from them in several respects. In a professional relationship the focus is limited to the achievement of specified goals while the objectives of a friendship relationship are more generalized and all-inclusive. But the social intervention relationship differs even from other, more limited professional relationships where clients have learned to be passive and to leave the problem-solving to the expert. When clients note that the social worker receives them in a friendlier and more relaxed way than many other professionals, they may mistake this approach for an invitation to a friendship relationship. However, they soon realize that the social worker does not function like a friend nor does he take over like the traditional expert whom they have met elsewhere. As a result, the new client may be confused or disappointed. But before the new client (or other participant) can participate effectively in the social intervention process, he must learn to understand both his role and that of the social worker. Without this basic understanding frustration and withdrawal will occur instead of participation and goal achievement. *Structuring* is the worker skill which can be used to help people obtain the necessary understanding.

One of the ways in which people learn what is expected of them is through the reactions of others. A child attempts to understand how others see him in order to know how to behave. This feedback information becomes a part of the self. If a teacher treats a child as if he were stupid, the child before long will accept this definition and will try to perform according to the teacher's expectations. In one experiment teachers were told that randomly selected first and second graders would "spurt ahead" academically within the year. And, indeed, the IQ scores of these youngsters showed dramatic gains, while those not identified as spurters did not gain (Rosenthal and Jacobson, 1968).

Adults do not hesitate to tell children that they did wrong nor are they reluctant to tell youngsters that their behavior was not acceptable. But often adults are reluctant to let other adults know that they have made a mistake or that they are behaving inappropriately. Critical feedback to adults is almost taboo in our culture, but this can make for problems when adults encounter a new situation for which they must learn a new role. Becoming a client is such a situation which requires learning new role behaviors. It will be helpful to provide first-time applicants with more feedback about their role behavior than is currently regarded as polite. But some social workers remain silent and passive because they believe that the client should set the direction for the engagement. They forego the opportunity of providing the client with helpful feedback. However, excessive worker passivity is not conducive to establishing meaningful engagement, especially in the beginning. This is what Julianna Schmidt (1969:81) may have had in mind when she observed that "unless a client knows clearly how his worker views their respective roles in determining interview content and direction, he is not free to make a choice." Structuring the relationship will strengthen rather than limit opportunities for self-determination.

The worker's notes on his meeting with MRS. CAREY present several examples of structuring:

### . . . *from the worker's notes of his first meeting with* **Mrs. Carey**

| | |
|---|---|
| *Timing* | The receptionist called at 10:30 to say that Mrs. Carey, my 11:00 appointment, had arrived and that |
| *Focusing* | she appeared nervous and upset. I told her not to |
| *Setting tone* | send Mrs. Carey to my office but that I would come to |
| *Activity* | the waiting room to greet her there. (I felt it important to do something to show Mrs. Carey from the very beginning that I wanted to help her.) |

In the waiting room I found Mrs. Carey, a pleasant looking, well-dressed woman in her early thirties. She appeared uncomfortable and nervous but responded appropriately to my greetings. On the way to my office she participated freely in small talk—the weather, traffic, parking. When we entered my office, she

*Setting tone* glanced at my diplomas but said nothing; however,
*Bridging gap* she did comment about the prints on the wall, saying that she had a similar one in her living room. I sug-
*Structuring* gested that she had not come to talk about fine art but about her son and the problem she was having with
*Focusing* him. I asked her to tell me about the problem she was having with her son. She told her story freely without any need for me to prompt her or to ask clarifying questions. [See Part III for a summary of Mrs. Carey's statement of the problem.]

After Mrs. Carey finished I told her that I understood
*Judge not* how difficult this situation must be for her. I said that this was the kind of problem situation in which the Family Service can be of assistance—but that there are
*Structuring* no easy ways to solve problems of this nature. Hard work on the part of Mrs. Carey and the other Careys would be required to resolve this problem. If she was interested, I was ready to help her and together we could do something about the problem. She said she

would like to try. I asked whether she would help me
become acquainted with Ben and the other family
members so that I could better understand the total
problem. She agreed to come back, together with
Ben, next week.

Almost at the beginning of their meeting Mrs. Carey
talked about their common interests, much as she would talk
to a friend or casual acquaintance, but this worker reminded
her that *she had not come to talk about fine art but about her son.*
This statement may have been somewhat blunt; a polite reply
(such as, "I'm glad that you also like prints"), followed by a
reminder about the purpose of their relationship, might have
been more appropriate. In his very next comment the worker
tried to clarify the structure of their relationship even
further—they were to talk about *the problem she was having with
her son,* not about her son and his problems. This may have
been an assumption on the worker's part; he may have moved
too fast by focusing on Mrs. Carey's problem when the problem may have been her son's. But he wanted her to know that
he was there to help with her problem. "I asked her to tell me"
gave Mrs. Carey the signal to start talking. Mrs. Carey was a
highly verbal client, and no additional structuring messages
were required to secure her verbal participation. With other
clients this might be necessary. But Mrs. Carey avoided talking
about her problem and described only her son's problem. The
worker sensed that Mrs. Carey, after presenting the problem,
wanted to withdraw and let the worker take over and solve the
problem. He tried to correct this mistaken expectation by telling her that her continued participation would be necessary:
*hard work on the part of Mrs. Carey and the other Careys would be
required.* His job was not to solve the problem, but *he was ready
to help her and together "we could do something about the problem."*
Perhaps the social worker assigned to the YOUNG ADULT
HIKING CLUB had his reasons for remaining in the background
during the early part of the group's first meeting. But structuring is also important when the client is a group. Unless

group members learn early in the group encounter what is expected of them, their participation may not be appropriate.
This can become a critical issue when the agency's goals remain hidden from the group members. At times a group is
formed as a "fun club" when the agency's real purpose is to effect behavioral changes, prevent delinquency, strengthen coping patterns, and so forth. Such a procedure not only raises
ethical questions, but also is of doubtful effectiveness.

    At times the worker is faced by an emergency which
requires immediate attention and worker intervention. Young
children have not had any food since yesterday morning because their family has exhausted all resources. Dozens of people are freezing because the furnace of a tenement building
broke down last Thursday and today the outside temperature
is below zero. The members of the Sultan Gang have vowed to
take immediate revenge for their comrade who just died as a
result of a stab wound inflicted by members of a rival gang. In
these and similar situations the worker faces a difficulty. On
the one hand he must take immediate action. But on the other
hand, by stepping in and doing things for people he may
structure the situation in a way which may be inappropriate
for professional engagement. Yet if he did not cope with the
emergency at once, future engagement might be altogether
impossible.

    Perhaps the difficulty is more apparent than real. Struc-
turing does not counterindicate worker activity. In fact, the
social worker who fails to act when his intervention is called
for does not fulfill his professional role obligation in a responsible manner. Structuring does mean that whatever a social
worker does or says should be done in a manner which will
facilitate, not discourage, further engagement. The social
worker must make sure that the children eat something even
before they leave his office, but menu planning and shopping
for supplies for the next few days should be done by the
children's mother or, if she is not ready to do so alone, by the
mother and worker together. From the very first moment the

worker will utilize every opportunity to structure the relationship so that the client will know exactly what is expected of him and what he can expect of the worker and of the agency. The families in the freezing tenement obviously need heat, but if their worker learns that it will take at least a week to repair the boiler, he can give each family an opportunity to decide whether to move in with friends, to go to a hotel, or to remain and heat the apartment with several electric heaters. In this instance the worker structures the situation by making realistic alternatives possible and by helping every family think through the advantages and disadvantages of each option. Even though in emergencies such as these the time for decision-making is brief, a beginning to mutual engagement must occur from the first moment of the encounter. The same approach must prevail in the threatened gang war; the worker's intervention will depend somewhat on any previous contacts which he has had with these gangs, but in any event he will structure the developing situation so as to provide opportunities for early meaningful engagement, even while intervening directly to prevent further bloodshed.

Structuring is especially important in the beginning phase of the social intervention process. It provides the client with timely direct and indirect feedback about his role and the worker's role. Structuring includes creating experiences in which the client can participate appropriately, encouraging the client to assume responsibility for his own fate, explaining what the worker can and cannot do, reinforcing suitable role performance, and disapproving incompatible role behavior. Structuring skills are also utilized in the later phases of the intervention process whenever client role behavior requires reinforcement or when new roles must be learned.

## Focusing

Whenever a person comes to a social agency for the first time, he exposes himself to several dangers. Firstly, he faces the danger of depersonalization, of being transformed into an impersonal number or into a case. Then there is the danger that the worker to whom he is assigned will impose his own objectives (or those of the agency) on the client while ignoring what the client wants. Herbert Gans (1962) spoke of the missionary aims of the caretakers and condemned those social workers who focused on their own agenda rather than on that of their clients. William Whyte (1955) also described the consequences of this approach. The great majority of the residents of Cornerville, the community studied by Whyte, did not participate in the activities of the local settlement house because the staff was more interested in facilitating upward mobility than in helping the residents improve neighborhood conditions; that is, the staff substituted its own goals for those of the residents.[2] Real engagement can occur only when the applicant or new client is convinced that the threat of these two dangers is not acute. By focusing attention on the client and his problems, the social worker can reduce this threat.

Several examples of focusing appear in the worker's notes of his first meeting with MRS. CAREY. Welcoming Mrs. Carey in the *waiting room* instead of having her search along strange corridors for his office was a deliberate attempt to personalize his contact with her. The *small talk* on the way back to his office was also meant to serve this purpose. But most important, giving Mrs. Carey a chance to talk about her problem as she saw it helped focus the interview on Mrs. Carey and her concerns.

Focusing, especially in the beginning phase, relies heavily on the worker's ability to listen and to respond. We will examine these skills in greater detail in chapter 12. Here we will discuss only the aspects of listening and responding that are especially relevant for engagement.

*Listening* requires preparation and concentration. But concentration is not natural when one is listening to someone

2. This approach is no longer characteristic of the contemporary settlement and neighborhood house (Hillman, 1968).

else. The more natural thing is not to pay too close attention since we can listen much faster than the other can speak. The listener's attention tends to wander because he can understand 300–500 words per minute while the average person speaks only 125 words per minute (Kadushin, 1972). As a result, many people listen with only half an ear while their thoughts wander off to other matters. Sometimes a worker thinks that he knows what the client will say after listening to the first few sentences; he has known others who have had a similar problem and he thinks that he can guess the ending before the client has told half of his story. A bored worker will find it difficult to pay attention to what the client is saying. Even when the worker does attempt to listen, his listening will be selective. Often he will hear only what he wants to hear or what fits his initial assessment of the situation (Sandifer, Hordern, and Green, 1970). Given these obstacles to listening, it requires purposeful preparation to remain attentive. Preparation is necessary even for a first meeting with a new applicant or with a new group whom the worker does not yet know. While he must be flexible and be guided by the other person's needs, the worker will want to use the first meeting to obtain certain information about the person and his problem. He will also want to spend some time on informing the person about the agency and the worker. What the worker can and cannot do must be part of the initial agenda. For later meetings, the content of the agenda will differ. But at all times, the focus must be on the client and on his concerns.

Clients are very much aware when workers do not listen. And this disturbs them and prevents their full engagement in the social intervention process. "Why should I become involved," they ask, "if my worker does not care enough to listen to me?" A worker must learn how to convey the impression that he is listening and paying attention. He can do so by asking relevant questions and by making comments which bear on the problems presented by the client. There may be a place for uttering "mmm" or for asking, "What do *you* think?" Unfocused responses like these do indicate that the worker is not asleep and they do give the client an opportunity to proceed with his story, but they fail to convey the worker's concern or his willingness to engage together in doing something about the condition. More appropriate responses will make reference to what the worker has heard from the client. The response may restate what the client has already said or the worker's comments may add a new dimension. Both types of response focus on the client and his problem.

When a member of the YOUNG ADULT HIKING CLUB asked the worker, "What do you think?" he probably was less interested in learning the worker's preferences than in knowing whether the worker was "with" the group. MRS. CAREY's worker carefully listened to her and avoided doing anything which might disturb her while she was telling her story. Since her statement was brief and quite complete there was no need to interrupt, but at the end he did ask a number of questions for clarification (not recorded in the summary). These verified that he had indeed been paying attention to Mrs. Carey. With a longer statement, or a less verbal client, the worker probably would have interrupted with a focusing question to indicate that he was really listening and to help the client tell the rest of her story. When meeting with a group the worker may have to help the members tell their story in a somewhat orderly way. If the participants have had no prior group experience, all members may want to talk at once, or one group member may dominate the conversation. Either way, the social worker can be helpful by "directing traffic" and helping everybody focus on the problem.

## Bridging Gaps

Differences between clients and workers may create difficulties for mutual engagement. Research findings are somewhat ambiguous on the effect of cultural differences, especially differences of race and class, but most published studies suggest that such differences widen the distance between client and worker and that the resulting gap handicaps the development of a meaningful relationship. Studies on the effects of social distance between client and social worker include Banks (1971), Barrett and Perlmutter (1972), Brieland (1969), Burns (1971), Dubey (1970), Kadushin (1972), and Vail (1970). Differences in age and sex may also have an impact on the worker-client engagement, though evidently these interfere less than ethnic and socioeconomoic dissimilarities. What is common about all of these differences is that they are objective differences; a worker cannot change his race or sex or age in order to facilitate engagement with his clients. Although a worker can change his class affiliation, this is hardly a realistic expectation in the American experience. However, this is precisely what has been suggested by some social workers in other countries, especially in France and Chile (Kendall, 1973). Even when the differences between worker and client are relatively small, they may block communication, interaction, and engagement. MRS. CAREY's background was similar to that of her worker, yet she made a point of observing that they shared a liking for the same kind of art prints. Her comment, though seemingly unrelated to the problem which brought her to the agency, may have been an attempt to establish that there was no gap between her and the worker. The worker, on the other hand, did not think that in this instance any worker activity was needed to bridge the gap.

Other differences that tend to limit engagement include experiential differences. Drug addicts often claim that a person who has never used drugs cannot understand what drugs are all about and that such a person cannot become an effective helper for a drug addict. Some parents resist bringing child-rearing problems to the attention of a childless professional, wondering how such a person can possibly know enough to help them. "You wouldn't understand . . ." is a frequently heard phrase in the social agency. Though it carries different meanings, one interpretation is that the gap between client and worker is too wide for meaningful engagement. In some agencies workers with the same experiential background as the client have been employed in a deliberate attempt to bridge this difference. Indigenous workers are assigned to work with the poor, former drug addicts meet with current drug addicts, veteran war widows counsel more recently bereaved war widows, and so on. However, the efficacy of this approach is far from certain (Goldberg, 1969; Jones, 1969; Loewenberg, 1968; Yablonsky, 1965).

In most settings differences between clients and workers continue to exist so that the challenge of finding ways to diminish or to span the gap remains. One school of thought holds that differences are not entirely dysfunctional. Georg Simmel, one of the pioneers of German sociology, taught that differences facilitate rather than block certain types of engagements because people who do not share the same characteristics or broad interests can be much more objective with each other. "People who have many common features often do one another worse or 'worser' wrong than complete strangers do . . ." (Simmel, 1955:43). Yet even Simmel would not deny that gaps between clients and workers need to be bridged; without a bridge, communication and engagement will not be possible.

Specific worker tasks for bridging or decreasing the gap include recognition of the differences, understanding the differences, accepting people despite differences, and maintaining authenticity. As a first step, the worker must stop denying those differences that do exist. Making believe that there are no differences merely reinforces the assumption that engagement is possible only when there are no differences between worker and client, though the operative assumption should be that engagement is possible despite differences. Barbara Shannon (1970), in a perceptive discussion of the implications of white racism for social work practice, observes: "To pretend that the color difference is not noted is to say, 'I will only like you if we are the same,' rather than, 'I like you in spite of our differences.' " Although acceptance rather than liking is the essential prerequisite for the professional relationship, Shannon's observation about racial differences applies equally to other cultural and experiential differences. But recognizing differences is only a first step. Recognition of differences can lead to a positive or a negative outcome. The virulent anti-Semite recognizes the difference between himself and the Jew even while he is not ready to engage in a helping relationship.

After recognizing the differences the worker must learn to understand and accept them. He must become acquainted with cultures and life styles different from his own. He must learn about the behavior patterns which are common in his client's community, though they may appear strange or even deviant to his eyes. Acceptance of these differences occurs when the social worker respects his client (and every person) as a human being who has the right to be different from other persons and when the social worker agrees that every client has the right to decide what he wants to do with his life, even when the worker thinks that this choice is unwise or impractical. The worker must support the client or strengthen him so that he can exercise this right in a way that makes most sense to him. The social worker can help by providing information and resources which will enable people to make choices appropriate to their life styles. Even if the worker himself would have made another decision, his professional obligation is to enable his client to actualize his own choice as long as this choice is legal and does not seriously interfere with the rights of others.

The parents of a brain-damaged child, for example, are thinking about keeping their child at home. Before making a decision these parents will need sympathetic help as well as information about other options. The worker must help them evaluate the "costs" of each of the alternatives; he must also direct their attention to the many consequences of each option. But once these parents have made a decision, the worker must support it to the extent that is consistent with his professional obligations. Once they have decided to keep their child at home, the worker should recruit resources that will make this decision manageable. Perhaps it is possible to arrange for a homemaker to assist the child's mother, or financial assistance can be provided to engage household help, so that the mother can spend some time with her other children. The worker must not use his power and position to veto the parent's decision by withholding resources or interfering with their plans.

Some social workers have attempted to bridge differences by talking or acting like their clients. At first glance this may appear to be an excellent suggestion, but experience indicates that this makes for more rather than for fewer problems. Not only is it extremely difficult, if not impossible, to duplicate a life style other than one's own, but the worker who pretends to be someone he is not is likely to misunderstand the worker-client relationship. This worker attempts to detach his professional role from the appropriate social system and attach it to another to which it does not belong. There are occasions when the judicious use of argot or jargon may be useful to indicate that the social worker is knowledgeable and does understand the other. Thus Kinsey (Kinsey, Pomeroy, and Martin, 1948) observed that by using a few terms from the specialized vocabulary of homosexuals and prostitutes he could quickly establish rapport with members of these groups who usually keep quite a distance between themselves and outsiders. While this technique may be effective for one-time interviewing, in ongoing relationships authenticity is preferable to make-believe. When William Whyte studied Cornerville he learned this lesson early (Whyte, 1955:304):

Trying to enter into the spirit of the small talk, I cut loose with a string of obscenities and profanities. . . . they all stopped to look at me in surprise. Doc shook his head and said: "Bill you're not supposed to talk like that. That doesn't sound like you." . . . Doc insisted . . . that I was different and that they wanted me to be that way. . . . I learned that people did not expect me to be just like them; in fact, they were interested and pleased to find me different. . . .

Social workers assigned to adolescent or young adult groups sometimes believe that the most effective way to bridge the gap is to become like one of the group members—talk like them, dress like them, act like them. This attempt often makes the worker look ludicrous and is usually counterproductive. For example, when one street-corner worker appeared in a pair of new stylish shoes, one of the gang members drew him aside and said, "I hope I ain't gonna hurt your feelings, but the shoes you are wearing . . . ain't right for you, they make you look like one of the kids" (Leissner, 1969:167). Being authentic means being oneself, being genuine, being natural, rather than pretending to be someone else. Worker and client roles are anchored in different social systems. Only when each remains authentic to his own system will they be able to meet and engage in the social intervention process.

To be authentic, to be oneself, may be especially difficult in situations where the difference between the client and the worker is small. When client and worker come from the same ethnic group or the same socioeconomic class, it may be tempting to establish a friendship relationship rather than a professional one. MRS. CAREY's worker resisted this temptation even though Mrs. Carey attempted to establish a casual relation between acquaintances. The young settlement house worker assigned to work with a young adult social club may think that he can best influence the group by participating like a group member. A friend or a group member can, of course, be enormously helpful, but his help differs from that of the professional worker. When we demand that the worker be authentic we ask that he be genuine both as a person and as a professional. Being professional should not require the submersion of the self, but neither must being authentic negate the professional role obligations. As Emanuel Tropp (1970) notes, "being oneself is not in contradiction with the performance of one's function."

Accepting differences and being genuine are important characteristics throughout the social intervention process, but they are especially crucial in the beginning phase when the social worker must interpret to the applicant the nature of their relationship, whether it is to be a dependent relationship (such as the client-patron or applicant-bureaucrat) or a mutual engagement of participants who, despite their differences, contract to cooperate in order to achieve jointly-agreed-to goals. Though there is wide agreement about the desirability of, and necessity for, acceptance as a prerequisite for engagement, this presents the social worker with a number of dilemmas in his day-by-day practice. Must he "accept" a client's decision even if the client will be harmed by it? What if the client wants to remain a heroin addict? What about the bedridden and helpless single older adult who refuses to move to a nursing home even though he can no longer take care of himself? Should a worker accept the decision of a parents' group which has voted to organize a school boycott in order to prevent the busing-in of black children into a previously all-white suburban school? There are those who have suggested that everybody has the right to make his own decisions, no matter what the consequences. But most social workers would argue that acceptance of a person does not necessarily mean approval of specific behaviors or agreement with every decision. However, it takes great skill to declare convincingly, "I like you but I do not agree with your decision." This is especially true in the beginning phase, before client and worker have really come to know each other.

## Timing

Time influences every aspect of modern life. Georg Simmel (1950:143) once observed that "all economic life and communication of the city would be disrupted" if clocks were off by only an hour. "Metropolitan life is unimaginable without the punctual integration of all activities and mutual relations into a stable and impersonal time schedule." Social agencies are also run by the clock. Workers are expected to arrive on time. Specific appointments are set aside for clients, and they are expected to come on time. But time may have an entirely different meaning for some clients. Their informal clock may tick more slowly than the official clock. Some people live without a single clock in their home. In many parts of the world, a forty-five-minute delay is as accepted as coming five minutes late is in middle-class America. Most foreigners and many Americans cannot understand how one's integrity and reputation depend on being punctual and completing work on time (Hall and Whyte, 1960).

It may be quite unrealistic to expect punctuality from a client who has never owned a watch. On the other hand, the way the worker uses time may not be in line with the client's expectations. A severely injured patient was looking forward to the daily visit of the hospital social worker. He was upset and felt abandoned when his worker failed to appear at the regular time one morning; he could not understand when the worker tried to explain later that an emergency with a new patient had prevented his coming at the regular time. A worker can learn much from the way a client uses time if he understands the meaning of time for that person. Thus, when MRS. CAREY arrived for her first appointment half an hour early, the worker had little question about the significance of this early arrival, especially since the more usual thing was for clients to come five or ten minutes late.

The calendar and the clock indicate one type of time dimension. The rhythm of the engagement process provides another. Sometimes a worker has the feeling that he has said the "right" thing at the "wrong" time. There is a thin line between making a tentative assessment and jumping prematurely to conclusions—but this line is an important one. A social worker, because of his experience, may be able to analyze a group's problem more quickly than the group members themselves. But if he is oblivious to the critical importance of timing, he may intervene too early and, as a consequence, lose the group. On the other hand, an overcautious worker may delay too long so that the clients will lose interest in the engagement. Sometimes a worker must anticipate developments so that he can act before a problem becomes too complex. An early warning to an adolescent may be far more effective than more intensive intervention at a later stage. A street-corner worker who watched the beginnings of a gang fight announced at just the right moment that he had to return to the office and asked if anybody wanted a ride to the community center, now. The timing was correct because the tension between the two gangs broke as soon as one of the gang leaders climbed into the worker's car. Irving Spergel (1966:130), who recorded this incident, noted that "the timing of the worker's action is critical in obtaining a successful outcome."

Timing is an important skill in every phase of the engagement process, but it is of particular significance during the termination phase. Here it becomes a question of *when* and *how* to end the engagement between client and worker. The natural tendency may be to end only after the problem has been entirely solved or completely removed, but this condition may be illusory since "life is an ongoing, problem encountering, problem solving process" (Perlman, 1970:139). If realistic goals were identified, termination should occur as the goal is approached without awaiting complete goal achievement. Lydia Rapoport (1970:302) put it well when she suggested that "termination can be achieved when the client *begins* to find solutions to his problems. This means that we do not expect him to work through all his problems, or even those parts of the problem that have been identified for focus."

The "right" time for termination may be when the client is ready to continue working on his problems alone without further assistance by the social worker. Misjudging the correct time for ending may result in a unilateral decision. The client may terminate his participation if he feels that further conduct is unproductive, or the worker, for his reasons, may end the engagement before the client is ready to do so. Termination at the "wrong" time may result in excessive client anxiety and regression, or it may result in a feeling of relief that "this is over." A mutual decision to terminate is always preferable. Such a decision is usually the outcome of a planned process which requires an astute sense of timing and an ongoing sharing of information. If a street-corner worker who has been meeting his gang every evening over a number of years suddenly announces that tonight is the last time he will meet with the gang members, he should not be surprised if there is some adverse reaction. At the very least, this worker should have gradually prepared the gang members for his departure, giving them ample time to adjust to life without his constant support. The question of when to start such termination preparations is again one of correct timing—neither too early nor too late is the general rule.

## Judge Not

The people with whom social workers come in contact are labeled by some as undesirable, deviant, even delinquent. But a social worker must not label people nor may he judge their behavior. He is not a judge of their innocence or guilt nor is it his function to determine whether the "accused" is responsible for his behavior. The social worker fills many roles, but judging is not one of them. This is fortunate since assigning blame and responsibility for behavior would interfere with establishing the type of relationship necessary for social intervention. Especially in the beginning phase people may be afraid to expose themselves to criticism from social workers. Emily Miller (1973) described her experiences with the members of a communal family who hesitated to get in contact with a social agency because of this very fear. This worker spent a great deal of time trying to convince them that her function was to help, not to judge.

Not judging does not mean, however, that the social worker is indifferent to what the client does or says, nor does it mean that the worker condones every kind of client behavior. Felix Biestek devotes an entire chapter of his book to this problem. He concludes that "the nonjudgmental attitude does not mean indifference to or rejection of value systems" (1957:93). The worker must not judge the client, but he may assess specific behaviors and their consequences. He can help a client understand why others think that he has done "wrong" or how his behavior hurts rather than helps him or those close to him. If goals have been clearly identified, this assessment of behavior can be in terms of its impact on goal achievement rather than in terms of right or wrong.

Most social workers agree that it is desirable, even necessary, to be nonjudgmental and nonpunitive. But this prescription poses a number of practical problems. For example, agency regulations generally define who is eligible for specific services and agency budgets determine the size of the assistance check a client will receive, yet many clients believe that their worker makes these decisions. Not a few think that the worker withholds services or reduces the amount of their check because he disapproves of their behavior or that he could give a more generous grant as a reward for their conformance. There may be workers who are punitive and who do make decisions on this basis, but most workers try to apply decision criteria objectively. Yet when clients believe that their worker is judgmental and punitive, meaningful engagement becomes difficult. When the worker scheduled one-hour weekly appointments for the parents of the communal family mentioned earlier, while their son was seen separately for two hours each week, they thought that the worker was punishing them (by withholding time) for their unconventional family arrangement. As long as they thought so, relations remained strained, and meaningful engagement was blocked (Miller, 1973).

Overcritical attitudes and unrealistic expectations are variants of judgmental attitudes, even when not intended as such. When a worker holds such attitudes or expectations, engagement tends to become problematic. A worker's overcritical attitude suggests that a client is not meeting certain standards of behavior or performance, even though these standards may not be applicable to this client. Criticism of MRS. WILSON for leaving dirty dishes all over her kitchen is based on the assumption that a clean and orderly kitchen is important for everyone and suggests that Mrs. Wilson has been lax in meeting this criterion. As long as the client does not share this assumption, such criticism will not get the dishes washed or result in a cleaner kitchen. Nor will such overcritical attitudes strengthen the engagement between the worker and the Wilson family. The group worker who told his teen club, "You guys played a great game but next time you should play as hard as the Eagles," may have wanted to encourage, but actually he told these boys that they were not playing as well as the best club in the league even though he knows that they will never play as well as that club. Even urging his boys "to try a little harder" may be unrealistic if they are already playing as hard as they can. In the same way, telling MR. WILSON that "with a little extra effort" he will certainly find a job may be unrealistic when there are no suitable jobs available for people without any skills. Such unrealistic expectations will not help solve Mr. Wilson's problem but only increase his alienation and sense of inadequacy.

Social workers must differentiate between expecting the "best" and expecting "the best a person is capable of under the present circumstances." The latter is constructive and helpful while the former is demoralizing, especially if the gap between the expectation and what the person can realistically attain is too great. Helpful expectations are goal-related and realistic in terms of the available external and internal resources. These strengthen the engagement because they direct the client toward achievable goals.

## Activity

Worker activity as an engagement skill has received little attention in the social work literature. This may have been due
to misgivings about too much worker activity and to the fear
that worker overinvolvement might cause or increase client
dependency. When worker activity is discussed, it is most
often in connection with "hard-to-reach" or "unmotivated"
clients who are not yet ready to engage fully in the social intervention process. It has been said, for example, that a group
worker's activity varies from "very active" with group
members who are "out of touch with reality" to "active when
asked" with group members who are "eager and competent to
participate" (Wilson and Ryland, 1949:68). The importance of
worker activity in initiating contact and helping people participate in social intervention activities has also been recognized
in work with lower-class and poverty groups. Here it may be a
question of outreach (unless the worker takes the first step
and reaches out there will be no contact and no engagement)
or of responding to the expectations of the clients. Lower-class
clients generally expect worker activity. Researchers have
found that in agencies serving such people client satisfaction is
highly related to worker activity; the more active a worker, the
greater the client's satisfaction (Mayer and Timms, 1970). And
Helen Northen (1969:123) cites a study of group work with
mental patients where higher improvement rates were related
to increased worker activity.

Worker activity is not mere activity for activity's sake,
"busy work," or doing things for the client because the worker
can do them better and more quickly. Instead, worker activity
must be viewed as a means to facilitate the engagement process and as a way to achieve the social intervention goals.
Viewed in this way, worker activity may be equally appropriate
with all kinds of people, not only with those who resist contact
or who have special problems. The specific type of activity and
its scope, of course, will vary from situation to situation, de-

pending on the worker's assessment of what is required. For example, when MRS. CAREY came for her first appointment, the worker left his desk and greeted her in the waiting room; here his intention was to demonstrate to the applicant that he was ready to help her—he did this, not by talking, but by doing.

Worker activity occurs in all phases of the social intervention process, but it is particularly important in the middle phase when the focus is on facilitating and maintaining engagement. George Homans (1950, 1961) developed the exchange theory of human behavior; this theory did not focus on social workers and their clients but considered all types of human relations. Yet his propositions tend to support the importance of worker activity as a means for strengthening engagement. Two of his propositions (1950:102, 243) bear directly on this discussion:

If the scheme of activities is changed, the scheme of interaction will, in general, change also, and vice versa.

The more frequently persons interact with one another, when no one of them originates interaction with much greater frequency than the other, the greater is their liking for one another and their feeling of ease in one another's presence.

The nature of the engagement between the client and the worker will change once the worker begins to be active. But, according to the second Homans proposition, the optimum relationship will develop only when there is a balance between client-initiated and worker-initiated activities. Both worker overactivity and overpassivity may be counterproductive because either will generate feelings of dependency and stress rather than feelings of ease and mutual participation. Admittedly, it is difficult to assess the correct amount of activity since there are no universal standards or objective measurements. The same amount of worker activity may be just right with one person and too much in another situation.

With overactivity comes overinvolvement. This occurs

when the client's problem becomes the worker's problem and when the worker is more concerned about the problem than is the person requesting the help. While the worker should be concerned, his concern must be appropriate to the problem and to his role. The worker must take an interest in the client and in his problem, but overinvolvement often leads to irrational and planless activity. Far from facilitating a professional relationship, overinvolvement usually leads to a personalized relationship where the worker's objectivity and judgment tend to be impaired. Whenever there is a great amount of worker activity without a corresponding amount of client activity, quick and decisive results are sometimes achieved, but these often miss the mark since they are likely to be solutions to the worker's problem and not necessarily responsive to the client's needs. Overactivity and overinvolvement may result in doing all kind of good things *for* the client without approaching goal achievement. In one example, reported by Rachel Levine (1970), a social worker placed an eight-year-old hyperkinetic boy in a therapy group and arranged for various medications, yet after more than a year of treatment there was little improvement. The worker was so involved in doing things for the boy that he overlooked the most important participant, the boy's mother. Only after the mother was given a chance to participate more actively in the social intervention process did the treatment become more relevant and begin to move toward success.

## Setting the Tone

Setting the tone may be the most essential of all engagement skills. For successful intervention it is crucial that the worker be perceived as someone who is able and willing to help. And it is important that this happens as quickly as possible. First impressions are especially important because they set the tone for the subsequent interaction. In one experiment college students were told that a substitute instructor was a "warm" person; these students participated in the class discussion twice as much as did their classmates who were told that the same instructor was a "cold" person (Kelley, 1950). It is likely that clients who perceive their social worker as a warm person will be more ready to engage and do so more quickly than those who think of their worker as a cold person. The social worker, therefore, must make every effort to set a warm, friendly, and relaxed tone, yet at the same time he must convey a sense of competence and ability.

The worker sets the tone by the way he uses his voice and body, especially his eyes and face. While there is not much he can do about being male or female, black or white, young or old, he can train himself in those skills which convey a warm voice, a relaxed body, a smiling face, and meaningful eye contact.

**Eye Contact.** When two people interact, no matter what the purpose of their interaction, they usually look at each other some of the time. At other times only one of them will look at the other, while at still other times neither will look at the other. When a client and a worker meet, there are four possibilities for eye interaction: (1) the client looks at the worker, but at that particular moment the worker does not return the glance since he is looking elsewhere; (2) the worker looks at the client while the client's eyes are focused elsewhere; (3) neither client nor worker looks at the other; they may both look out of the window, stare at the ceiling, or keep their eyes closed; (4) the client's look at the worker is reciprocated by the worker's look at the client. Eye contact occurs only in the fourth alternative. When one person speaks to another he generally looks at him between 30 percent and 60 percent of the time, but the listener's eyes do not always respond when he is looking. Actual eye contact is effected for only ten to thirty seconds out of every minute of conversation, typically in intervals of about one second. Eye contact is equally crucial when working with groups. Though a worker cannot be in eye contact with each group member as frequently as in the one-to-one situation, he should deliberately try to establish eye contact with *every* group member. Focusing his eyes on only one or two members would be an error.

The significance of eye contact differs in various cultural settings. In parts of the Far East eye contact is (or was) taboo during conversation. Eye contact is also avoided by many American Indian and Spanish American children, especially when they are scolded by their elders. But in most Western cultures the total avoidance of eye contact would be regarded as a sign of rudeness or mental disturbance. The precise meaning of eye contact depends on the accompanying facial expressions, the sequence of the interaction, the setting, and other factors. Prolonged eye contact (we call it "staring") followed by a hostile expression has an entirely different meaning than the staring which is combined with the longing expression of two lovers.

Several observations about eye contact are particularly relevant to this discussion about engagement skills. Eye contact occurs more often between people who like each other or who have established a positive relationship. And a client will feel that a worker is more believable, more confident, and more positive in his attitude toward him when the worker accompanies his speaking with looking at the client. Eye contact can be a useful technique in establishing engagement. But too much eye contact may not be effective because it may become unpleasant or even embarrassing.

People who wish to conceal their emotional state or some aspect of their personality often attempt to avoid eye contact and may even interpret the worker's attempt to initiate eye contact as an invasion of privacy. Clients who want to conceal part of their problem or who want to withhold specific information will tend to reduce eye contact to a minimum since eye contact tends to pressure persons into making disclosures. Eye contact evidently is perceived differently by men and women. Women, especially when talking with other women, engage in more eye contact than do men. Also, women tend to look at the other more when speaking while men look more often when listening. This might suggest that social workers must make a special effort to establish engagement when the client is from the opposite sex.[3]

**Facial Gestures.** The face is an important organ in human interaction. We speak of "losing face" when others publicly reject a person's self-definition. When meeting friends, or even strangers, the face gives a clue about how one is feeling; a frowning face or one contorted in pain sends a different message than a smiling face. Clients who report that their new worker looks "mean" will find it more difficult to engage in the social intervention activity than those who feel that their worker looks friendly. A facial smile is one way to convey a friendly interest. The right timing, of course, is important. While in Japan a smile is customary when bringing bad news, in America a grin would be an inappropriate response to a client's tale of woe. Other facial gestures may be suitable in one culture but not in another. Sticking out one's tongue is a sign of apology in parts of China, a mark of deference in Tibet, but an indication of extreme disrespect in the United States and most Western countries (Argyle, 1967). But the worker can do much to set the tone for effective engagement by using his face purposefully.

**Body Language.** The idea of body language has become popular only in recent years, but social workers have been familiar with nonverbal communication for a long time. A person who is scared of another can communicate his fear without talking about it. A worker can convey his interest or lack of interest in the client by the way he sits. When a children's club meets in a classroom the group leader will often sit on top of the teacher's table or in a student's chair to demonstrate visually

3. This discussion is based on the research and writing of Argyle (1967) and of Exline, Gray, and Schuette (1965).

(but without words) the difference between himself and the teacher. Earlier in this chapter we noted that the distance between people can facilitate or hinder engagement; the actual physical distance between two people can be shortened when the worker leans forward, just as the separation can be made greater by the worker putting his feet on his desk and thus erecting a barrier. By being relaxed, yet attentive, the social worker attempts to share with the client his interest and his confidence in being able to help.

**Space.** Space can also facilitate engagement. "Space communicates," wrote Edward Hall (1959). Office interviews which take place in small, open cubicles offer little privacy and may suggest an industrial rather than a professional setting (Seabury, 1971; Wasserman, 1970). The desk between the worker and the client may become a barricade to effective communication: it emphasizes the difference in power and status between those who sit on each side of the desk. Yet this same desk can also provide the security that some people need when facing a difficult situation. In one study clients and workers were shown photographs of different office seating arrangements; the arrangement preferred by most respondents (clients and workers) was the one where the two chairs were placed at right angles around the corner of the desk (Haase and DiMattia, 1970). Welcoming a client in the waiting room, as happened to MRS. CAREY, is another way of using space to tell a client that the worker is interested in her as an individual.

But space has different meanings for various people. A home visit may indicate to one client that the worker is really interested, while another client may interpret this same home visit as snooping and an unwarranted interference in his private life. The identical distance between two people can facilitate or block engagement, depending on the cultural meaning assigned to distances. Hall (1959) indicated that in America the normal distance between two people who exchange infor-

mation of a nonpersonal nature is four and a half to five feet
while for personal subject matters it is from twenty to thirty-
six inches. But these norms evidently do not hold for all population groups. Lower-class residents in New York City when
observed in casual conversation on the street were observed to
stand from eighteen to thirty inches from each other, or closer
than the norms reported by Hall (Jones, 1973; Willis, 1966).
Every social worker must learn the distance which his clients
consider proper. If he sits too close, the client may feel threatened; if he sits too far away, the client may think that the
worker is not interested.

## Summary

Social intervention requires the participation of client and
worker. The first task facing the worker is to actualize the
client's participation; that is, to engage the client. In this
chapter we have discussed seven different engagement skills:
structuring, focusing, bridging the gap, timing, "judge not,"
activity, and setting the tone. In practice it will be difficult to
assign any one skill to a specific action or phase since they tend
to occur simultaneously. The social worker who can appropriately utilize these skills has a far better chance of effecting
meaningful engagement than one who cannot.

# chapter eleven

# Assessment Skills

Social intervention activities will be effective only if workers understand their clients and correctly identify their problems. The process which leads to this understanding and identification is called assessment or diagnosis. Assessment is not preliminary to the social intervention but is an integral part of it. Helen Northen (1969:112) defines assessment as "an ongoing process as well as a first step in practice [which] leads quite logically and naturally to planning for what should be done to enable a client system to improve its functioning." Even though assessment is discussed here separately, it must be remembered that it is an ongoing activity throughout the social intervention process.

The assessment process can be divided into three phases, each of which makes different demands on the social worker and requires different skills. These three phases are: (1) exploration and collection of information; (2) analysis and interpretation of information; and (3) decisions about information. Information is important because intervention possibilities are limited if data are missing or inaccurate. For example, if no information is available about his home situation, a chronically ill patient may be sent home from the hospital even though there is no one in his home who can take care of him. Without information or with inadequate information, the worker must accept someone else's definition of the problem without knowing to what extent that definition is accurate. It will not be possible to develop an intervention strategy for the specific problem if insufficient information is available to identify the problem accurately. Instead, the worker must rely on standard plans which may or may not be effective. Planning a strategy with insufficient information about the problem is like giving a soldier a gun without telling him where the enemy is located.

Insufficient information is one problem; collecting too much information can also be a problem. It is neither possible nor desirable to collect *all* the facts about a problem situation. When all kinds of relevant and irrelevant data are collected without reference to their future use, analysis and interpretation become difficult if not impossible, and the implementation of the intervention activities is delayed until it may be too late.

## Exploration and Collection of Information

How much information should a social worker collect during the assessment process? It is difficult to answer this question with any degree of accuracy or precision, but a general guide might read: collect as little information as possible but as much as necessary in order to understand the person, his environment, and his problem. Useless and unnecessary information will interfere with problem assessment and analysis—and during the time it takes to collect this extra information the problem may grow bigger and more complex. The time and effort used for assembling nonrelevant information are better spent on other, more useful aspects of the social intervention. Admittedly, it is not always easy to know in advance whether a given item of information will be helpful. What appears to be an insignificant bit of information may become the key to understanding the problem. Perhaps the very question asked at the beginning of this paragraph is misleading since it suggests incorrectly that information-gathering is a one-time activity when really it is an ongoing process. The alert social worker looks for additional information throughout the social intervention process, not only during the first weeks, and constantly uses this information to revise his assessment and review the strategy. Without a continuous flow of information the social worker cannot determine whether his first impressions were correct, nor will he know whether the initial strategy was adequate. The sequence of events recorded in the summary of the CAREY FAMILY illustrates the need for ongoing information-gathering. The worker's initial impression that there was more to Ben Carey's problem than mere misbehavior was confirmed by information which was obtained from other members of the Carey family during the months after the initial meeting with Mrs. Carey. Though the worker's first assessment of a problematic parent-child relationship was confirmed, subsequent information indicated that there were also other serious family problems which would require the worker's attention if he was to be of real help to the members of this family.

**Client Involvement.** Information-gathering is an integral part of the social intervention process which should be undertaken by the social worker himself and not delegated to a special intake worker. This is important because the relationship established during the early meetings between the applicant and the social worker sets the tone for the entire social intervention process. Obtaining information is important, but how this information is obtained is often even more important. Information-gathering, as part of the social intervention process, is not detective work nor should it resemble a court room cross examination. Instead, it should be a cooperative worker-client activity. But the client must understand from the very beginning why information is important, lest his participation be reluctant. Sometimes it may seem simpler for the worker alone to gather the necessary information. However, the involvement of the person with the problem in the information-gathering phase is as crucial as his involvement in the other phases of the social intervention process.

One frequent dilemma facing the social worker is that many persons come to the social agency with the expectation of receiving immediate help or instant solutions. Often they do not even state a problem but immediately ask for a specific service: Can you help me find an old age home for my aged mother? I want to put my baby in a foster home. We want the auditorium for a fund-raising dance. But the social worker, even though he genuinely wants to help, cannot do so until he understands the problem. Admission into a home may not be the best solution for the aged mother; a foster home may help neither the baby nor the natural parents; and a dance at this time may harm rather than help solve the problems of this group of young adults. The person who requests the help, on the other hand, wants to hear the social worker say, "Yes, I can help, and this is what I will do now." Instead, he generally hears him say something about wanting to help but first needing various kinds of information, a message which often sounds like a polite stall since the applicant does not understand the need for information.

This is the time for the social worker to be both positive and purposeful. He can tell the applicant that he does indeed need some help with the problem which brought him to the agency and that he, the social worker, is ready to join him in doing something about the problem (provided the problem is of a type for which social intervention is relevant). The first thing that they must do together is to look at the problem and gain a better understanding of it in order to decide exactly what kind of help will be most effective. This approach is not a ploy which uses different words to say the same thing. Instead of the bureaucratic model of information-gathering where the worker asks questions and records the other person's answers, we are suggesting that the applicant and worker *together* evolve a plan of action, decide *together* the type of information they need in order to understand the problem better, and determine *together* how and where this information can best be obtained. Information-gathering is not only for the worker's benefit, it should also benefit the person who has the problem.

Client participation in information-gathering does not mean that worker and client must do exactly the same thing. Each has his functions, just as each brings his own strengths and skills to the social intervention process. Client participation does mean that the person with the problem is appropriately involved. Such involvement starts at the very beginning and must include steps which are often thought to be routine. Thus, in some agencies every applicant is asked to sign a medical information release form during the first interview; sometimes the applicant is told that his signature is required if he wants to receive service or he is told that his signature on this form is a mere routine. At times a social worker will hurriedly explain the purpose of the form, but often the applicant fails to understand why medical information might be relevant to his application for service. Putting a signature on a form that is not understood is only token or ceremonial involvement. Appropriate involvement in information-gathering requires that the applicant understand the relevancy of the information and that he himself locate or suggest sources where additional medical information may be available. He may be able to suggest which hospitals and doctors have information that is relevant and then sign the release form.

Sometimes the social worker receives information on a confidential basis from another agency or from another person. Appropriate involvement does not mean that the worker must share everything with the client. The worker must not abuse the trust put in him by others. Confidential information must remain confidential and cannot be shared even if the worker thinks that the client should know about it. For example, the worker cannot tell MRS. CAREY that her husband has been running around with other women if he received this information confidentially. But he may urge Mr. Carey to tell his wife. Sometimes a group member tells the social worker some confidential information about himself and another member of the group. Joey related how he and Jeff were planning to run away from home next week. Even if this information is correct (and it may only be a figment of Joey's imagination), it would not be wise for the worker to confront Jeff with it. Neither would it be right to run to Joey's parents with this news. The worker may counsel with Joey. He may urge him to have Jeff talk with the worker. He may discuss "running away" in general terms with the group, hoping that there will be a more specific follow-up once he has opened the subject. But the worker should not tell Jeff that Joey revealed their secret plan unless he is willing to risk the trust and confidence which Joey and other group members have placed in him. The source of the confidence really makes no difference; whether it comes from an outside source or from another member of the family or a group member, confidential information is meant to remain confidential between the source of the information and the worker. The worker does not have the right to reveal it to a third party.

**Contradictory Information.** Most social workers readily understand why it is not appropriate for a worker to reveal a husband's extramarital activities to his wife, but they are not always sure what to do when information received from a collateral source does not agree with the information given by the applicant himself. MRS. CAREY said that her son's teachers had never complained about him, but when the worker visited the principal he learned that Ben had been expelled from school several times during the past year. If Mrs. Carey knew that the worker had been in touch with the school (and the worker should not have taken that step without her prior knowledge), it will not be too difficult to bring up this discrepancy next time they meet. While the worker must not reveal confidential information, he can tell Mrs. Carey that he spoke

with the principal and that he had received a different picture
of Ben than the one she had given him. The worker might ask
why she thinks that the principal sees things differently than
she does. Or he might indicate that he knows that it is not
always easy to discuss problems with strangers, especially if
these reflect on one's children. The worker must not accuse
her of lying; instead, he should make it easy for her to provide
additional and perhaps more correct information.

The client should be kept aware of all information
sources approached by the worker. If there is objection to
making contact with a certain person or a specific agency, the
worker must not make that contact. Instead, he should explore the reasons for this refusal and the possibility of alternate sources. But he must respect the right of every person,
including clients, to withhold information about himself. Far
from questioning this right or limiting it, social workers must
support it because it is a basic pillar in strengthening the inherent human dignity of the individual. The active involvement of the applicant in developing information sources and
his right to withhold information do not mean that the social
worker must play a passive role. He can and should suggest
information sources which the applicant may have overlooked
or does not know. And by asking the right questions at the
correct time, the worker can help guide the applicant to clarify
his problem and his condition. However, these questions must
be asked in a way that will avoid imposing the worker's preconceptions and biases.

There are situations where it will not be possible to involve those who seek service in the ways described here. These
situations occur most often when the person who needs help is
unable to request the intervention of a social worker. An abandoned infant needs help but is in no position to become actively involved. Similarly, a very disturbed teen-ager may not
be able to participate in the information-gathering phase or in
other parts of the assessment process until he has calmed
down a bit. There may be good reasons for not delaying the

initial information-gathering. However, instances where the social worker proceeds without the client's participation should be the exception, not the rule.

**Information Needed.** What information should the social worker collect? Earlier books, including Mary Richmond's classic *Social Diagnosis* (1917), presented detailed schedules of questions which social workers could use under various circumstances. There was one questionnaire for use with unmarried mothers, another for a "child possibly feebleminded," and one called an "inebriety questionnaire." But Richmond herself was aware of the limited usefulness of these questionnaires and warned (1917:373).

. . . the purposes and limitations of these questionnaires are bound to be misunderstood by some who attempt to use them, no matter how clearly it is set forth that none are sets of questions to be asked of clients and that none are schedules the answers to which are to be filled in by anyone.

The purpose for which the information is gathered and not the printed questionnaire should guide the choice of questions. What is important in one situation may be of little importance in the next. Information about a person's developmental history may be crucial when the problem concerns a child's interaction with his parents but will be quite unimportant when making plans for a bedridden older adult. Detailed information about an applicant's adolescent years may or may not clarify his current problem. If information will not increase understanding and lead to action, it should not be collected. Information about a group's pattern of organization (who are the leaders? the followers?) is almost always relevant when working with a group, but a detailed history of the group's beginnings may or may not be important, depending on the present problems and goals of the group.

An awareness of the theoretical framework upon which the assessment and the subsequent social intervention will be based directs attention to the type of information which will be useful and relevant. In the framework suggested here, based on the proposition that most human problems result from the faulty interaction of man with his environment, the social worker must collect information which will help him understand not only the *problem* and the *person* who has the problem (or the person who has requested help), but also how this person *interacts* with other people and how he participates in social systems which impinge, directly or indirectly, on the problem condition. The worker also will need to gather information on those social systems which make up the *environment* in which the action and the human interaction occur. For example, when working with a boy whose behavior has created problems in the classroom, the social worker will not limit his information-gathering to the boy's personality or his behavior in the classroom but will also want to know how the boy gets along at home, with his friends, on the playground, in the community center, and elsewhere. At the same time he will try to obtain information on what is happening in the classroom, how the teacher relates to this boy and to other boys, what demands are made of these students, and so on. But data about this boy's weaning and toilet training do not appear relevant to the present problem and therefore will not be collected.

In addition to interaction and environmental data, the worker must assemble information about the client and his problem and about the factors which brought the client to seek help from this agency at this particular time. Information about the client's coping capacity and modalities is crucial if an effective intervention strategy is to emerge from the assessment process. It is of some importance to establish how this person expresses himself when faced by other critical problems, how he deals with conflict, how he defends himself against external and internal threats, and similar information. These are the potential strengths on which the intervention strategy may be based.

How the client identifies the problem will also make a difference in planning the intervention strategy; this information must therefore be gathered during the assessment process. The client's description of the problem may be correct, biased, or incorrect, but it represents *his* view of the problem and, as such, it becomes an important input. The social intervention can be effective only when the goals and the strategy are relevant to the problem which the client has identified. Thus, intervention activities designed to improve the interaction skills of the members of the YOUNG ADULT HIKING CLUB will meet with little success as long as they believe that their problems with girls are due solely to the community's failure to provide adequate facilities for frequent social events. The problem identified by the client at the beginning need not be the final problem; the worker may have other ideas and introduce them for joint examination; or in the course of the assessment process, the client may begin to recognize other problems in addition to, or instead of, the original problem. The general direction in information gathering should be problem-solving rather than collecting historical data. As Mary Richmond (1930:487) observed, "Our examinations of the yesterdays and the todays should be with special reference to the client's tomorrows."

**Information Sources.** Where does a social worker obtain relevant information? The specific details will vary from situation to situation, but the primary source is almost always the person who has presented the problem or who has the problem. His perception may not be accurate, but his point of view and his understanding of the problem situation are always important for problem-solving. A visit to the home or the neighborhood where the person lives or works is often (but not always) a good way of beginning to gather information. It is more natural and easier to observe human interaction in a normal environment. How people get along with each other, what roles they fill in their various social systems, how they participate in decision-making—these are information data which cannot be acquired in the worker's office. An understanding of the quality of the client's life requires more than the client's answers to a few questions. In the office, MRS. CAREY appeared to be a pleasant and poised housewife, appropriately concerned about her children's welfare, but a different picture emerged when the worker observed her and the other Careys in their living room. The manager of the KENNEDY HOUSES was most cooperative when Mark Ortego, the community worker, met with him in his office; Mark could not believe that it was the same person whom he observed the following evening at the meeting of the Tenants' Council.

A home visit may be a good way to secure information, but its limitations must be kept in mind. For one thing, the presence of the worker is anything but normal. His visit adds a new factor to the family constellation, and the family members will not behave as they usually do. Their change in behavior need not be conscious, though at times there may be an effort to impress the worker or "put something over" on him. But even if these changes are minimal, a home visit will reveal only a small slice of the twenty-four-hour day of family life. Nevertheless, a home visit can be valuable and should be considered, unless counterindicated by the nature of the problem. Home visits should be made only with the consent of the client since otherwise they might represent an unwarranted invasion of his privacy.

There was a time when social workers relied on relatives and neighbors for information about the person who requested help. These people may sometimes be in a position to provide additional information, but they should not be approached routinely because such routine contacts suggest that the worker does not believe the client or thinks that he is incapable of providing correct information. If the applicant suggests that the worker talk with specific people for the purpose of obtaining information, the worker should do so. If the worker has reason to doubt the client's information, he should share these doubts with the client and ask him to bring further information which may support his statements or to suggest ways in which the worker's questions can be clarified. Should a worker want to visit a particular neighbor or relative to gain a better understanding of the problem, he must make this visit only with the applicant's permission. The primary purpose of information-gathering, it must be remembered, is to help the participants in the social intervention gain a better understanding of the problem—not to catch the applicant in an untruth. Even where there is a legal requirement to establish eligibility, the investigation need not be done behind the applicant's back. Involving him is not only the responsible way of proceeding but will result in a more positive worker-client relationship which, in turn, will facilitate all subsequent phases of the social intervention process. Often additional sources of information will be uncovered which would not have come to light if the applicant had been kept in the background during information-gathering. But perhaps most important, early involvement will help the client learn more about himself, his problem, his environment, and how to cope with these.

Organizations and systems which are significant for the problem or for the person who has the problem are other sources of information. Thus, the school is a social system which has relevance for BEN CAREY who is believed to have the problem. If, on the other hand, Mrs. Carey had stated initially that she wanted help with a marital problem, Ben's school probably would not be considered a prime source of information.

Information comes not only from individuals but also from official records. Medical records and case records from other social agencies with whom the person had previous contacts may provide significant information. School records, employment records, and occasionally even police records may help give a better picture of the person and his problem.

There is one caution that must be remembered when using official records. Their value and validity are no greater than the person who wrote them. And since we usually do not know the person who wrote a particular document or entry, we must be cautious in using such information. An observation written by an unknown welfare worker ten years ago, that a child appeared to be retarded, must not be taken as proof that the adolescent in trouble today is retarded. But such a notation might suggest one avenue for further exploration. Repeated entries by a number of different workers about a marital problem in a client's family would alert a worker to the possibility that this problem might still be unresolved, but no such entry can replace a current assessment of the family situation.

An initial assessment should be arrived at quickly, and even a more definitive assessment should not be unduly postponed. There are those social workers who accept the client's presenting problem as *the* problem and who therefore have no need for a specific assessment phase. Most social workers, however, feel that there is importance in providing for an assessment or diagnostic phase but caution against its undue prolongation. Exploration is essential for problem-solving, but collecting information should not be used as a rationalization for delaying the implementation of the social intervention strategy. The specific contents of the assessment statement is discussed later in this chapter.

## Analysis and Interpretation

In the second phase of the assessment process the emphasis is on analyzing and interpreting the data. *Analysis* comes from the Greek root for dissolving or breaking up a whole into parts in order to find out the nature, purpose, or function of the whole. Analysis is particularly important because problems almost never are simple or isolated but come in sets and are usually highly complex. *Interpretation* comes from the Latin word for agent, broker, or interpreter; it signifies to explain the meaning of something or to make it more understandable.

Before a social worker can be helpful in developing meaningful goals and effective social intervention strategies, he must understand how the various parts of a problem set are related to each other and what they mean. Analysis and interpretation always occur together, with one making possible the other. If, for example, juvenile delinquency is viewed as the consequence of socioeconomic or cultural factors, the analysis of juvenile delinquency data will be concerned with housing, community values, employment opportunities, and similar factors; on the other hand, the focus will be on interpersonal and intrapsychic factors if a psychological interpretation is given to juvenile delinquency. In this case, as so often, interpretation guides the analysis.

Information about the problem and about the person who suffers from the problem is important, but not all information is of equal importance. The fact that MRS. CAREY is 5'2" tall probably is not terribly important in connection with the problem which she presented. But her residing in a new suburban community, settled mostly by professional people and industrial managers, may be significant. However, this one item of information by itself has little meaning until it is connected with other bits of information into a meaningful interpretation of the situation. Often a social worker is faced by an assortment of information and does not know what to do with it. Data will become useful and informative only when they are relevant and when they are organized into a meaningful and understandable pattern. Selecting relevant information and giving it meaning are the essence of analysis and interpretation. Selected entries from the social worker's notebook about George Winter, a member of the Peanuts Gang, illustrate the importance of skillful analysis and interpretation of data.

George was brought to the attention of the juvenile court by the police. They identified him as a member of the Peanuts Gang, a group of juvenile delinquents who were terrorizing neighborhood storekeepers. Social workers undertake a study of every juvenile brought before the court in order to assist the juvenile court judge to understand the youngster and his problems. The following are some of the data collected by the social worker assigned to study George Winter:

Age: 15 years, 2 months
Born in Community Hospital
Dropped out of school three years ago when in grade 6
Curly red hair; 5′ 8″; 125 lbs.
Black
Family lives in nicely furnished apartment in Harlem
Reportedly smokes marijuana and known to have experimented with heroin
Father employed as bank security guard; mother a schoolteacher
Youngest of three brothers
Brothers do not have police record
Father high school graduate; mother graduated teachers college
Oldest brother in grade 12; middle brother in grade 10
Grandmother lives with family
Sloppy dresser
Almost illiterate
Rarely at home, not even for meals
Had rheumatic fever at age 6 years; no other illnesses reported
Wants to become a dentist or a numbers runner
Weaned from breast at age 2 months, from bottle at 31 months
Likes rock music, ice cream, and hot dogs
Claims that he has no friends in neighborhood; says that his friends live in the Bronx (members of his gang??)
Family not known to any social agency

All of the information collected about George (and there is more than is reported here) may be interesting, but in its present raw form it will help neither the social worker nor the judge to understand the boy or his problem. To make sense out of this collection of information, the social worker must first analyze it. Analysis of data involves the following activities, though not always in the order indicated:

*Ordering.* The worker must arrange the information into the more and the less relevant. For example, the color of George's skin is much more relevant than the color of his hair.

*Discovering.* An attempt must be made to discover relationships between various relevant items. There may be a significant relationship between living in Harlem, becoming a school dropout, and using narcotics. At this point in the analysis, the focus is on discovering relationships and not on trying to establish causal factors.

*Exploring.* The meaning of the information must be explored in terms of the cultural setting in which it occurred since identical behaviors or events often have different meanings in different settings. Dropping out of school in Harlem may not have the same meaning or the same consequence as it does in Ogden, Utah, or in Southfield, Michigan.

*Identifying.* Factors which might cause the problem or which may alleviate it must be identified. Without this step it will be difficult to plan an effective intervention strategy.

The social worker's knowledge, wisdom, and imagination are important throughout the assessment process, but they are especially crucial in the analysis and interpretaton phase. It is not possible to make effective plans if the information is incorrectly analyzed or if a false interpretation is offered. Were the social worker to conclude that ecological factors in the Harlem community were most important in the development of George Winter's delinquent behavior, the intervention strategy might focus on relocating the Winter family, perhaps in a suburban community. But if damaged family relationships were the real source of the problem, a move to suburbia (where families often must assume additional functions and carry new responsibilities) might aggravate rather than reduce the problem.

**Values and Biases.** Interpretation and analysis are never routine. In a sense, one can say that they constitute a very personal process. Every social worker brings his unique personality and his life experiences so that no two workers will approach the same data in exactly the same way. Because a worker's personal values and even his biases play an important part in anlysis and interpretation, they must be recognized as elements which tend to influence the data analysis and, at times, even distort the interpretation. Certain precautions may be desirable lest social intervention be transformed into an emotional experience instead of the professional activity that it must be. For one thing, the worker must be fully aware of his own values and his biases so that he can make allowances for them. Most social workers, for example, disapprove of the use of hard drugs, but they must be aware of this attitude (valid as it is) when working with heroin addicts, lest their intervention becomes punitive or hostile.

One way to reduce distortion in analysis and interpretation is to expose one's own values. Sharing the preliminary interpretation with the person requesting help is another way to limit the impact of one's biases and values. This sharing should occur at various times in the assessment process, beginning even before the worker has formulated a definitive interpretation. It will require skill and tact to involve the client in a way that will facilitate the interpretation process and at the same time strengthen the developing relationship between worker and client. Questions are often better than statements, but even questions must be appropriately phrased so that the client can understand and handle them. The question, "Have you ever thought that your child might be mentally retarded?" requires a more or less accurate understanding of mental retardation, yet many parents lack this understanding. Instead of clarifying the situation and providing a check on the worker's tentative interpretation, a question phrased in this manner might trigger all kinds of guilt feelings.

A social worker must know with whom he is talking. In many cases it is necessary first to provide basic information before the worker's questions or messages can be understood, or it may be necessary to use simple language. Parents not familiar with the concept "mental retardation" may be asked instead whether they have noted that their child learned to do things at a somewhat later age than other children. Sometimes people may not be ready to cope with the preliminary assessment information. The members of the YOUNG ADULT HIKING CLUB had experienced repeated failure; they may need to have some successful experiences before they can usefully handle information which reflects their problematic heterosexual development.

**Simplification.** Most problems which come to the attention of social workers are far from simple. Yet a reasonable degree of simplification is helpful, even necessary, to understand a problem situation. It is not possible to deal with all aspects of a problem at once nor is it feasible to analyze every implication of a problem at the very same time. Partialization is a valuable and often a desirable step in the problem-solving sequence. Instead of dealing with the total problem or all of the problems brought by the client, the worker and the client deliberately and thoughtfully select one part of the problem or one aspect of the problem situation.

Mrs. Dwight came to the welfare office with an eviction order in her hand. She also told the worker that there was no more food in her kitchen, that her husband has been out of work for over a year, that her oldest boy was arrested last week for stealing a car, and that she was three months pregnant. Mrs. Dwight and her worker must identify those emergency problems which require priority attention. Getting food to the seven Dwight children will have the first priority—but what comes next?

Prior to planning the next steps in the social intervention process, the social worker must analyze and interpret the information available to him about the Dwight family and its problems. Whenever a problem situation is complex, there is a strong temptation to simplify things because complicated situations are generally disconcerting, even to professionals. Simplification is helpful and necessary, but oversimplification can be perilous because it is misleading. Oversimplication tends to occur whenever the analysis and interpretation are prepared in an impulsive manner without sufficient consideration of the available information. Several kinds of inappropriate worker activities can result in oversimplification. These include stereotyping, labeling, overgeneralizing, identifying simple causes, and being rigid.

*Stereotyping.* This occurs whenever one attributes a characteristic to a person merely because he is a member of a group about which certain things are believed. For example, the worker would be stereotyping if he thought Mrs. Dwight was lying because "all people on welfare lie to their worker." It is true that some relief recipients lie, as do some people who do not receive welfare assistance. It may even be true that Mrs. Dwight is not telling the truth. But when the worker called Mrs. Dwight a liar merely because she was on relief, he was using a stereotype.

*Labeling.* When stereotyping, we tie a person to a group characteristic merely because he belongs to that group. In labeling, we attach an individual to a characteristic. Some labels are merely descriptive ("he is tall"), but others involve value judgments ("he's lazy") or contain derogatory information ("he's a thief"). Labels can be particularly vicious because the person labeled rarely has an opportunity to defend himself. While it will make little difference whether the social worker describes Mrs. Dwight as tall or short, the moment he designates her as lazy, he forecloses a number of intervention possibilities.

*Overgeneralizing.* This activity is similar to stereotyping. A social worker who has had many clients report that their children were starving when in fact the families had concealed income may believe that all clients with a similar story, including Mrs. Dwight, will lie. Stereotyping involves faulty deductive thinking while overgeneralization consists of faulty inductive thinking. Overgeneralization is more difficult to guard against

than stereotyping because a reasonable degree of generalization, based on a worker's knowledge and experience, is desirable and helpful. However, the worker must exercise caution when extending conclusions and interpretations to people
who seem similar but who may be quite different. Unemployment, for example, has different consequences for different
people and at different times. Being unemployed in a neighborhood where everybody is out of work is different from
being unemployed at a time when practically everybody is
working. Generalizing from one situation to the other can lead
to serious mistakes if the worker does not exercise caution.

*Identifying simple causes.* One danger which every social
worker must try to avoid is that of identifying single factors as
the cause of complex problems. In today's complicated world
there are few areas where simple cause-and-effect relationships can be established. Yet many people continue to look
for one-factor explanations because they tend to be uncomfortable when they do not understand why certain things are
happening—and one-factor causes are easier to understand
than more complicated ones. Mr. Dwight's continued unemployment may have many causes, including his lack of market-
able skills, the elimination of nearly all unskilled labor by machines, a change in marketing procedures, the unprofitability
of small industry, a change in tax laws, his own laziness and
unreliablility, and so forth. Instead of trying to find *the* cause
for a client's unemployment, a social worker must train himself to analyze behavior from various aspects. One scheme of
analysis, as proposed in chapter 5, is based on the proposition
that human behavior is best understood if it is analyzed on
four levels: biological, psychological, social-structural, and cultural. Such a formulation or a similar approach will help social
workers avoid identifying spurious causal factors or limiting
their choice to single factors when many are involved.

*Being rigid.* The significance and meaning of information
changes over time. Most social workers are aware that the
same event or behavior has different meanings in different

cultures and in differing social classes. But workers need to remember that changes in meaning also occur over time within the same culture or within the same class. For example, many in the middle class no longer proscribe premarital sex relations as they did a generation or two ago. In these circles, having and keeping an out-of-wedlock baby means something quite different today than it did twenty years ago. Social workers who work with unwed mothers must be aware of these changes if they want to offer relevant and effective intervention services. Changes in the significance of high school graduation provide another example of the need to avoid rigidity. Fifty years ago only one out of every six seventeen-year-olds completed high school while today eight out of every ten receive a high school diploma. When interpreting the significance of dropping out of school, social workers must keep in mind not only the social setting of the school leaver but also the over-all societal setting in which this behavior takes place. Applying yesterday's norms to today's problems is not helpful.

**Validity of Interpretation.** How does a social worker know whether he has correctly analyzed and interpreted the information available to him? There is no simple answer to this crucial question. The one definitive test of the validity of the interpretation comes from the results achieved. If the results are successful, the interpretation can be considered valid, but even with a valid interpretation mistakes in the implementation may cause failure. A "yes" answer to the following questions does not guarantee a valid interpretation but will increase the probability that the analysis and interpretation are correct.

Has the interpretation been shared with the client and with others who are participating in the social intervention?

Does the interpretation seem plausible in view of everything known about the problem, the participants, and the setting?

Do professional colleagues agree with the interpretation?

Lack of consensus among colleagues does not invalidate an interpretation but does suggest the need for further analysis.

Many young social workers (and even some more experienced ones) resist making an interpretation because they feel that they do not yet have enough information upon which they can base a scientific explanation of the problem. Their desire to postpone the interpretation until more data have been collected is understandable because additional data may make their job easier and less chancy. Nevertheless, there are a number of reasons why repeated postponement of arriving at an interpretation is usually inappropriate. It is never possible to know everything about a person or a problem. There will always be one more item that is missing. Early analysis and tentative interpretations can identify what it is that is missing. Instead of gathering additional unrelated data, early assessment may indicate specifically the type of additional information needed. But there is a danger of prematurely foreclosing alternative interpretations by defending, consciously or unconsciously, one's initial preliminary interpretation. In fact, Sandifer (Sandifer, Hordern, and Green, 1970) found that professionals tend to collect only the type of information that will support their initial interpretation, whether or not it is correct. This must be avoided.

It must be remembered that analysis and interpretation do not constitute an event that happens once and then never again. It is an ongoing process which starts at the very first contact and should continue throughout the social intervention activity. Early in the assessment process, analysis and interpretation are more akin to preliminary trial attempts, while later the interpretation will assume a more definitive shape. Note that we said "more definitive" and not "final" because in social intervention every interpretation is always subject to revision (even to rejection and replacement by another) if new information or a new analysis of the old information suggests this. Delaying assessment and interpretation hinders rather than helps the development of the social intervention activity.

## Decisions about Information

The focus in the third phase of the assessment process is on decisions which lead to intervention strategies. While a consultant may confine his activity to analysis and interpretation of data, a practitioner must translate what he knows and what he has learned into decision options that lead to action. Many of the activities in goal-setting and strategy formulation have been identified and discussed in earlier chapters. Here we will examine briefly the assessment skills relevant for these areas.

When the objectives of a social agency are specific and clear, goal-setting may not appear to require much thought since applicants (if they want to receive service) must accept the agency's objectives as their own goals. When youngsters join a community center, they must accept that agency's socialization and mental health goals even when their only purpose is "to have a good time." When a pregnant teen-ager, alone and scared, applies for help, the goals of the social intervention may depend on the objectives of the particular agency and not necessarily on what is best for this girl or for her as yet unborn infant. In case she happens to apply to an adoption agency, she may have to agree to give up her baby if she wants to receive service. The phrase "if she wants to receive service" is often a euphemism which disguises the fact that many social agencies are monopolies. Sometimes a person, such as a probationer or a parolee, is compelled by law to come to the social agency, but more often an applicant has no choice because of his circumstances. When a destitute family applies for aid to the welfare department, it usually does so because there are no alternative services to which it might turn. As long as financial assistance and social services were integrated in one public welfare program, such clients had no choice but to accept the goals and services offered by the worker if they did not want to starve.[1] Even though these ex-

1. Separation of income-maintenance and social service functions has been required for all state and local public welfare agencies since 1973, but prior

amples portray conditions which still exist in many communities, they are examples of poor social work practice and not of "specific and clear agency objectives." Every responsible social agency, even one which offers only one type of service, should make sure that prospective clients receive the service most suitable and most effective for them. Exploration of a client's problems and goals, together with an attempt to determine the suitability of what the agency can offer, is or should be an objective, at least an implicit objective, of every agency. For a social worker to do less is irresponsible.

**Goals.** Often a client needs the worker's help in identifying goals and objectives. There are times when an applicant requests specific help without being overly concerned about the nature of his problem or the possible outcomes. Aside from emergency situations, the worker deceives such an applicant if he accepts or rejects his request without first helping that person critically assess his problem and possible outcomes.

Mrs. Russell, a recent widow, requested that her two children be placed in a foster home so that she could go to work. If her social worker would take time to help her clarify her goals and explore the possible consequences of placement, both for herself and for her children, Mrs. Russell might realize that a foster home was not really what she wanted and needed at this particular time. Or such clarification might support the validity of her request. When the members of the YOUNG ADULT HIKING CLUB wanted help in running a big dance, the worker did not automatically process their request but instead explored with the group members how this activity, at this particular time, would help them achieve what they wanted to achieve.

to that time these services were usually offered by the same public welfare worker. See U.S. Department of Health, Education and Welfare, "The Separation of Services from Assistance Payments," Washington, 1972 (Publication No. SRS 73-23015).

Even though the emphasis in goal-setting is on the applicant's goals, the social worker must also participate. His professional experience and expertise add an important ingredient. He can help the applicant assess whether the desired outcomes are feasible or possible, given the person's and the community's resources. In most instances applicant and worker will be able to agree, or at least reach consensus, on a set of appropriate intervention goals, but there will be times when they cannot agree on what is best or what is possible. When the parents of a brain-damaged child insist that they want their child to become a physician, the worker need not accept this as the goal for the intervention activity. Even though the parents and the social worker may be able to agree on more immediate objectives, the worker must help these parents understand why their long-range vocational goal is unrealistic and what other alternatives are available for them. But no matter what their final decision, he must make it quite clear that he and his agency cannot help them prepare their brain-damaged child for a medical career. Differences between the applicant and the social worker concerning goals should be dealt with openly during the assessment process. If these differences are ignored or "pushed under the rug," they will reappear later under various guises. And later on these differences will often present more serious problems than at the beginning of the process.

Goals, as noted earlier, should focus on attitudinal, behavioral, or structural changes which are attainable through social intervention. Sometimes the goal identified by the applicant and the worker is reasonable in terms of the problem but requires the intervention of a professional other than a social worker. When a wife, physically abused by her alcoholic husband, comes to a social worker and requests help in obtaining a divorce, the worker must help the applicant test the reality and validity of this goal, making sure that she understands the various consequences of a divorce for her and for her children. But if after this exploration she wants to continue with the divorce, the worker should help her obtain the legal help necessary for achieving this objective. At the same time, the social worker may want to explore whether other services, including social intervention services, are indicated and desired—but there is little purpose in prolonging contact with an applicant who neither requires nor wants the assistance of a social worker.

**Strategy.** Once agreement, even tentative agreement, has been reached on the problem to be attacked and on the goals to be achieved, attention focuses on the intervention strategy. Here the skills and experiences of the social worker will be decisive, even though client participation is still important. The social worker must have a thorough knowledge of available resources and how these can be used most effectively. A worker who is familiar with only a few community resources will not become an effective social intervention agent. The search for the most effective and most efficient strategy option will remain an empty phrase if the worker's knowledge of resources is limited to those which his agency offers. But knowledge of community resources is only one of the necessary assessment skills. The worker must also be able to assess the client's motivation, capacity, and readiness to participate in the social intervention activity. A well-planned strategy may fail if the client is not ready or able to complete the tasks assigned to him. While motivation and readiness are not static (and workers must develop skill in extending these client characteristics), the ability to assess the client's current status is a prerequisite for effective strategy development.

## The Contract

*Contract* is a popular word in today's social work vocabulary. It expresses the idea that the client (be he an individual or a group) must know what will happen to him and what is expected of him before the social intervention activity starts. Anthony Maluccio (1974) defines the social work contract as "the explicit agreement between the worker and the client concerning the target problem, the goals, and the strategies of the social intervention, and the roles and task of the partici- pants." Even David Macarov (1974), who questions the ef- ficacy of contracts, notes that many social work teachers and practitioners consider the contract as "the *sine qua non* for suc- cessful treatment . . . logic, theory and practice wisdom all seem to support the importance of mutually-agreed goals, and the attempt to arrive at them often becomes an important dy- namic in the worker-client relationship." This service agree- ment, or "plan of care" as it is often called in the child welfare field, need not be formally negotiated or put into legal lan- guage like a business contract. While it need not be in writing, it is a contract which the applicant or client can accept or reject.

The social worker must make sure that the client really understands the terms of the contract before he accepts or rejects them. Sometimes a client is scared or confused and says "yes" because he thinks this is what the social worker wants to hear. Only later, after much time and effort have gone into the social intervention, does it become clear that the initial "yes" was really a "no" or a "maybe" or a "I don't understand." Testing the client's initial reaction, probing whether he fully understands the terms of the service agreement, raising ques- tions, presenting alternatives—these are far better worker re- sponses than quickly accepting the first nod to, "Is this okay with you?"

**Written Contract.** In many social agencies the contract is a written document which both the worker and the client sign. Sometimes all family members sign the contract so that every- body will understand what will happen during the social inter- vention activity. In group service agencies, usually all members of the group sign the contract. There is merit to a written document because it tends to minimize misunder- standings. But there are social workers who believe that a written contract is too formal a procedure, one which interferes with the informality characteristic of the positive client-worker relationship. No matter whether the contract is written or oral, there must be clarity and agreement about the conditions of service, the goals of intervention, and the respective roles of client and worker. Both must understand that every contract is subject to renegotiation when circumstances change. Either has the right to request reconsideration of the contract terms at any time. Some workers have even suggested a compulsory review of the contract at stated intervals to make sure that it is still relevant. Perhaps more important than a formal review clause is the social worker's constant alertness to the possibility that the original contract terms need revision. And when that need arises, there is no advantage in delaying the contract renegotiation.

One of the benefits of a contract is the introduction of accountability into the social intervention process. The client can no longer remain a passive subject upon whom or for whom certain operations are performed, nor can the social worker continue to do as he pleases. Both have contracted to engage in certain specified activities in order to achieve designated objectives and goals. Both are accountable to each other (and to society) for their activities and both will be evaluated on the basis of reaching or not reaching these objectives. A fringe benefit, noted by Alan Keith-Lucas (1974), is the general reduction of client hostility toward the agency as a result of having a contract which clearly spells out what the client can expect from the agency and from the worker. Thus a contract can provide greater security for a child in a placement since he now has a written confirmation of his rights and obligations.

## Preparation of Assessment Statement

Assessment is a dynamic and ongoing process in which all social workers engage. Even routine social services cannot be provided without first making some kind of assessment about the person requesting the service and his problem. Yet many social workers try to avoid putting this assessment into writing. There may be something too definite about writing such a statement when the worker himself still has many questions about the problem or about the person. So long as the assessment is only in the worker's mind, changes (even major changes) are easy, but many workers feel thay are "trapped" or "stuck" once they put the assessment on paper.

However, these workers fail to take account of the dynamic nature of the assessment process and the fact that in social work any written statement is necessarily tentative and subject to revision as new information becomes available or as new developments occur. Changes and revisions, far from indicating an error or a failure, are a sign of a worker's strength. Some social workers have found it helpful to utilize two types of written statements: (1) a preliminary statement early in the assessment process; and (2) a more complete statement later on.

**Preliminary Statement.** The preliminary statement is often written immediately after the first interview or meeting. It will contain the worker's first impressions and thoughts about the client and his problem. A crucial part is the preliminary assessment where the worker will assemble the early results of his data analysis. Hunches and guesses are permissible in this preliminary statement but must be identified as such. Another important part of the preliminary statement is the section on "next steps." What action must be taken right away? What tasks will the client carry out? What tasks are the worker's responsibility? What additional information is needed? Following is a topical outline of the areas usually covered in a preliminary statement. The order of the topics and the topics noted are suggestive only; in any given situation, additional areas may be covered or certain points may require more attention.

## Preliminary Statement

1. Identifying Information *
   Name, address, phone, age, marital status
   Short physical description
   Employment and education data
   Family composition
   Behavior while presenting problem
   Previous contacts with agency, if any

2. Presenting Problem and Request
   What is the complaint?
   What service or help is requested?

3. Information Relevant to Problem and Request *
   What information is known now?
   What additional information is necessary?
   How and where can additional information be obtained?

4. Worker's Preliminary Assessment
   What seems to be the nature of the real problem?
   Does the applicant seem ready to work on the problem?
   What other people and systems should be involved?

5. Next Steps
   What are the plans for the immediate future?
   How will the applicant cope with the problem (if it is an emergency)?
   Has another appointment been arranged? With whom? For what purpose? When?
   Is worker/agency taking any steps (other than further assessment) at this time?
   Has applicant agreed to any responsibilities between now and next appointment?

* When the client is a group, section 1 will contain identifying information on each group member, including his role in the group; section 3 will also contain information about the group as a social system, its structure, culture, method of operation, and so forth.

**Assessment Statement.** Once the goals for the social intervention activity have been formulated and the intervention strategy developed, it is time for the worker to prepare a complete assessment statement. This statement serves several purposes: (1) summary and review of the assessment process as it has developed until this point; (2) operational guide for the implementation of the intervention activity; and (3) point of departure for the evaluation. This statement, like the preliminary statement, is not fixed and unchangeable. On the contrary, whenever circumstances require a change in goals or strategy, this statement should be revised. Nor is it essential that workers wait to prepare this statement until the strategy has evolved; often it is more useful to prepare the assessment statement prior to strategy development.

### Assessment Statement *

1.  Identifying Information (as in the preliminary statement)

2.  Assessment of Problem
    Presenting problem
    Environmental and ecological factors relating to problem
    Client's characteristics relevant to problem
    Other factors bearing on problem
    Current assessment of problem

3.  Resources for Problem-solving
    Applicant's coping capacity and modes of coping with previous problem situations
    External resources: family, agency, community, other barriers and constraints impeding problem resolution or problem reduction
    Assessment of change potential—with client(s), environment, others

4.  Intervention Goals

5.  Targets of the Social Intervention

6.  Intervention Strategy

* When the client is a group, this statement will be modified along the lines suggested in the preliminary statement.

The assessment statement is also known as the *diagnostic statement*. It should be much more than a mere recital of facts and bits of information. The focus must be on an analysis and synthesis of the information which the worker and the client have gathered. The emphasis of the analysis will be on the future: what meaning does it have for goal achievement? Some social workers prefer to write sections 1–4 of the assessment statement first and use this as a basis for developing the strategy. This is a matter of individual work habits and personal preference. It should be remembered that in the day-by-day work the various phases of the assessment process do not occur sequentially but simultaneously. Often it is not possible to know whether, at a given moment, a worker is engaged in goal-setting or in a strategy development.

Every worker should prepare an assessment statement for every problem, but each worker will develop this statement according to his own personal style. It is not important how the statement looks or whether it follows some outline, such as the one suggested here for illustrative purposes. What counts is that the document represents the outcome of an assessment process during which the problem was skillfully analyzed and interpreted and that, at the same time, the statement provides clear guidance for the subsequent intervention activity.

## Summary

Assessment is an activity which occurs throughout the social intervention, though it is particularly important in the beginning phase. In this chapter we examined three component phases of the assessment process. In the first phase the emphasis is on *collecting information* which will help both the client and the worker understand as fully as possible the problem situation and the person requesting help.

*Analysis* and *interpretation* of the information constitute the core activities during the second phase. Here an attempt is made to understand how the various parts of the problem are related to each other and what they mean. Analysis of the information involves ordering the data, discovering relationships between various items, exploring the meaning of the data, and identifying the factors which might cause the problem. In the third phase, client and worker make *decisions* about the information, decisions which lead from assessment to strategies of intervention.

# chapter twelve

# Communication Skills

Communication occurs whenever two or more people interact and exchange information, ideas, emotions, and so forth, by means of symbols. Communication can also take place between a person and a machine, such as a computer, as well as between two machines. In this chapter our emphasis will be on those communication skills which are particularly relevant to social intervention. We will first explore the general background of communications and then apply this material to specific intervention situations.

Communication takes place whenever two or more people interact, even when their interaction is at the most minimal level and there is almost no contact between them. The airplane passenger who stares straight ahead or who buries his nose in a newspaper "tells" the person in the next seat that he does not wish to be disturbed. And generally his neighbor understands him and will respect the message. In the presence of others it is virtually impossible not to communicate. Paul Watzlawick (Watzlawick, Beavin, and Jackson, 1967:49) wrote, "activity or inactivity, words or silence, all have message value: they influence others and these others, in turn, cannot *not* respond to these communications and are thus themselves communicating."

Most people think that communication is one of those simple processes which almost every adult has mastered. Yet all around us we find evidence of communication failures and breakdowns. Husbands misunderstand their wives; and wives, husbands. Parents have difficulty in communicating with their children and vice versa. Bloody battles between teen-age gangs have erupted because messages were misunderstood, and nations have been pushed into wars by misunderstanding each other's intentions. Effective communication is far from simple. It requires a higher level of skill than many have mastered. Communication is a basic process in every phase of the social intervention, no matter whether the strategy is based on one of the talking therapies or on some other intervention modality. Whenever a social worker presents himself and his ideas to others, he must use communication skills. Worker and client depend on communication skills to gather the information necessary for assessment. Intervention goals are identified and strategies developed only when worker and client communicate effectively. Communication need not be verbal nor does it always make use of formal language. Important messages can be transmitted without speaking and without writing. The social worker who repeatedly forgets what he promised to do clearly informs his client that he is not interested in helping him, no matter what his verbal explanation may be later on. And the client who inevitably forgets his appointments sends a similar message without using any words.

## Elements of Communication

The three basic elements of communication were identified by Aristotle over two thousand years ago: (1) the person who speaks or sends the message; (2) the message that he produces and transmits; and (3) the listener or recipient of the message. This Aristotelian model, like every model, simplifies a very complex process in order to make it more easily understandable. The model applies to all types of messages and all types of media. Even though some have identified additional elements, this is the basic model for understanding all communication processes. Its major limitation is that it depicts only one fragmentary segment or message when actually communication is sequential and consists of an almost infinite chain of messages. The Aristotelian model also suggests that communication travels in one direction only when actually it is a two-directional or multidirectional process. Communications flow not only from A to B but also from B to A. More complex communication models, such as Barnlund's interpersonal communication model (1970), incorporate additional elements in order to overcome these limitations, but for our purposes the simpler model (with one additional element which will be introduced in the next paragraphs) suffices

A model diagrams the communication process without concern for the quality or consequences of the communication. In real life, however, the social worker is vitally concerned with the effectiveness of his communications. A communication is effective only when the recipient interprets it in the way it was intended by the sender and when it produces the effect desired by the sender. But the recipient can respond appropriately only when he correctly receives the message directed toward him. Our consideration of communications must, therefore, also take account of the factors which result in messages being received incorrectly or not at all, which happens all too frequently.

In our revised model we will include one additional element to account for the distortions in communications which make for imperfect reception. This additional element we call *noise.* There are several distinct types of noise which interfere with effective communication. Each type requires different efforts for overcoming or reducing it. *Mechanical noise* includes real noises, such as an airplane flying overhead, a loud radio or TV, a lawnmower outside the window, and other noise-producing situations which make it physically difficult for the recipient to hear the message accurately. Static on the telephone or a sudden disconnect on the telephone are other examples of mechanical noise which interfere with the communication process.

*Organic noise* refers to those pathological conditions of the organs (particularly those connected with speaking and hearing) which interfere with sending and receiving messages. Speech disorders, such as lisping, and hearing difficulties, especially uncorrected deafness, limit the chances for effective communications.

*Psychological noise,* like organic noise, may be a characteristic of either sender or receiver. Fear, worry, preoccupation with other matters, are conditions which may prevent concentration on the current communication. Many a client is so concerned with his problem that he literally does not hear what the worker is saying. Or the worker may be mentally reviewing a particularly difficult problem of another client with which he will have to deal later in the day and not pay attention to the person with whom he is talking now.

The complete elimination of all noise may be an ideal condition that is not achievable. In human communications there will always be some distortion so that no message is ever understood exactly as it was intended by the sender. Nevertheless, the reduction of noise is one of the most important ways of increasing the effectiveness of communications. Specific steps for accomplishing this will be discussed in a later section of this chapter.

## Verbal and Nonverbal Communication

Human communication uses both verbal and nonverbal symbols. *Verbal communication* employs word symbols which can refer to concrete objects (such as money, bread), concepts (eligibility, poverty), feelings (anger, love), people (Mrs. Simpson, Bill), or activities (speaking, working). Verbal symbols are based on language and can be transmitted orally or in writing. Symbols not based on language are called *nonverbal symbols.* These include facial expressions, eye contact, body gestures, tone of voice, and so on. A laugh, the type of clothing worn, nodding one's head, the distance between two people, coming on time—these are examples of nonverbal symbols which are frequently used in the communication process. Some communication situations rely exclusively on nonverbal symbols while others use both verbal and nonverbal language. But it is not possible to communicate only with verbal symbols.

When a social worker is in the middle of an important telephone call, the tone of his voice indicates the importance or urgency he attaches to the communication. This is the nonverbal message which accompanies his verbal message. At the same time, he may use other nonverbal symbols to communicate with a person who suddenly rushes into his office and thrusts a piece of paper in front of his eyes. The worker may put his finger over his lips and shake his head from side to side. The newcomer stops, drops his hands to his sides, and nods his head up and down. Though this scene lasts only a few seconds, several messages are exchanged without using any words or making any sounds. Had verbal symbols been used, the conversation might have run as follows:

"Mr. White, I just got this notice in the mail. What does it mean?"

"Hold it. Can't you see that I am busy talking on the phone. Relax, sit down, and I'll be with you in just a little while."

"O.K. I understand."

These two people understood each other because people who grow up in the same culture interpret nonverbal symbols in similar ways.

When people grow up in different cultures, nonverbal communication is not always understood correctly. A social worker who is working with recent immigrants may have as much difficulty understanding their nonverbal communications as their language. Take the recent Chinese immigrant who in the middle of a "talk" with his social worker (with the help of an interpreter) scratches his ears and cheeks; the worker might think that these gestures indicate embarrassment or puzzlement, but in the traditional Chinese culture this nonverbal movement symbolizes happiness (Klineberg, 1938).

The following incident of misunderstood nonverbal communications (Panitch, 1974:328, citing Thomas Kochman; italics added) might have occurred in any of our metropolitan areas:

In an urban classroom an Anglo teacher is reproaching a Puerto Rican child. Part of his response includes the *lowering of his eyes.* The teacher *moves toward the child, lifts his chin,* and even *more harshly* than before scolds, "You look me in the eye when I'm talking to you." The child is hurt and bewildered.

We have italicized the nonverbal messages which so obviously have been misunderstood because teacher and student grew up in different cultural environments. Lowering one's eyes in response to being scolded is the "correct" Puerto Rican reaction, signifying shame and a willingness to accept responsibility. But the teacher interpreted avoidance of eye contact as a sign of withdrawal and evasion of responsibility. The teacher's moving toward the child and touching his face was meant to be a symbolic threat, but in the student's culture body contact under these circumstances was symbolic of extreme humiliation.

It was hardly accidental that both teacher and student relied heavily on nonverbal communications in an effort to get their message across. Experimenters have found consistently that people put more emphasis on nonverbal communications than on verbal messages. Jack McCroskey and his associates (1971) reported on the basis of experimental findings that less than 35 percent of the meaning of messages was communicated by verbal symbols. And Albert Mehrabian (1968) concluded that the impact of an oral message depended 55 percent on the sender's facial expression, 38 percent on his tone of voice, and only 7 percent on the verbal content of the message. Even in written communications the nonverbal characteristics of the sender are often more important than the text of the message. When college students were given excerpts from newspapers and magazines about controversial questions, they generally accepted the communications that were attributed to trustworthy sources but rejected these same excerpts when they were attributed to biased sources, such as *Pravda* (Hovland and Weiss, 1951).

What a person says or writes is usually less important than the nonverbal cues which accompany the verbal message. How often does it happen that we listen to a person and think that he does not really mean what he says? We base our decision whether to believe what another says on our interpretation of the accompanying nonverbal symbols since we assume that it is harder to pretend nonverbal communications than to distort verbal ones. A neighborhood worker may tell people to get in touch with him whenever they have a problem, but the way he tells them clearly signals his intentions. The nonverbal signal may say, "Do come!" or it may read, "Don't bother me!" Whenever there is an apparent contradiction between the verbal message and the accompanying nonverbal message, the decision to accept or reject the communication is generally based on the nonverbal cues.

Nonverbal communications are effective for managing social relations, for supporting verbal messages, or for replacing verbal messages. Men do not need words to tell women that they find them sexually attractive; the whistle is only one of several nonverbal techniques for communicating this sentiment. Attitudes about others can be transmitted effectively through nonverbal messages. A speaker will "tell" others how he feels about them or about the relationship between them by using different styles of speaking or different speech codes. A client can usually tell quite early what his social worker thinks of him by noting how he speaks to him. As one client once put it, "It isn't *what* he said but *how* he said it."

The effectiveness of nonverbal communication has also been verified experimentally. When shown photographs and short written statements collected during stressful interviews, most judges were able to match the photograph with the verbal statement (Ekman, 1964). In another experiment an actress was able to convey various emotions, such as anger,

nervousness, and happiness, by reciting the alphabet in different voice tones (Davitz and Davitz, 1959). Even though these
experiments produced statistically significant results, they also
underscore the ambiguity and inexactness of nonverbal symbols. In the real-life interview or group meeting the meaning
of nonverbal symbols is much clearer than in the experimental
situations since the listener does not depend on an isolated
cue. Instead, he assesses the meaning of any message on the
basis of an entire set of nonverbal symbols, so that the accuracy of interpretation is potentially much greater in the real
situation than in the experiment. But the accuracy is reduced
when sender and receiver come from different cultural backgrounds, as is often the case in social agencies. Under these
circumstances misinterpretation will continue to occur
frequently.

The utilization of nonverbal messages as a replacement
for verbal messages is probably less important in social work
than in many other contexts. In a noisy factory commands
may be given by hand signals because voice communication is
not possible. Occasionally, social workers do use nonverbal signals when other types of noise make verbal communication
impossible. Thus, when an interpreter must be used because
the worker cannot speak the language of the client, the
worker will attempt to supplement the verbal translations by
using direct nonverbal signals. Similarly, he will be able to receive nonverbal responses from such clients.

**Silence.** The pause between two oral messages is known as
silence. Even though no verbal communication takes place
during periods of silence, communication continues on a nonverbal level. The meaning of silence is often misunderstood,
especially in America where silence is viewed with disfavor.
Most people try to avoid silence, associating it with something
undesirable or stigmatized. The "silent treatment" is considered a particularly harsh form of peer discipline, used only in
the most serious instances of status deviation. In conversation

the silent pause is thought to be awkward, and every good conversationalist knows how to avoid it. However, social workers sometimes use silence to encourage clients to participate. Some workers deliberately remain silent during the beginning phase of an interview or during the first few meetings with a group in order to permit clients to disclose their reason for coming. But silence is an ambiguous communications technique. It fails to give direction and it does not specify what the sender wants the recipient to do. At a time when the worker's active intervention may be vital to structure the interaction, his silence is dysfunctional since it communicates the very opposite of what he intended. Often clients misinterpret the worker's silence as a lack of interest. Or they may be confused since they do not understand the meaning of the worker's silence. Only when clients clearly know what they want and how they can utilize the agency's services will worker silence serve a constructive purpose.

Many social workers are puzzled and do not know what to do when a client is silent and does not participate in the interview or in the meeting. Some have suggested that a worker who talks more than one third of the time is too active and prevents client progress toward goal achievement (Kadushin, 1972:187). But worker silence, as noted, may not always serve a useful purpose. Moreover, a worker may feel threatened by a client's continued silence, especially if he feels that this nonparticipation is due to his shortcomings as a worker. In an attempt to reduce his feelings of anxiety and insecurity, this worker may increase his verbal activity but later feel guilty about talking too much. Effective social intervention requires that this vicious circle be interrupted. The worker must try to understand the meaning of the client's silence. The silence may mean many different things, but it always contains a message. Silence may indicate that the client is confused about the purpose of the interview and uncertain how to respond. Or silence may be the result of a physical handicap (deafness prevented the client from hearing the worker's question) or lack of an adequate vocabulary with which to respond. Silence may indicate a refusal to participate. The client may have decided to withhold certain information, or he may be so ashamed about having to ask for help that he cannot participate. Each of these silences (and there are others) communicates a certain message and calls for a different worker response. It is important that the worker attempt to understand what the client is trying to "say" when he remains silent.[1]

Basil Bernstein (1964) has argued that the social structure is a major factor in determining a person's ability to enter into various types of interpersonal relationships. Persons raised in middle-class families have learned to speak freely and easily, while those raised in lower-class homes have a smaller vocabulary and less facility in verbal communication. Speech is the key for social interaction. People with a limited speech pattern find it difficult to relate to others on any but a formal basis. These differences in speech patterns also affect the social intervention process. The silence of a taciturn manual laborer who rarely speaks a full sentence has an entirely different meaning from the silence of a young executive's wife who ordinarily never stops talking. Social workers must not expect the same type and amount of participation from clients who come from various backgrounds. The nod or the smile of one client may be as significant as ten minutes of speech from another. With some clients it is best to utilize nonverbal interaction modalities. Just as play therapy has been found useful with young children, so various types of activities will be effective as intervention strategies with adolescents and adults who lack verbal facility. Often a silent client is eager to participate and will respond positively to specific tasks which the worker assigns to him. He may not be able to tell much about his childhood or his activities last week but he is more than willing to collect and bring in pay stubs, letters, the family

---

1. Basso (1972) presents an interesting attempt to interpret various meanings of silence among the Western Apaches.

Bible, and other items which may supply the needed information.

In summary, the principle of not talking more than one third of the time is not a law but only a bit of generalized practice wisdom which is not always applicable. There are times when the worker must be more active, just as there will be times when the worker will be less active. Worker silence (and its meaning to the client) does not depend on any rules. In deciding whether to speak or to remain silent, the worker must consider how the client will perceive what he does. Whenever a client equates worker silence with lack of interest, it will be best to minimize silent pauses. But if the client interprets worker silence as an invitation for him to become more involved in the social intervention, then the "one-third guide" will be useful.

## Effective Communication

An effective communication is one which the recipient interprets in the way intended by the sender and one which produces the effect desired by the sender. When a worker asks his supervisor a question but the latter thinks that he is criticizing him, the communication is ineffective because the worker did not receive the information he requested and because the worker-supervisor relationship was changed in a way not intended by the worker. The last-minute refusal of a natural mother to give up her baby for adoption, even after the social worker has made all the necessary arrangements, must have been preceded by a series of ineffective communications. There are many reasons why a natural mother might not want to give up her baby, even at the last moment. But if prior communications had been more effective, the social worker would have had earlier clues of the mother's ambivalent feelings or of her true intentions. Another example of less than effective communication occurred when the question, "Can your mother help you when you feel that way [temporarily depressed]?" received a response of, "No, she doesn't have any cash to spare." The answer indicates that the word "help" had different meanings for the sender and the receiver (Komarovsky, 1964). And different meanings make for ineffective communications.

A communication which is not accepted by the recipient is only half a communication. It matters little whether the communication was not accepted because the receiver misunderstood it or because he did understand it but did not wish to comply. A communication can be accepted only when the recipient understands it as the sender intended it. But this is only one of the requirements for an effective communication. Other characteristics that make for effective communications include an effective communicator or sender, an appropriate message, reduction or elimination of noise, and a proficient receiver. It is not accidental that these four characteristics mirror the four elements of our revised model of communication. We will now review these four characteristics in some detail in order to help social workers utilize more effective communication skills. Since every sender is also a receiver of communications, we will examine the first and fourth characteristic together.

## The Effective Communicator

**Credibility.** *Who* says something may be as important (and sometimes even more important) as *what* is said. It will matter little what the social worker says if he is perceived as aloof, insincere, cold, or hostile. On the other hand, when a worker is believed to be trustworthy, knowledgeable, and interested, it is likely that his message will be accepted and acted upon. Credibility is not so much a question of moral character and good will (important as these qualities are), but more of how the communicator is perceived by others. When a client has confidence in his worker and believes that the worker can help him, the worker has high credibility, no matter whether this perception is factually correct. Even a confidence man enjoys, at least for a limited time, high credibility among his victims because he has succeeded in portraying himself as trustworthy, knowledgeable, and interested in others.

The example of the confidence man suggests that there are specific ways through which anyone can enhance his credibility. The worker who is bored by his clients or afraid of them or the worker who fails to focus on his clients' problems because he is preoccupied with his own will not merit credibility and will fail to become an effective communicator, as will the social worker who is dishonest or ambiguous. Though one would think that every social worker was aware of such obvious and elementary considerations, research has shown that these very conditions often are the cause of communication blockages and unsuccessful intervention efforts (Truax and Mitchell, 1971). Honesty, warmth, a sense of humor, and attentiveness are necessary for any person who wants to help others. Social workers must learn how to demonstrate these characteristics so that they will be accorded credibility by those whom they serve.

**Honesty.** Honesty requires that the worker's verbal and nonverbal messages are complementary and that the worker's activities are in agreement with his communications. A worker must never say one thing and do another—and expect that his client will continue to believe in him. A worker should not engage in an activity which affects a client without first discussing this with him. In the best of circumstances there will be agreement about all worker and client activities, but even in situations where the worker is obliged to act without the client's consent, the worker's actions must not come as a surprise to his client. The juvenile court social worker, for example, is required to share information with the judge. In many jurisdictions the social worker also makes recommendations to the court about the disposition of the complaint against a juvenile. This sharing of information and the gen-

eral trend of the worker's recommendations should be known
to the youngster before he learns of it from the judge. Otherwise, it may happen that the youngster will feel betrayed and
abandoned by the social worker who he thought was a friend.
*Warmth* and *good humor* can be conveyed by the tone of voice
and the content of a message. The social worker who takes
himself too seriously probably will not come across as a warm
person. *Attentiveness* does not always come naturally and may
require an extra effort, especially when the client's story resembles that of many others.

But there is more to credibility than this. The social
worker must also be aware of the obstacles to credibility that
arise out of common practice situations. Seymour Halleck
(1963) identified seven practice patterns or "lies" which social
workers tend to employ, consciously or otherwise, when working with disturbed adolescents:

1. *The lie of adult morality.* Workers condemn immature
behavior and ask the teen to behave more maturely. But
adults themselves do not always live up to the behavior standards demanded of teens. And adults are not punished when
they behave in ways for which adolescents are punished.

2. *The lie of professional helpfulness.* Although claiming to
want to help the adolescent, workers are not always in a position to do so because they have prior obligations toward the
community. When the needs of the community and of the adolescent are in conflict, most social workers give priority to the
community's requirements even if this results in neglecting the
adolescent.

3. *The lie of confidentiality.* Despite their promises, social
workers cannot guarantee the confidentiality of the information which they received from adolescents since they must
often share it with others.

4. *The lie of rewards for conforming behavior.* Though workers promise that a change of behavior from deviant to conforming will be for the youngster's own good, the new behavior pattern may not be functional and may not be rewarding.

The real beneficiary of the conforming behavior is the community, not the adolescent.

5. *Denial of real limits.* Social workers may set goals which are far beyond the capacity of the adolescent, especially if he comes from a lower-class background. Impossible expectations result in frustration and in loss of faith in the worker and in self.

6. *"Open up; trust me and all will go well."* The social structure of the worker-client relationship does not permit true intimacy between equals, even though many workers try to achieve this. Workers who themselves are subject to bureaucratic constraints cannot assure their clients a long-term relationship since they may be transferred or may leave their present job for another at any time.

7. *"I like you but not your behavior."* Despite this platitude, which is frequently heard, Halleck maintains that it is almost impossible to work with adolescents without periodically becoming angered.

Most adolescents are aware of the reality situation and are not taken in by the worker's "lies." The net effect of this type of professional dishonesty, therefore, is to confuse and infuriate adolescents, to produce more rebellion, more unwanted symptoms, more psychic pain—and a reduction of worker credibility.

These practice patterns are not unique to social intervention with adolescents, for they are also common in work with other age groups. As long as the worker is unaware of these behavior patterns or if he pretends that the client is ignorant of them, communication will be less than effective. The social worker may believe that he is motivated only by the client's best interest, but most clients are not ready to accept the worker's intentions when these do not match his performance. Effective communication requires open and honest communications. When there is a conflict between client needs and community requirements, this should be recognized by both worker and client. When worker and client have different priorities, these differences should be acknowledged and discussed. Communication can be effective even in situations where agreement is not reached, provided the conflicts and differences are handled honestly. A client may not like it that the information he will provide will be repeated to the worker's supervisor or to the judge, but he will appreciate the honesty of the worker who tells him about this early in their relationship.

**Stages of Credibility.** Jack McCroskey and his associates (1971) have suggested that credibility is not a one-time phenomenon but a condition which needs continual attention by the social worker. According to McCroskey, there are several distinct credibility stages. *Initial credibility* refers to the perception which the receiver has of the communicator before the communication process actually begins, even before there is any direct contact between sender and receiver. Initial credibility depends on such factors as the sender's reputation, his appearance, his social group, and so on. An applicant or a client about to meet a new social worker has certain preconceived impressions even before he enters the social agency office for the first time. His initial decision to accept (or not to accept) the worker as a trustworthy person may be based on the opinions of friends who have had experiences with social workers, on his own contacts with other social workers, on the image of social workers projected on television or in the movies, or of his own imagination, prejudices, or stereotypes. Though the image of the social worker may be vague, every client has some preconceptions about the credibility of the social worker whom he is about to meet. This initial image will be confirmed (or changed) by such factors as the appearance of the waiting room, the manner in which the receptionist greets him, and the way the worker's office looks. All this takes place before any messages have been exchanged between the worker and the client.

    *Derived credibility* refers to the level of trust that results from the actual interaction between two persons. It depends on the impression which the worker makes on the client during the social intervention.

*Terminal credibility* refers to the client's final assessment after the social intervention activity has been completed. Terminal credibility of today may become the basis of an initial credibility tomorrow.

The social worker who talked with MRS. KING enjoyed high initial credibility because Mrs. King had confidence in the neighbor who had told her that a social worker had once helped her. But Mrs. King's reactions during the first interview were mixed. The worker seemed nice and friendly, but he talked most of the time and actually did little to help her. The derived credibility (reflecting Mrs. King's feelings during and immediately after the initial interview) was considerably lower than the initial credibility, so much so that the effectiveness of the intervention became endangered. However, in subsequent interviews this social worker was able to enhance the effectiveness of his communications by demonstrating his competence and interest in Mrs. King's problem. Half a year later, when Mrs. King discussed her experience with a friend, she spoke warmly about the social worker who had helped her so much just when she needed someone to help her. Because the intervention was successful the worker's terminal credibility was rated as high. Various techniques and different skills are needed to enhance the three types of credibility. A social worker may think that there is little he can do about initial credibility since this does not seem to depend on his personal characteristics or his own efforts. Yet this is undoubtedly the most crucial credibility stage. Without high initial credibility later attempts to enhance credibility may be all but impossible. When high initial credibility is maintained, a successful outcome is generally assured, regardless of what the worker does.[2]

2. Gallimore and Turner (1969) utilized initial credibility (which they called "faith in the therapist") to explain why the intervention efforts of many different types of practitioners, including social workers, psychiatrists, witch

There are, of course, factors other than initial credibility which influence the outcome of the social intervention process. Yet benefits rarely accrue to those clients who initially do not trust their worker. Social workers must, therefore, increase their efforts to assure initial credibility. Old strategies must be reviewed and new ones created to achieve this important objective. Fee-charging may be a strategy appropriate for increasing initial credibility of middle- and upper-class clients who think that whatever is free cannot be good. Making sure that the waiting room and the office appear pleasant and efficient may add to initial credibility. Diplomas on the wall and professional books on the bookshelves may "testify" to the competence of the worker. Efforts to develop more positive relations with the media are important since many people learn about social work from magazines and television. These are more or less routine suggestions which nevertheless merit attention because they are often overlooked.

There are also a number of innovative ideas which deserve attention and thought. Arnold Goldstein (Goldstein, Heller, and Sechrest, 1966) suggests placing a confederate in the waiting room to "share" positive information about the social worker with others who await their appointment; however, this suggestion raises a number of ethical questions and, therefore, cannot be recommended. But the waiting room does offer opportunities for providing client services, and these, indirectly, may enhance the worker's credibility. Some agencies have employed former and current clients as hostesses; their job is to make those waiting more comfortable, answer their questions (and thus reduce some anxiety), play with children, watch infants while their mothers meet with the social worker, and generally convey an atmosphere of friendliness and efficiency.

Street-corner workers, whether they work with groups or

---

doctors, and quacks, seemed to result in almost identical levels of successful outcomes. Disturbed people who believe in their therapist seem to get well, no matter what his credentials. And when people have no faith in their practitioner, they will not be helped, no matter how competent he may be.

individuals, cannot rely on such props as waiting rooms or diplomas to strengthen their initial credibility. Social workers who work with groups often use facilities over which the agency has no control (school buildings, churches, and so forth). Aside from advance word-of-mouth publicity, these workers are completely on their own. How they handle themselves, what they do, what they say, is important for all social workers, but it is especially crucial for workers who operate away from their home base.

While initial credibility is important, credibility must be maintained throughout the social intervention process if a successful outcome is to occur. Credibility will be maintained only when the client's expectations are matched, more or less, by the worker's activities. The worker's credibility, for example, will decline if the East Side Neighborhood Council had been looking forward to an aggressive community worker who would tell everybody what to do and the new worker, on the contrary, was unwilling to take a lead but insisted on the full participation of everybody. When an applicant expects a worker to assume a "white coat" medical role but the worker follows an entirely different intervention model, a reduction of worker credibility may result. The seriousness of this problem is suggested by a number of studies which report that the expectations of clients vary widely from the actual role behaviors of social workers (Chilman, 1966; Mayer and Timms, 1970; Silverman, 1970).

To counteract this discrepancy and increase worker credibility, some have suggested that workers take into account and utilize role models with which clients are already familiar. It is argued that the worker will not be helpful if he insists on using verbal therapy techniques with clients who expect more active problem-solving or more direct advice. At one time most social workers would have rejected such a suggestion out of hand, but today many agree that intervention modalities must fit both the problem and the people involved. If it is important to develop an ongoing relationship, then the worker must start where the client is.

Even though the full involvement and participation of every client may be desirable, a worker may decide to utilize a more active and aggressive intervention strategy in the beginning in order to enhance his credibility. New intervention techniques have been developed to supplement the more traditional ones. For example, some social workers have all but abandoned the formal one-to-one interview when working with welfare mothers. Instead, they have found that task-focused groups, concerned with achieving relevant objectives, such as securing additional benefits from the welfare department or making toys for their children, provide a much more effective vehicle for meaningful communications than the formal interview. Similar experiences have been reported by those working in other settings and with various age groups. A hospital social worker, assigned to a diabetic ward, found that patients accepted communications about dietary restrictions and activity limitations more quickly once he substituted group sessions for individual interviews. He felt that in a group he could relate more naturally to the patients, and that as a consequence his credibility became greater.

**Listening.** Being a good listener is another crucial characteristic of the effective communicator. Listening is not a passive activity, as many believe, but a skill which requires activity on the part of the listener. And listening is not a natural talent, but a skill which must be acquired. Many people, including some social workers, are poor listeners. Some clients complain that their social workers do not listen to them. And when a social worker does not listen to his clients, the communication process cannot be effective. Many think that listening is the opposite of talking, requiring only that the listener close his mouth and open his ears to the message which someone else sends. But not talking does not necessarily result in hearing, nor does listening always follow hearing. Hearing is a physical process which is not limited to the human species; many animals can hear better than most humans. Listening, on the other hand, is a mental and cultural process which is encountered only among humans. It is first learned during childhood but must be relearned during later stages of the life cycle. One of the reasons that listening is so difficult is that we hear only what we want to hear and what we expect to hear, regardless of what the other person said. When listening to a client, the social worker tends to pay attention to those items of information which confirm his first tentative assessment while overlooking other information which might lead in different directions.[3]

The effective social work communicator must make every effort to listen attentively to his clients' communications. The object of listening is to understand what the other person is really trying to communicate. This total listening requires that the listener uses not only his ears but all of his senses. He must focus attention on what is said and how it is said, as well as on what is not said. Total listening means hearing verbal messages with the ears, observing body gestures with the eyes, using the hands and eyes to send back nonverbal messages to encourage further communication, and involving the entire body of the listener in the communication process. This kind of listening takes time and skill, but it does solve one communication problem. Thought, as noted earlier, is much more rapid than speech so that ordinarily the listener's attention tends to wander. The person who listens only with his ears may become bored or begin to think about his own problems, but when the "extra" time is used for total listening, there will be hardly enough time to notice everything that should be observed.

Learning to become a good listener requires learning new skills. Without the right techniques, the attempt to demonstrate good listening sometimes achieves the very opposite. One social worker who was trying to encourage his client's communication told him sympathetically, "I know exactly how

3. Selective listening, that is, listening to only part of a conversation, is a common phenomenon. Sandifer and his colleagues (1970) experimentally confirmed this selective listening pattern for psychiatrists.

you feel." Even though this client may have appreciated the warm response to his initial statement, he did not relate further details about his problem since he believed that the worker already knew how he felt. But the social worker still did not understand the client's problem. Another response, perhaps "tell me more," might have been better since it would have conveyed both the worker's interest and his encouragement for further communication. Further communication generally is desirable both for the client and for the worker. The worker must learn more about the problem before he can participate fully, and the client will be helped by having a thoughtful listener to whom he can talk about his problem. The way in which a worker receives client communications is important. One way to demonstrate attention, interest, and concern is by gestures. Another way is through such comments as, "I see" or "uh huh" or through friendly remarks, such as, "I don't quite understand," and questions, as "Did you mean . . . ?" In the long run, however, a worker demonstrates his interest by what he does rather than by what he says.

**Communication Styles.** Another characteristic of the effective social work communicator is his ability to reduce client anxiety and ambiguity. The less anxious the receiver of the message and the less ambiguous the situation, the greater the chances of his being able and willing to receive the communication. Client anxiety and ambiguity depend, at least in part, on what the communicator does or does not do. Earlier we noted that an appropriate amount of worker activity has a beneficial effect in reducing anxiety, while too little or too much tends to increase client anxiety. We also indicated that the worker is responsible for structuring the intervention relation so as to reduce client ambiguity.

The choice of an appropriate communication style may also affect the level of client anxiety. Donald Hansen (1965) identified two communication styles, calling one the *personal influence style* and the other the *positional influence style*. Some communicators use only one of the two, regardless of the situation, while others are able to vary their style to meet the demands of a particular situation. The positional influence style emphasizes the structural elements of the worker-client relationship ("As your social worker I urge you to consider a foster home placement for your baby"; or, "Do as I suggest. Trust me, for I have dealt with problems like yours for many years . . ."), while the personal influence style focuses on the receiver and his feelings ("How would you feel about placing your baby in a foster home?"; or, "I can't make this decision for you because you are the person who will have to live with it . . ."). Positional influence relies on the communicator's status, while personal influence, as its name implies, relies on the interpersonal relationship. Positional influence is more concerned with the consequences of an action, while personal influence pays more attention to intent and process.

These two communication styles are not limited to the client-worker interaction but are found throughout life in every transaction, starting with the mother-child relationship. Hansen suggests that the use of the positional influence style may put the client under less tension than the use of the personal influence style. However, this may depend on the prior socialization experiences of the message receiver and on the content of the communication. For persons whose early socialization was largely by way of personal influence, the personal influence style may be less anxiety-provoking and more effective than the positional influence style, while the opposite would be true for clients whose socialization was largely on the basis of positional influence. The personal influence style may be more suitable for certain types of problem-solving, while the positional influence style may be most effective for various persuasion techniques and commands. But, above all, the effective communicator must be flexible. He must be comfortable and proficient in using both influence styles, selecting the one appropriate for a given situation and a particular client.

## The Effective Message

*Who* says something is important, but *what* is said is also important since no communication can be more effective than its message. An ineffective message is likely to be misunderstood or ignored by the intended receiver. The effective message is characterized by five traits: (1) congruence; (2) intelligibility; (3) comprehensibility; (4) multichannel repetition; and (5) compatible punctuation. The more pronounced these traits, the more effective will be the social worker's communications.

1. Messages are *congruent* when the verbal message agrees with or is compatible with the nonverbal messages that accompany it. We noted earlier that a verbal message will be received only if it is reinforced by accompanying nonverbal messages. Most people can accurately judge whether or not verbal and nonverbal messages are compatible. In most social situations, for example, there is little doubt about the meaning of "come and visit me any time" when it is accompanied by a distinct look of disinterest. And when social workers *say* that they want to help but *do* nothing, most clients understand that they are not really interested in helping them. Merely saying something is not sufficient to get a message across if the accompanying actions and gestures do not reinforce the verbal message. When the verbal and nonverbal messages are in conflict, the nonverbal message is the one which receives priority attention. As noted earlier, people are more likely to accept emotions and gestures as true since they believe that these are more authentic than the spoken word.

2. The *intelligible* message is one which is simple and specific. The receiver will not be able to accept a message unless he can understand it. Many social workers are frustrated because they seem to be unable to communicate with their clients. One worker, assigned to a group of released prisoners, reported that even though he and they were using the same English words they seemed to be talking two different languages, and he could not understand them. Basil Bernstein

(1971) noted that many of those who grow up under conditions of early deprivation and extreme poverty develop only a limited verbal capacity and tend to avoid abstract concepts. On the other hand, college graduates, including social workers, are highly verbal and skillfully use complex abstractions. Under these circumstances it may not be realistic to expect lower-class clients to understand the social worker's ordinary language. Instead workers must try to send simple and specific messages.

3. The effective message must be *comprehensible;* that is, it must be compatible with the receiver's life style so that he can know what the sender meant. People who believe that everything in life is preordained or that they are completely powerless will not understand and will not accept messages which suggest that they do something about their situation. The social worker failed to convince Josef GUSTAMENTA about the importance of his daughter's education because the message was not comprehensible. Mr. Gustamenta came from a different background and used a frame of reference quite different from that employed by the social worker. Effective communication became possible only after the social worker discovered ways to make his message more comprehensible to Mr. Gustamenta.

Messages which do not violate or contradict the receiver's beliefs are more likely to be received than those which do. If a client has very strong feelings about something he will be less likely to accept a message about this subject than about another matter about which he has not yet made up his mind. For example, a woman who has definite ideas against abortions will usually be unwilling to accept a message suggesting this possibility. But if she has no strong feelings about abortions or has never thought about the subject, there is a greater likelihood of her listening. We are not suggesting that the social worker say only those things which a client likes to hear. Often he must send messages which he knows the client would rather not receive. The point is how best to communicate such messages so that they can be as effective as possible. Those messages which are compatible with the receiver's life style and which do not clash with his belief system are more likely to be effective. A social worker would do well to communicate unpleasant or touchy subjects in a way which recognizes this principle. A client may have strong feelings about using contraceptives, but she may have equally strong feelings about giving all her children a good start in life. While birth control may be an unacceptable topic for this client, family planning and spacing may be a compatible and comprehensible area for discussion.

4. Advertisers have long known that the effectiveness of a message can be increased if it can be given repeated exposure in different media. Seeing the merits of a new detergent on television, reading about it in the newspaper, and hearing about it from a neighbor will be more convincing than receiving this message from one source only. Students of communications theory, and particularly those concerned with attitude changes, have come to similar conclusions. Though the pioneer research of Kurt Lewin (1943) dealt only with the greater effectiveness of group discussions in changing traditional food habits, later researchers identified the utility of *multichannel* messages. Herbert Menzel and Elihu Katz (1955) studied the adoption of new medical products by physicians. They found that advertisements in medical journals and visits by drug company salesmen brought information about new products to a doctor's attention but that the decision to prescribe a new drug occurred only after the doctor talked with his medical colleagues who were already prescribing the new drug. Later Katz (1957) formalized this process as the "two-step flow of communication" theory. He postulated that the sender of the message activates social pressure and social support for its acceptance by using various channels, especially mass media and interpersonal relations.

Social workers can learn much from Katz's two-step flow theory. If they utilize only single-channel messages and forego the support and pressure coming from mass media and other people significant in the client's social network, their message will probably receive only minimal attention. On the other hand, they can activate social pressure and receive social reinforcement in support of their messages if these are echoed by the media, if they reflect the normative stance of the client's environment, and if they are supported by the client's family and friends. If perchance a popular television star comes out with a similar statement, the effectiveness of a worker's communication will be even greater. While a social worker cannot be expected to arrange for radio and television support, effective social intervention does require work with significant others in the client's social system. When working with a group of delinquent teen-agers, the social worker cannot limit his attention only to these boys; work with their families, their employers or teachers, the policeman in the neighborhood, storekeepers, and others, may be as important if not more important. One of the reasons for the importance of working with these people (who are not clients) is the greater effectiveness of multichannel communications.

Multichannel communications make for more effective communications, but redundancy must be avoided. Repetition of a message may be desirable at times, perhaps even necessary, because the receiver may have failed to hear the message at first (due to selective attention or excessive noise). Redundancy occurs when the repetition becomes pointless and counterproductive. An ineffective message will not become more effective merely because it is repeated many times. If a message has proved ineffective, the sender should rephrase it before sending it again rather than merely repeat it.

5. The effectiveness of a message can be reduced, even voided, by incompatible *punctuation*. Punctuation is generally thought of only in connection with written communications, but it is also a characteristic of other forms of communication. Punctuation gives specific meaning to messages that otherwise would be ambiguous and equivocal. Thus, different punctua-

tions give opposite meanings to the words *don't jump*. Depending on the punctuation, a message with these two words can mean "Don't jump!" or the very opposite, "Don't [wait]! Jump [now]!" When considering the total communication exchange rather than only a single phrase, we face an almost endless series of interchanges between two or more people, where each is both sender and receiver of messages. It is the punctuation which gives meaning to this exchange of communication. By altering the punctuation, the meaning and significance of the messages are changed. And when sender and receiver use different systems of punctuation, communication problems arise. Let us say that a couple has a marital problem to which the husband contributes symptoms of passive withdrawal and his wife, nagging criticism of her husband. He claims that his withdrawal is a defense against her nagging, while she claims that her active behavior is the result of his passivity. She says, "I nag because you withdraw," while he counters, "I withdraw because you nag." The facts are the same, but the punctuation differs. The crucial question here is not who is right but how can the social worker help both to alter their punctuation so that they can begin to understand each other once again (Watzlawick, Beavin, and Jackson, 1967). The social worker himself will increase the effectiveness of his messages if he pays attention to the client's punctuation. Is the client responding to something the worker has said or done? Or is this something new which the client is presenting because of some other reason? Is the group's inattentiveness a response to something the worker has said? Or has something happened outside the group-worker interaction?

## Reduction of Noise

Reduction of noise is perhaps the most important way to increase the effectiveness of communications. The sender of messages has little control over some types of noise, but he can control or reduce others. A receiver's deafness is a fact which the sender cannot change, at least for the immediate present. This is an *organic noise* which cannot be corrected during the present interaction. But a social worker can reduce some types of organic noise. For example, distinct diction instead of a hesitating and faltering manner of speech will make for easier reception of messages. This is a communication skill which the social worker can acquire through practice.

*Psychological noise* can be reduced or controlled if it is recognized as such. A client who does not know with what to pay tomorrow's rent may be unable to engage in a discussion about his son's problems at school. Communication effectiveness will be enhanced by starting with the problem which the client feels is most pressing and only later talking about the problems which the social worker believes must be faced. When the social worker who has been meeting once a week with a group of pre-adolescent boys tried to resume a discussion about homosexuality, started a week earlier, he noticed that the boys seemed completely uninterested. He assumed (correctly) that noise was interfering with effective communication. Some probing revealed that just an hour earlier, report cards had been distributed, and many of the boys were concerned with how to approach their parents with a poor report card. This worker did not try to stick to his plan, even though the agenda had been worked out earlier with the group members. Instead, he refocused the discussion on the problem of parents and report cards, holding the original discussion for a later meeting. A different kind of psychological noise blocked effective communication between the social worker and MRS. HILL. In this case the problem was the worker who because of the lateness of the hour was more concerned about getting home than about listening to what Mrs. Hill had in mind.

*Mechanical noise* often makes normal communications difficult. A quiet private office may be an ideal which every social worker dreams about but not all achieve. But quietness is a relative concept. Some of the most meaningful conversations with clients have occurred in noisy cafeterias, on busy street corners, in speeding automobiles, and in the bleachers of a ball park. Though it is not possible to overcome every noise, it is desirable to reduce mechanical noise whenever possible. A few drops of oil will quiet a noisy fan or a squeaky door. Shutting the window or closing the door will reduce outside noise. Turning down a loud radio or television will reduce the decibel level. These are a few simple steps which a social worker can take to increase opportunities for more effective communications.

A club room is rarely a quiet place, especially if the group is composed of adolescents. Youngsters are often noisy, and the last thing a social worker would want to do is to quiet their natural, though noisy enthusiasm—as long as such noise is appropriate. Under these circumstances the social worker bears a special responsibility to ensure that messages to and from the worker, as well as messages between group members, are received with a minimum of distortion. The worker may have to raise his voice so that he can be heard, he may ask another to speak louder or ask him to repeat what he has said—all this as a way to compensate for the *natural noise*. But at times the situation demands a degree of quiet to permit more effective communication. Now it would be a mistake to try to outshout the noise; instead, the worker will use his normal voice but repeat his message until he is sure that everyone has heard it.

## The Purposes of Communication

In the preceeding sections we explored communication skills in general terms. We considered the generic characteristics which identify the effective social work communicator and the effective message. In this section we will focus on different types of communication used by social workers and note some of the distinctive functions and characteristics associated with each type. Unless a worker is consciously aware of the different purposes for which he uses communication in the social intervention process, he may utilize inappropriate techniques. Developing a greater awareness of the different types of communication purposes may also help social workers gain a better understanding of what they are doing. One study found that even experienced caseworkers were not using as many advanced therapeutic techniques as they thought they were but were largely engaged in securing information about their clients' problems and then feeding these data back to them (Reid and Shyne, 1969). If workers had a more accurate perception of what they actually do, they would presumably be more ready to sharpen their intervention skills.

Seven purposes of social intervention communications will be discussed here briefly: (1) exploration; (2) structuring; (3) clarification; (4) encouragement; (5) information; (6) advice; and (7) commands.

This classification is according to the purposes imputed to the message by the social worker, no matter whether this purpose is successfully achieved and regardless whether the receiver of the message understands the purpose. The purpose may not always be conscious, though it is hoped that social workers who use themselves purposefully will be conscious of their objectives and of the purposes of their communications.

Two general comments must be made before examining in further depth this typology of communication purposes. First, a message may and often does have more than one purpose. A command, for example, almost always includes (at least implicitly) a structuring message which defines the relationship of the one who issues the order to the one who is to receive it. The social worker may say, "You sign here *because I, the expert, tell you to do so.*" The italicized phase usually is not verbalized because it is self-understood, but whenever there is a doubt about the relationship, it will be stated explicitly. Similarly, an advice message may also contain words of encouragement. The social worker may say, "It would be a good idea if you signed up for the training program because I know that you will become a first-rate carpenter."

The second general comment is that the specific communication technique not only is determined by the type of communication, but depends also on the characteristics of the receiver, on the nature of the problem, and on the relationship between the sender and the receiver. In fact, several different techniques may be suitable for delivering a given type of communication, depending on the factors just cited. When, for example, the situation calls for a clarification communication, the social worker must consider the effectiveness of various approaches, including logical discussion, confrontation, supplying additional data, or some other technique. The decision concerning which approach to utilize will depend on the purpose of the communication, the readiness of the receiver, the nature of the problem, and the phase of the intervention process.

1. *Exploration.* The purpose of exploration is to investigate the problem and to discover potential goals and strategies. Exploration communications will be used both with individuals and with groups. A client may know that something bothers him or that something is amiss but may not know exactly what the problem is, or he may not be able to communicate accurate information about it. Usually, the client is the principal informant in exploration, but there are times when others can provide more information. Exploration usually is a high-priority activity in the beginning phase, but it will continue on a reduced scale in the middle and ending phases of the social intervention process. The purpose of exploration is to secure information which the social worker does not have but which he needs before he can participate fully in developing a relevant social intervention strategy. The goal is only to secure the information and no more (see also chapter 10).

2. *Structuring.* When the purpose is to clarify the respective roles of client and worker and their mutual relationship during the social intervention activity, we speak of structuring communications. The more spontaneous and natural a rela-

tionship between two people, the less the need for structuring messages. But the social intervention relationship is far from natural or spontaneous and therefore, requires a relatively large amount of structuring communications. Social workers err if they think that every client is familiar with his own role as a client or with the worker's role. Research findings from many different studies underscore the ambiguity of the client-worker relationship and the need of most clients for direction as to what is expected of them. But structuring is used not only with clients. It is also useful when communicating with others. Structuring may be the primary or auxiliary purpose of a given message. For example, when a social worker attempts to obtain information (*exploration*) from a probation officer, he first must identify himself and describe his interest in the particular person, about whom he wants information (*structuring*). Or when a social worker gives testimony before a Congressional subcommittee which is investigating the public housing program (*information*), he must first present his credentials and establish his expertise (*structuring*). Structuring is especially important in the beginning phase, but the dynamic nature of the relationship between client and worker suggests that structuring communications will also be useful in later phases (see also chapter 10).

3. *Clarification.* These communications are designed to help a client (or other person) better understand himself, his problem, and/or his environment. The efficacy of clarification is based on the assumption that a person who understands can participate better and more adequately in problem solution than one who does not understand. Feedback of information secured from the client and from other sources is one technique which is often effective in clarification, though there is much more to clarification than merely echoing data. Another technique suitable for clarification is for the worker to interpret to the client what he (the worker) perceives. However, the worker must remember that merely listening to what a worker thinks will rarely help people understand themselves

better. Understanding involves activity, at least intellectual and emotional activity, and involvement. Effective clarification communications must lead to activity on the part of the receiver. Helping a person who has been avoiding reality face what others think about him or his problem may be an effective technique in some cases, but confrontations of this kind must be utilized with caution and only when the worker is certain that the recipient can cope with this type of information.

This technique also can be effective with groups. Some unemployed ex-convicts were very despondent because they had been unable to find jobs despite weeks of looking for employment. They felt that employers discriminated against persons with criminal records. The social worker who met with them did not deny that there was some truth to their conclusion, but at the same time he wanted them to understand that nowadays everybody without skills has difficulties in finding jobs. In this example, clarification involved more than supplying statistics about unemployment. By directing the group's attention to what they knew already but had conveniently forgotten, by helping members share information with each other, by helping to make connections between various known data, and by supplying additional information when needed, the worker helped this group move from its initial, only partially correct problem definition to a more realistic perception of the problem so that, in turn, a realistic action strategy could be developed. During this phase of the communication process the worker's purpose was clarification. Whereas exploration plays a primary role during the beginning phase, clarification is more common during the middle phase.

In therapeutic intervention clarification is utilized to help people gain insight into their own behavior. But clarification can also serve other purposes. Often the objective is more immediate and limited to helping a person better understand the real problems which he faces. MRS. CAREY, for example, consistently refused to acknowledge the many problems of her family, other than Ben's stealing. The worker's clarification communications focused on helping Mrs. Carey accept the reality of these problems rather than on having her understand why she had evaded them in the past (see also chapter 9).

4. *Encouragement.* This type of communication is designed to support a client's present behavior. Whenever a worker attempts to reinforce a person's coping and problem-solving skills, he is encouraging him. This type of communication is not intended to increase the person's understanding but instead tries to support what he is already doing or is about to do. A smile, a nod of the head, saying "good," are some of the ways used to encourage. Longer messages, such as, "I knew all the time that you could do it" or "That was a good beginning; now try doing it again at home" or "You have been successful before; I just know that you can do it again" are also ways in which social workers encourage. Encouragement communications are based on the belief that people will repeat doing those things that result in favorable responses and positive reinforcements. For the most part, social workers have not shown great interest in using encouragement as a social intervention technique because they do not quite understand how support of present behavior can lead to goal achievement. Yet there are social workers such as Robert Brown (1973) who have argued that "providing supportive information, such as bringing out the client's strengths, is surely a viable facet of producing change." Social workers who use behavior modification techniques know about the usefulness of encouragement in producing change (Arkava, 1974). Encouragement should be equally as effective when used by social workers who follow other intervention models.

KEVIN MINTON has had a very difficult time since his release from the state penitentiary. Unable to find a job, he sat around at home, unhappy and morose, while his wife worked to support the family. One day he told his social worker that he had begun to work as a janitor in the neighborhood bowling alley. Even though this job paid little, it meant that Kevin had made a beginning step in rehabilitating himself. The worker greeted his statement with, "That's great. I am especially proud that you found this job yourself. I know this is only a beginning, but the beginning is probably the hardest part!" Kevin looked relieved at the worker's encouragement and smiled broadly. Weeks later he told the worker that after the first day in the bowling alley he wasn't sure whether to continue but that the worker's encouragement helped him decide to keep working until a better job came along.

However, encouragement is not a panacea which will produce successful results in every situation. Its use must be limited to occasions when the worker can and should encourage the continuation of current behavior. While every person has some desirable characteristics which can be encouraged, encouragement is not always functional for problem-solving. For example, encouragement would be counterindicated when it could result in complacency instead of activity. Or encouragement may not be relevant because a person or a system other than the client may need to change. It would probably be inappropriate for the social worker to encourage MRS. LEFFERT to continue the great job she has been doing in taking care of all of her family single-handed. This situation needs a radical change, not encouragement, if Mrs. Leffert is to avoid a nervous and physical breakdown. Similarly, a social worker must not encourage a child to put up just a little longer with his psychotic parents who have repeatedly injured him in the past. Nor must a social worker encourage a person to keep on trying to achieve an objective which he knows cannot be achieved by this person.

5. *Information.* One of the characteristics of living in today's complex world is that people often lack the information they need to make decisions or to cope with problems. Communications intended to offer relevant information are classified as information. MRS. KING needed various types of information: information about child-care facilities, information about her husband's condition, and information about a job

for herself. MRS. EVANS asked her worker where she could get birth-control information. And some of the tenants of the KENNEDY HOUSES wanted to know what they could do about their terrible housing conditions. Often a request for information also contains a request for other types of help. The social worker must do more than merely give Mrs. Evans the address of the nearest family-planning clinic—but first he must provide the requested information.

Most information messages are in response to specific or nonspecific requests for information, but at times a worker will provide information without being asked for it. Thus, the social worker told the HERMANS about the upcoming meeting of parents interested in making plans for their retarded children. And MR. RIOS's daughter was given information about nursing homes which might be able to provide a solution to his problem. A social worker spends much of his time providing information, so much so that he may overlook the fact that there are limits to this type of communication. Information is most appropriate and useful when there is general agreement on the nature of the problem, the goals, and the immediate strategy. While agreement in every last detail is not necessary, lack of general agreement will make it likely that the information will be rejected. Information communications may be dysfunctional and interfere with the attainment of the social intervention goal if the client is not able to handle the information or if the information negatively reinforces his self-image. Telling MRS. EVANS that she can obtain birth-control pills at a clinic which can be reached only by private car or taxi will not really be helpful. Here the worker must provide the information and assist the person to utilize the information. Informing an unemployed person about a job for which he obviously is not prepared will not be helpful, especially if that person already suffers from an inferiority complex. Information which fits the receiver and the problem is appropriate in every phase of the social intervention process.

6. *Advice.* Suggestions or advice are used in com-

munications which are intended to influence the decisions of others in specific directions. Many social workers do not favor the use of advice since they believe that it encourages dependency. They also feel that advice is of dubious value since people follow it only when they like it. Research findings indicate, however, that many clients, and especially those coming from the lower classes favor advice communications and would like to receive more (Mayer and Timms, 1970; Reid and Shapiro, 1969). Advice may be of value even when clients do not follow it since it often provides normative direction which may have an indirect influence. OBADIAH WILSON was not yet ready to accept the social worker's advice about enrolling in adult classes, but at least he heard that society expected adults to know how to read and write. Perhaps later on he will be ready to act on this advice. Advice is most appropriate when there is a degree of consensus over goals but no agreement (or even disagreement) over strategy. Advice on technical matters or on non-controversial questions is generally more acceptable than other kinds of advice (see also discussion on AID, chapter 9).

7. *Commands.* These are communications designed to transmit certain decisions which others are expected to carry out. Commands or orders may utilize threats of force, subtle pressures, or status differences. To be effective, the command must be accepted by the other person as a command. If the other person ignores the command or laughs at it, the communication is ineffective and it would have been better had it not been made. Social workers generally try to avoid command communications since they are contrary to the spirit of social work, which emphasizes democratic values, client participation, and self-determination. Yet there are occasions when every social worker will use commands. KEVIN MINTON was told that he must report to his probation officer every Monday morning. Mark Ortego, the community worker assigned to the KENNEDY HOUSES TENANTS COUNCIL, was notified by his agency director that he must not organize the protest rally against city hall. In some settings, especially institutional settings, the use

of command communications will be more frequent than in others. But no matter where he works, commands must never become the social worker's usual mode of communication because their use signals that the social intervention process is still a very long way from successful completion.

## Facilitating Communication

Usually communications are viewed as a tool for problem-solving. The problem is identified by one or more verbal messages. Through discussion, the goals and strategies are developed. Language is used to present information and advice. But sometimes faulty communication is itself the problem. Or lack of sufficient communication skill can make a problem situation even more complex. In these situations, the goal (or one of the goals) of a social worker's intervention will be to facilitate communication. Worker activity which facilitates communication can include stepping up weak signals, stepping down strong signals, redirecting messages, and asking for elaborations. These activities may occur during an office interview or a home visit, in a group meeting room or on the street corner, or in connection with any other type of interpersonal engagement (Shulman, 1968).

A weak signal is a message, a tone of voice, or even a facial expression whose meaning is not clear to those for whom it is meant. It needs to be stepped up before others can understand it. The person who employs weak signals may have something important to say but he needs help in expressing himself. One worker noticed during a home visit that the father had a funny smile on his face whenever his oldest daughter was talking. Picking up on this facial gesture (which was not noticed by other family members), the worker asked the father why he was smiling. The purpose of this question was not to gather information but to assist the father in expressing himself better so that others could know what was on his mind.

Strong signals, such as shouting, an angry tone of voice, sarcasm, and certain facial expressions, can distort the message they accompany. Often a message is misunderstood because of the tone of voice in which it is delivered. Instead of responding to the communication, the recipient responds to the signals which accompany the message. For example, Willie, a fourteen-year-old boy, had been crying since he arrived in the detention home two days ago. Eric and Ron, fellow residents, finally barked at him and told him to stop whining or they would beat him up. Willie winced and cried even harder because now he was afraid of receiving a beating, in addition to being homesick. At this point the social worker intervened to help Willie understand the message. He told him that the other boys were upset by his constant crying and wanted him to stop. Without the strong signals Willie was able to understand the message and was able to comply.

At times a worker is asked to serve as a middleman. A person will try to talk to the worker when he really should be talking directly to the other person. One social worker, assigned to a group of teen-age girls, was told by Kitty that she had heard rumors about Dianne's planning to run away with her boyfriend. The worker wondered why Kitty did not ask Dianne directly if this was so. In this kind of situation the worker would not have been helpful if he had served as a middleman. Instead, he should point out that messages can be communicated directly with greater efficiency and greater effectiveness.

One common way in which a worker can facilitate communication is by asking for elaborations. Sometimes a client is not quite sure whether it is appropriate to discuss a certain problem with the worker. The client might drop a hint or make a brief reference to the problem to test the worker's reaction and response. Asking for additional information will encourage further communication. Alyce Lewis, for example, began to cry in the middle of the intake interview and, between tears, told the worker that lately everything seemed to be going wrong for her. The worker, sensing that she needed some encouragement to communicate, asked her if she could tell him what had been happening to her.

The social worker has a responsibility to help clients and others with whom he comes in contact to communicate more effectively. The ways just described are some of the techniques which can help. The particular tactics used will depend on the specific problem and on the persons involved. At times the worker may use a feedback mechanism to check whether everybody really understood a message which was somewhat ambiguous. He may need to point out to a communicator that his message was not understood, or was misunderstood, by others. The social worker may make comments or ask questions in order to invite further responses by the original communicator or by others. He may request further amplification. He may notice points of disagreement and help bring these into the open so that they may be explored by the participants. He may restate an idea in order to verify his own understanding. Above all, the social worker must always serve as a model and an example of the clear, direct, and honest communicator.

## Summary

Communication occurs whenever two or more people interact. Because the purpose of communication is to inform or influence others, it is a key skill in the social intervention process.

Human communication includes both verbal and nonverbal signals. No verbal message is possible without a simultaneous nonverbal message. Whenever there appears to be a contradiction between the two, more attention is paid to the nonverbal message. Nonverbal meanings, like verbal ones, are learned. Therefore, people who come from different cultural backgrounds may attach different meanings to the same signal.

Silence does not signify the absence of communication

since nonverbal signals continue during periods of silence. Some social workers attempt to use silence in order to encourage clients to talk, but this is not always an effective technique since the meaning of silence can be quite ambiguous. And many clients misinterpret a worker's silence as a sign that he is not interested in them.

An effective communication is one which the recipient interprets in the way the sender wanted him to understand it. Such a communication requires an able communicator, an absence of interfering noise, an understandable message, and a willing recipient. The social worker who wants to be an effective communicator must be an honest and warm person and an attentive listener. Initial credibility, that is, the impression the client has about the social worker before the first contact, is crucial for effective communication. But unless a positive initial credibility is maintained during the subsequent worker-client contacts, the effectiveness of the communication process will suffer.

The communication style used by the social worker must be suitable to meet the demands of the particular situation. Whether to use the "personal influence" style or the "positional influence" style will depend on the nature and purpose of the message and on the background and other characteristics of the recipient. But whatever style is used, the message must be congruent, intelligible, comprehensible, and compatible. A message which is sent over more than one channel will be more effective than a single-channel message.

# Part Three
# Exemplars and Vignettes

# Introduction

Social intervention practice cannot be learned from a textbook alone. Field learning must accompany classroom learning. Field learning gives the student an opportunity to test what he has learned in the classroom, to see if the theory he has learned can actually be applied, and to find out what knowledge or theory elements the book or his instructors have overlooked or not yet taught. It is in the field that the student will find the best and the most relevant illustrations for the principles which he hears about in the classroom. And the field is the place where the student learns to perfect his practice skills.

However, a student's practice opportunities are limited, especially in the first year of his social work studies. In the very beginning he may only assist another social worker or take over a case previously carried by his field instructor; he may not have an opportunity to become involved in initial assessment or in some of the other activities connected with the first intervention phase at the very time when he studies these in class. Or his assignment may be with a teen-age group in a settlement house, and it might be a while before he comes in contact with a family. Learning in the field never occurs in exactly the same sequence as the process unfolds in the textbook. For these reasons some social work practice teachers prefer to use "case records."

At one time, model case records were very popular. Intended to be examples of excellent practice, many became quickly outdated, and few were able to convey the dynamics and excitement of real practice. It is almost impossible to convey within a few (or even many) pages the flavor of an actual social work relationship. Nor were these model records generally taken from the type of practice situations in which beginning social work students were involved. The beginner faces "simple," almost mundane bread-and-butter problems, while model records tend to deal with difficult, complex problem situations which often demand a very sophisticated level of practice. Many a student became discouraged by the gap between his own practice and the advanced level of practice portrayed in some of these case records.

No claim is made that the exemplars and vignettes presented here are examples of excellent practice. Instead, we have tried to select samples from actual situations in which students and beginning social workers were involved. Several of the exemplars include some of the social intervention activities undertaken by the social worker. The way the social worker handled the situation is not always the best way. Analysis by teachers and students will suggest other, perhaps more effective ways. Practice episodes for some of the exemplars are found throughout the text to illustrate specific principles (see Index of Exemplars and Vignettes). In the shorter vignettes we have presented only the problem so that the student may have an opportunity to sharpen some of his practice skills. It is hoped that these exemplars and vignettes will be supplemented and before long replaced by examples from the students' own learning experiences in the field.

# chapter thirteen

# Exemplars and Vignettes

## Cynthia Bennet

Mrs. Bennet, a mother of three young children, recently was deserted by her husband and left penniless. When she applied for welfare assistance she told the intake worker that she thought it best for her children if she stayed at home and remained a full-time mother. Her worker, on the other hand, recommended a job-training program which would prepare her for a position as a nurse's aid. In this way she would be able to earn a good living within a short time. While Mrs. Bennet was enrolled in the training program she would receive enough money to get by.

The worker also told Mrs. Bennet that he was ready to make arrangements for the day care of her children while she attended the training program. Seeing that the worker really thought it would be a good idea for her to get a job, Mrs. Bennet agreed reluctantly to enroll in the job-training program. The worker made all the necessary arrangements. All Mrs. Bennet had to do was to show up for the first class.

Subsequently, the social worker learned that Mrs. Bennet dropped out of the job-training program at the end of the first week, claiming that her children were not properly taken care of while she was at school.

## Carey Family

A woman identifying herself as Mrs. Carey from Rosewood Heights, a middle-class suburban community, called the New City Family Service to ask if she could obtain help for her eight-year-old son who was having some difficulties at home. She was given an appointment with a social worker for Thursday morning, two days hence.

Elaine Carey, a well-dressed woman in her early thirties, came to the office half an hour early. The receptionist informed the social worker that Mrs. Carey appeared quite nervous while waiting, leafing through many magazines apparently without reading any. The social worker met Mrs. Carey in the waiting area and walked with her back to his office. After Mrs. Carey sat down, he asked her to tell him about the problem which brought her to the agency. This is what she told him:

Ben, her eight-year-old son, had a normal childhood and seemed to be a happy boy who got along well with everybody. He was now a third-grader in the county elementary school; his grades were just below average, but his teachers had no real complaints about him. He had many friends and several hobbies. He was an average, all-around boy and until recently he had been no problem at home. But during the past four or five months Mrs. Carey had noticed that Ben always seemed to have much more money on him than he received for his allowance. At the same time she began to miss small amounts of money from her purse. But she did not connect these two occurrences. When asked to explain how it happened that he had so much money, Ben gave a variety of answers: he had saved money from his allowance; he had found money on the street; he had won it pitching pennies. Even after his father beat him, he did not change his story. Three days ago Mrs. Carey missed a fifty-dollar bill from her pocketbook. Later that night she went through Ben's pants pockets and found the bill there. She was so upset by this discovery that she had not told her husband or spoken to anyone else about it. In desperation she had called the Family Service. What do we suggest she do?

The social worker explained that he understood how upsetting an experience this must be for Mrs. Carey. And he noted that this is the kind of a problem in which the Family Service can be of assistance. He was ready to help her work through this problem but first Mrs. Carey would have to help him become acquainted with Ben and the other members of the Carey family. Before the end of the first interview, Mrs. Carey told the worker about her other children, Charles (age fifteen) and Cheryl (age thirteen), and about her husband, who was the manager of an insurance agency in town. The worker arranged for an appointment with Ben on Saturday and with Mr. Carey for the following Tuesday afternoon.

In his initial assessment the worker noted that there may be a

link between Ben's stealing and problems in the parent-child relations. The worker made this tentative interpretation on the basis of
the information which Mrs. Carey had shared with him (but which
was not reported in the above summary of the first meeting). Further information secured in the following weeks from Mr. and Mrs.
Carey and Ben seemed to support the initial interpretation. After
appropriate involvement of the Carey family in goal-setting, an intervention strategy was developed which called for rebuilding the
relationships between Ben and his parents.

During the following months the worker met weekly with Ben
and in separate sessions with either his father or his mother. Attempts to arrange for joint meetings with all family members proved
unsuccessful. During these weekly meetings the worker gathered additional information which proved to be significant in the further
evolution of the intervention strategy. He learned that Cheryl, Ben's
thirteen-year-old sister, was six months pregnant; that Charles, his
older brother, had a long history of encounters with the police and
with the juvenile court; and that in Ben's peer group stealing was
viewed as a test of skill, with honors accorded to the fellow who stole
the most. The worker also learned that the relationship between
Elaine Carey and her husband had been a very poor one for many
years; that they had been on the point of divorce or separation many
times. It began to appear that the children's problems were all that
held this family together. With this additional information, obtained
at various times from different members of the family, as well as
other data obtained from supplementary sources suggested by Mrs.
Carey, the social worker gained a new understanding of Ben's problem and of the problems of the Carey family. The worker now realized that there was need to revise the initial assessment, as well as
the original goals and social intervention strategy.

## Georgia Evans

Georgia Evans is the mother of two children, fourteen months and
three months old. Her husband, an unskilled laborer, has been unemployed for the past year. The welfare worker, who tries to visit
the Evanses every other month, was impressed by the cleanliness of
the small apartment and by the way Mrs. Evans was raising her
children.

At the last visit, Mrs. Evans asked her worker to help her not
have any more children.

## Carla Gustamenta

Carla Gustamenta, the fourteen-year-old daughter of a farm worker, has had a history of irregular school attendance. During the past year she did not attend school at all. Carla's social worker thought that it was important for Carla to go back to school, at least long enough to learn to read and write properly. Carla agreed that reading and writing were important. She did not want to be like her mother, who couldn't even sign her name. She told the worker that she was ready to go back to school if her father agreed. But it soon appeared that her father really did not want Carla to go to school, and Carla was not willing to act against her father's wishes.

In a discussion between Mr. Gustamenta and the social worker it became clear that Carla's father believed that a girl's place was at home, in the kitchen. School, he said, was dangerous nonsense. He got along without it, his wife did not need it, and why should Carla be exposed to all those temptations that are part of the modern school? When the social worker attempted to tell him how important it was for Carla to know how to read and write, Mr. Gustamenta simply got up and left the room, muttering, "No woman is going to tell me what to do with my daughter."

Even after meeting with Mr. Gustamenta, the social worker thought that it would be best if Carla returned to school. But obviously a different strategy was needed to achieve this goal. Since her father was unable to see the importance of continued school attendance and was unwilling to accept the social worker's definition of the problem, it was desirable to locate someone to whom he would listen.

The social worker knew that Mr. Gustamenta was a regular churchgoer and that he thought highly of his minister. The worker, therefore, arranged a meeting with this minister to discuss with him Carla's problem and her father's refusal to send her back to school. The minister did not need to be convinced that education was important, but he confirmed that irregular school attendance was a fairly common problem in this part of the county. He promised to devote his next sermon to the importance of giving children a proper education. The social worker was pretty sure that Mr. Gustamenta would pay attention to what his minister had to say. But he wanted to make sure that Mr. Gustamenta understood the message; therefore, she did not rely solely on this one approach.

The social worker knew that Mr. Gustamenta was very eager to obtain a better-paying job. Some weeks earlier she had arranged for him to see an employment counselor at the State Employment Service. In checking back with the counselor she found out that a second appointment had been scheduled for the following week. The counselor was not very optimistic about finding a better job since Mr. Gustamenta did not read or write. The social worker discussed Carla's problem with the counselor and observed that Mr. Gustamenta probably did not realize the importance of a good education. She asked whether the counselor would help in conveying this message. The latter thought he could by showing Mr. Gustamenta a number of good jobs which were available but for which he could not qualify because he lacked minimal reading and writing skills.

The messages communicated by the minister and by the employment counselor evidently hit the mark. Two weeks later, on the social worker's next visit to the Gustamenta home, Carla ran out and excitedly told her, "Dad registered me in school yesterday!"

## Tootsie Herman

Tootsie is the three-year-old daughter of Ruth and Phil Herman. Mr. Herman is an elementary school teacher. Prior to the birth of her oldest child, Mrs. Herman worked as a secretary in a large company. The Hermans have two other children in addition to Tootsie: George is five years old and Cathy, thirteen months. Mrs. Herman is again pregnant and expects to deliver in about three months.

Mrs. Herman came to the Community Family Service to request help in placing Tootsie in an institution. She explained that Tootsie was severely retarded and that they could no longer keep her at home. She and her husband had been aware for some time that Tootsie was not developing like other children. Their fear that their daughter was retarded was recently confirmed by their family doctor. She and her husband had considered Tootsie's problem from all angles. They wanted her to have the best training possible so that she could enjoy as much of life as possible for her. At the same time, they wanted to raise their other children without the handicap of having a retarded child at home. They felt that a placement in a good institution would be the best answer to the problem.

The worker, who had dealt with several similar cases in the last half year, had to advise Mrs. Herman that there was no such institution in their community or in their state. But he did tell her that a group of parents had scheduled a meeting at the agency for next week to discuss what could be done for their retarded children. He invited Mr. and Mrs. Herman to come to this meeting.

## Laura Hill

Mrs. Hill was scheduled to enter the hospital for a lengthy period. Prior to her hospitalization her doctor referred her to the hospital social service department to make arrangements for her family while she was in the hospital. The social worker noted that there were two children (age seven and five) in the family and that Mr. Hill, a taxi driver, did not come home from work until late in the afternoon.

Mrs. Hill and the worker discussed at length various things the seven-year-old could do after school until his father came home. The plan developed called for the intensive use of the nearby community center plus the hiring of a high school girl for a few hours each afternoon.

The hour was already late when the discussion turned to the five-year-old boy. Mrs. Hill and the worker agreed that some arrangement outside the home would have to be made for him. To speed things up, the social worker recommended a temporary foster home. Even though Mrs. Hill had planned to ask her sister to take in her boy, she kept quiet and agreed with the worker's suggestion for a foster home, feeling that the worker must know best what to do.

## Charles Johansen

Charles Johansen was brought to the attention of the school social worker because he frequently fell asleep in class, seldom completed his homework, and generally did not get along with the other boys in the second grade. In talking with Mrs. Johansen the social worker learned that she, her husband, and their four children lived in a one-room cold-water flat. On a home visit the social worker discovered that Mrs. Johansen was a poor homemaker, that there was only one bed for the entire family, and that the television seemed to be going constantly.

## Kennedy Houses Tenants Council

Mark Ortego, a community worker employed by the local antipoverty agency, helped organize the Kennedy Houses Tenants Council eight months ago. This was done at the specific direction of his agency supervisor. Initially, Mark made little progress because of a general lack of interest by the tenants, but during the past three months more than 50 percent of the 118 families who live in the project began to participate. The deteriorating situation in the proj-

ect and the modest gains which Mr. Ortego had helped the Tenants
Council achieve accounted for the increase in participation.

Four months ago a young child was killed when she fell down
an elevator shaft. The defective door of that elevator has not yet
been repaired, despite frequent complaints by the tenants. Garbage
collection had become more and more irregular in recent months;
some residents claimed that in many buildings rats already outnum-
bered tenants. Drugs were sold openly throughout the project. Ap-
peals for police protection seemed useless. It had been weeks since
the last policeman was seen in the project. Thefts and holdups were
daily occurrences which people no longer bothered to report to the
police. But the tenants were shocked when last week an elderly
widow was beaten brutally by unknown persons.

At an emergency meeting of the Tenants Council it was decided
to conduct a series of activities, spaced at one-week intervals, to call
attention to their desperate situation. The plan decided upon included the following four steps: (1) a news conference to dramatize
the plight of the tenants and to alert the community to the future actions planned by the tenants if they received no relief; (2) a protest
rally at city hall, demanding the immediate intervention of the
mayor on their behalf; (3) legal action to force the city housing authority to live up to its undertakings, and finally, if the previous
steps did not produce results; (4) a rent strike until effective measures were taken to remedy their complaints. Mark Ortego had
played an active role in this important meeting and helped the tenants formulate their demands and their strategy. Now the tenants
expected that he would help them implement this strategy.

As soon as his supervisor heard about this action plan, he called
Mr. Ortego to his office to remind him that he was a social worker,
not an agitator or political activist. The agency, he pointed out, was
dependent on the good will of the community and especially of city
hall. It could not afford, therefore, to be identified with this type of
militant action program.

A little later in the morning, Mark received a call from city hall.
The mayor was calling a meeting to discuss the problem of the Kennedy Houses and wanted Mark to attend. But when he was told to
come alone, without any representatives of the tenants, Mark refused. He indicated that he could attend only if the tenants could
also come. The meeting was canceled.

Next came a call from the police department, requesting that
the site of the rally be shifted to a neighborhood park in order to
avoid a traffic jam downtown. In the meantime, some of the tenant

leaders were exposed to similar pressures. They asked for another meeting of the Tenants Council to reconsider the wisdom of the earlier decisions.

## Betty and Jim King

Jim King, age twenty-six, married and father of three young children (age three, two, and one year) was suddenly hospitalized three weeks ago. He does not know exactly what is wrong with him, but the doctor has told him that he may not be able to work again.

Jim has worked regularly at various unskilled jobs ever since he quit school in the eighth grade; for the past three years he has worked at the vegetable counter of a neighborhood supermarket. Although he has always earned enough to support his family, he had no savings and no insurance.

Betty King, his wife, is five years younger than Jim. They eloped when Betty was in the ninth grade. For a while Betty worked as a cashier in a department store, but she quit just before her first child was born and has stayed home ever since.

Jim's hospitalization has brought about many changes in the King family. With no income of any kind, Betty had to borrow money to buy groceries and pay the rent. This was the first time she ever had to borrow money. She does not think that her relatives can let her borrow much longer; soon she will have to go to work. But how can she go to work and leave her children for whom she now is both mother and father? Even more troublesome is the uncertainty about Jim; nobody can tell her what is the matter with him or how long he will be incapacitated.

Betty is worried and does not know which way to turn. A friend told her to see a social worker at the County Welfare Department. "That's where people like you can get help," she said.

## Sophie Leffert

Sophie Leffert is the mother of three children, three, two, and one year old. Her husband was disabled by an industrial accident over a year ago. Her senile mother also lives in their four-room apartment.

Until now Mrs. Leffert has been able to handle all the demands made by her three children and by the two dependent adults. But without any outside help she has carried more than her share. Frankly, she can no longer cope with all that is required and she is about to have a nervous breakdown.

## Sally McPherson

Sally McPherson is only thirty-two, but she easily looks ten years older. She is hard of hearing and may be slightly retarded. Her poor management habits made it difficult for her and her three daughters to live on the semimonthly welfare check. For the last five or six days of each half-month the family lives virtually on bread and water. Mrs. McPherson's common-law husband, the father of her three daughters, disappeared many years ago.

The oldest daughter, Joan, is fifteen years old. Two years ago she gave birth to a blind boy. Before birth her social worker arranged for the adoption of the baby, but because he was born blind, the adoption arrangements were not completed and the baby has been in an institution ever since birth. Joan has never taken an interest in the son whom she has never seen.

Mary, age fourteen, is currently pregnant but claims that she does not know who is the father of her child since she has had relations with many men. She suffers from malnutrition, and the clinic is concerned whether she can carry to full-term. Lana, age twelve, has asthma. She was expelled from school for experimenting with drugs and for promiscuous behavior.

An eviction order has been served on Mrs. McPherson because she has not paid the rent for her one-room flat for the last three months.

## Kevin Minton

Kevin Minton, age thirty-three, came home five weeks ago after spending the last two years in the state penitentiary. His former employer was unwilling to take him back, and so far he has not been able to find a job. His wife is continuing to function as the family head and provider. His two teen-age sons are ignoring him because he cannot give them money like other fathers. Kevin is becoming increasingly morose because he appears to be a complete failure, both as a father and as a husband.

Even though there seem to be a number of underlying problems in this family, no doubt aggravated by Kevin's enforced two-year absence, the immediate problem is his continued unemployment. Since Kevin has no skills which are in demand, the worker felt that he should enroll in a job-training program. But the social worker is certain that Kevin will be back in jail long before the training program is completed unless some meaningful short-range goals can be achieved in the very near future in order to give Kevin some self-confidence. In discussions with Kevin the following crucial short-range goals were identified: resumption of employment and being once again the head-of-family.

## Julian Rios

Julian Rios, an eighty-two-year-old widower, lives in a furnished room in a run-down residential hotel, inhabited primarily by poor single pensioners like himself. He is losing his eyesight rapidly, suffered a heart attack some months ago, and has been advised to restrict his diet severely because of overweight. Since his Social Security check, his only source of income, is insufficient to meet his special needs, he has been receiving supplementary aid from the county welfare department since the beginning of this year.

His case has just been assigned to a new worker who learned from reading the case record that the previous worker visited Mr. Rios only once, six months ago.

## Alice Samora

Alice is thirty-two years old and single. She lives at home with her aged and sickly parents. Alice is paralyzed from the waist down, the result of an accident when she was four years old.

Alice is always at home. She has no friends and, aside from watching television, no interests. Her life is completely dominated by her parents. She makes no decisions without asking them what they would advise her to do. Though her parents mean well, she has become completely dependent upon them, psychologically as well as physically.

The last time Alice left her parents' apartment was five years ago when she took a bus to the river which runs through her town. There she tried to commit suicide by drowning herself.

The family have been public welfare recipients for many years since they have no resources and the father is too sick to work regularly. Until recently the social worker's focus had been on the parents and their need for economic support. A few months ago the family was assigned to a rehabilitation worker with a request to service Alice.

In the rehabilitation worker's early meetings with Alice he found her to be passive, almost lethargic. She indicated without any real convictions that things were "O.K." When asked what she would like to do instead of watching television all day long, she giggled and said "make money." The worker interpreted this as a request for employment and decided to involve Alice in some work activity. Since she was paralyzed from the waist down, he thought it best to provide her with homework, his usual strategy in these cases. The worker did not examine alternate strategies and failed to consider the possible effect of homework on Alice's other problems.

## Obadiah Wilson

There are eight people in the Wilson family. Obadiah, the father, is twenty-five years old; he is an unskilled laborer, generally out of work. He can barely sign his name or read street signs. Obadiah spends most of his days and evenings with his friends on a nearby street corner. Ella, his wife, is twenty-three; she left school in the seventh grade when she became pregnant for the first time. She has not worked since the birth of her third child five years ago. The four older children (ages eight, seven, six, and five years) attend elementary school, more or less regularly. The youngest two (ages three years and six months) are at home. Ella Wilson is again pregnant. The family has been receiving welfare assistance for the past five years.

The Wilsons live in a dilapidated two-room apartment on the edge of the city's worst slum. Their home is always dirty. Two beds, one table, and three broken chairs make up the total furniture. The kitchen is almost always filthy, with unwashed dishes all over the sink. The children generally look unkempt. During the past winter the two youngest boys were treated for rat bites.

The physical condition of the apartment reflects the mood of the Wilsons. Apathy and lack of ambition are in evidence everywhere. Dependence on the welfare check has become a way of life for them. They no longer even try to make it any other way.

## Young Adult Hiking Club

A number of young adult men found it difficult to establish and maintain satisfying relationships with young women. Most of their friends were already married or going steady, but somehow they had lost their way. They could be seen at every dance in the community center but usually were found on the sidelines or in the lobby. They would regularly "cover" all of the town's night spots but usually alone or together with other men. They rarely dated girls, some because they did not know how to ask a girl and others because they were almost always refused.

The community center social worker became acquainted with several of these men and invited them to meet with him to discuss the organization of a young adult group at the center. Twenty men showed up for the initial meeting as a result of word-of-mouth publicity only. At this meeting the men were quite explicit about their problem: they saw themselves as failures when it came to girls. Many hoped that this group would solve their problem.

When the discussion turned to the group's activities, there was an even division among those present. Half wanted only social programs, since this was their problem area; but the other half, perhaps afraid of further failures, opted for other types of activity. One young man mentioned that his cousin in a distant city belonged to a co-ed hiking club where there were opportunities for doing things *and* for meeting girls. Some thought that this was a good idea. Others presented various arguments against this suggestion. Finally, one of those present turned to the social worker, who had remained silent until now, and asked him, "What do you think?"

# Bibliography

Allport, Gordon W. 1955. *Becoming*. New Haven, Conn., Yale University Press.

Anderson, Claire M., and Thomas Carlsen. 1971. "The Midway Project on Organization and Use of Public Assistance Personnel." In Robert L. Barker and Thomas L. Briggs, eds., *Manpower Research on the Utilization of Baccalaureate Social Workers*, pp. 17–28. Washington, U.S. Government Printing Office.

Argyle, Michael. 1967. *The Psychology of Interpersonal Behavior*. Baltimore, Penguin Books.

Arkava, Morton L. 1974. *Behavior Modification: a Procedural Guide for Social Workers*. Missoula, Mont., University of Montana.

Banks, George P. 1971. "The Effect of Race on One-to-one Helping Interviews." *Social Service Review* 45:137–46.

Barnard, Chester I. 1938. *The Functions of the Executive*. Cambridge, Mass., Harvard University Press.

Barnlund, Dean C. 1970. "A Transactional Model of Communication." In K. K. Sereno and C. D. Mortensen, eds., *Foundations of Communication Theory*, pp. 83–102. New York, Harper & Row.

Barrett, Franklin T., and Felice Perlmutter. 1972. "Black Clients and White Workers: a Report from the Field." *Child Welfare* 51:19–24.

Bart, Pauline B. 1968. "Social Structure and Vocabularies of Discomfort: What Happened to Female Hysteria?" *Journal of Health and Social Behavior* 9:188–93.

Bartlett, Harriett M. 1970. *The Common Base of Social Work Practice*. New York, National Association of Social Workers.

Basso, K. H. 1972. " 'To Give Up on Words': Silence in Western Apache Culture." In Pier P. Giglioli, ed., *Language and Social Context*, pp. 67–86. Baltimore, Penguin Books.

Berelson, Bernard, and Gary A. Steiner. 1964. *Human Behavior—an Inventory of Scientific Findings*. New York, Harcourt, Brace & World.

Bergin, Allen E. 1966. "Some Implications of Psychotherapy Research for Therapeutic Practice." *Journal of Abnormal Psychology* 71:235–46.

Bernstein, Basil. 1964. "Social Class, Speech Systems, and Psychotherapy." *British Journal of Sociology* 15:54–64.

—— 1971. *Class, Codes and Control.* London, Routledge and Kegan Paul.

Bernstein, Saul. 1960. "Self-determination: King or Citizen in the Realm of Values." *Social Work* 5(1): 3–8.

Biestek, Felix P. 1957. *The Casework Relationship.* Chicago, Loyola University Press.

Billingsley, Andrew. 1964. "Bureaucratic and Professional Orientation Patterns in Social Casework." *Social Service Review* 38:400–407.

Bingham, Walter V. D., and Bruce V. Moore. 1924. *How to Interview.* New York, Harper.

Bisno, Herbert. 1969. "A Theoretical Framework for Teaching Social Work Methods and Skills." *Journal of Education for Social Work* 5(Fall):5–17.

Blank, Marion, and Frances Solomon. 1969. "How Shall the Disadvantaged Child Be Taught?" *Child Development* 40(March): 47–61.

Blau, Peter M., and Richard W. Scott. 1962. *Formal Organizations.* San Francisco, Chandler.

Boehm, Werner W. 1958. "The Nature of Social Work." *Social Work* 3(2):10–18.

—— 1959. *Objectives of the Social Work Curriculum of the Future.* New York, Council on Social Work Education.

—— 1968. "Common and Specific Learnings for a Graduate School of Social Work." *Journal of Education for Social Work* 4(Fall):15–26.

Briar, Scott, 1971. "Family Services and Casework." In Henry S. Maas, ed., *Research in the Social Services,* pp. 108–29. New York, National Association of Social Workers.

—— and Henry Miller. 1971. *Problems and Issues in Social Casework.* New York, Columbia University Press.

Brieland, Donald. 1969. "Black Identity and the Helping Person." *Children* 16:170–75.

Brown, Gordon E. 1968. *The Multi-Problem Dilemma.* Metuchen, N.J., Scarecrow Press.

Brown, Robert A. 1973. "Feedback in Family Interviewing." *Social Work* 18(5):52–59.

Burns, Crawford E. 1971. "White Staff, Black Children: Is There a Problem?" *Child Welfare* 50:90–96.

Caldwell, Bettye. 1969. *Inventory of Home Stimulation from Ages Zero to Three.* Syracuse, N.Y., Children's Center, Syracuse University.

Chilman, Catherine S. 1966. "Social Work Practice with Very Poor Families: Some Implications Suggested by the Available Research." *Welfare in Review* 4:13–22.

Clausen, John A. 1966. "Mental Disorders." In Robert K. Merton and Robert A. Nisbet, eds., *Contemporary Social Problems,* pp. 26–83. New York, Harcourt, Brace & World.

Cloward, Richard A., and Lloyd E. Ohlin. 1960. *Delinquency and Opportunity.* New York, Free Press.

Cohen, Jerome. 1964. "Social Work and the Culture of Poverty." *Social Work* 9(1):3–11.

Cohen, Nathan E. 1964. *Social Work and Social Problems.* New York, National Association of Social Workers.

Coleman, Lee. 1941. "What Is America? A Study of Alleged American Traits." *Social Forces* 19:492–95.

Commager, Henry Steele, ed. 1967. *Lester Ward and the Welfare State.* Indianapolis, Bobbs-Merrill.


Davitz, Joel R., and Lois Davitz. 1959. "The Communication of Feelings by Content-free Speech." *Journal of Communication* 9:6–13.

Dittmann, Laura L., ed. 1968. *Early Child Care: the New Perspective.* New York, Atherton.

Dubey, Sumati. 1970. "Blacks' Preference for Black Professionals, Businessmen, and Religious Leaders." *Public Opinion Quarterly* 34:113–16.


Ecklein, Joan L., and Armand A. Lauffer. 1972. *Community Organizers and Social Planners.* New York, Wiley.

Ekman, Paul. 1964. "Body Position, Facial Expression and Verbal Behavior During Interviews." *Journal of Abnormal and Social Psychology* 68:295–301.

Elkin, Robert. 1969. "Framework for Decision-making—Applying PPBS to Public Welfare Program Structure." *Public Welfare* 49:157–66.

Epstein, Laura. 1973. "Is Autonomous Practice Possible?" *Social Work* 18(2):5–12.

Erikson, Erik H. 1950. *Childhood and Society.* New York, Norton.

Exline, Ralph, David Gray, and Dorothy Schuette. 1965. "Visual Behavior in a Dyad as Affected by Interview Content and Sex of Respondent." *Journal of Personality and Social Psychology* 1:201–9.


Fine, Sidney A. 1967. *Guidelines for the Design of New Careers.* Kalamazoo, Mich., W. E. Upjohn Institute.

Fischer, Joel. 1971. "A Framework for the Analysis and Comparison of Clinical Theories of Induced Change." *Social Service Review* 45:440–54.

—— 1973. "Is Casework Effective?" *Social Work* 18(1):5–20.

Foucoult, Michael. 1965. *Madness and Civilization.* New York, Pantheon.

Fried, Alfred. 1969. "The Attack on Mobilization." In Harold H. Weissman, ed., *Community Development in the Mobilization for Youth Experience*, pp. 137–62. New York, Association Press.

Fromm, Erich. 1947. *Man for Himself.* New York, Holt, Rinehart & Winston.


Gallimore, Ronald G., and Jim L. Turner. 1969. "Faith and Psychotherapy." In Donald A. Hansen, ed., *Explorations in Sociology and Counseling*, pp. 93–116. Boston, Houghton Mifflin.

Gans, Herbert J. 1962. *The Urban Villagers.* New York, Free Press.

Geismar, Ludwig L. 1969. *Preventive Intervention in Social Work.* Metuchen, N.J., Scarecrow Press.
—— 1972. *Early Supports for Family Life: a Social Work Experiment.* Metuchen, N.J., Scarecrow Press.
—— 1973. *555 Families.* New Brunswick, N.J., Transaction Books.
Ginsburg, Benson F. 1966. "All Mice Are Not Created Equal: Recent Findings on Genes and Behavior." *Social Service Review* 40:121–34.
Glueck, Sheldon, and Eleanor Glueck. 1950. *Unraveling Juvenile Delinquency.* Cambridge, Mass., Harvard University Press.
Goffman, Erving. 1959. *The Presentation of Self in Everyday Life.* New York, Doubleday.
—— 1961. *Asylums.* New York, Doubleday.
—— 1967. *Interaction Ritual.* Garden City, N.Y., Anchor Books.
Goldberg, Gertude S. 1969. "Nonprofessionals in Human Services." In Charles Grosser *et al.,* eds., *Nonprofessionals in Human Services,* pp. 12–39. San Francisco, Jossey-Bass.
Goldstein, Arnold P., Kenneth Heller, and Lee B. Sechcrest. 1966. *Psychotherapy and the Psychology of Behavior Change.* New York, Wiley.
Gordon, William E. 1962. "A Critique of the Working Definition." *Social Work* 7(4):3–13.
—— 1965. "Towrd a Social Work Frame of Reference." *Journal of Education for Social Work* 1(Fall):19–26.
Greenleigh Associates. 1965. *Study of Services to Deal with Poverty in Detroit, Michigan.* New York, Greenleigh Associates.
Gross, B. M. 1969. "The New Systems Budgeting." *Public Administration Review* 29:113–32.
Grosser, Charles F. 1965. "Community Development Programs Serving the Urban Poor." *Social Work* 10(3):15–21.
Gummer, Burton, Jane Kronick, and Felice Perlmutter. 1972. *The Evaluation Study of the APWA Model for Social Service Delivery as Implemented by the County Board of Assistance in Delaware.* Bryn Mawr, Pa., Bryn Mawr College.
Gurin, Gerald, Joseph Veroff, and Sheila Feld. 1960. *Americans View Their Mental Health.* New York, Basic Books.

Haase, Richard F., and Dominic J. DiMattia. 1970. "Proxemic Behavior: Counselor, Administrator and Client Preference for Seating Arrangement in Dyadic Interaction." *Journal of Counseling Psychology* 17:319–25.
Hall, Edward T. 1959. *The Silent Language.* Garden City, N.Y., Doubleday.
—— and William F. Whyte. 1960. "Intercultural Communications: a Guide to Men of Action." *Human Organization* 19:5–12.
Halleck, Seymour. 1963. "The Impact of Professional Dishonesty on Behavior of Disturbed Adolescents." *Social Work* 8(2):48–56.
Hamilton, Gordon. 1958. "Foreword." In Herman D. Stein and Richard A. Cloward, eds., *Social Perspectives on Behavior,* pp. xi-xiv. Glencoe, Ill., Free Press.
Handler, Joel F., and Ellen Jane Hollingsworth. 1969. "The Administration

of Social Services and the Structure of Dependency: the View of AFDC Recipients." *Social Service Review* 43:406–20.

Hansen, Donald A. 1965. "Personal and Positional Influence in Formal Groups." *Social Forces* 44:202–10.

Hearn, Gordon, ed. 1968. *The General Systems Approach: Contributions toward an Holistic Conception of Social Work.* New York, Council on Social Work Education.

Hillman, Arthur. 1968. *Making Democracy Work—a Study of Neighborhood Organization.* New York, National Federation of Settlements and Neighborhood Centers.

Hoehn-Saric, R., *et al.* 1964. "Systematic Preparation of Patients for Psychiatry." *Journal of Psychiatric Research* 2:267–81.

Hollingshead, August B., and Frederic C. Redlich. 1958. *Social Class and Mental Illness: a Community Study.* New York, Wiley.

Hollis, Florence. 1964; 2d ed., 1972. *Casework, a Psychosocial Therapy.* New York, Random House.

—— 1970. "The Psychosocial Approach to the Practice of Casework." In Robert W. Roberts and Robert H. Nee, eds., *Theories of Social Casework,* pp. 33–75. Chicago, University of Chicago Press.

Homans, George C. 1950. *The Human Group.* New York, Harcourt, Brace & World.

—— 1961. *Social Behavior: Its Elementary Forms.* New York, Harcourt, Brace & World.

Horney, Karen. 1939. *New Ways of Psychoanalysis.* New York, Norton.

Hovland, Carl I., and Walter Weiss. 1951. "The Influence of Source Credibility on Communication Effectiveness." *Public Opinion Quarterly* 15:635–50.

Hughes, Everett C. 1963. "Professions." *Daedalus* 92:655–68.

Jackson, Jesse. 1968. Cited by Alvin L. Schorr in Editorial. *Social Work* 13(3):2.

Janis, Irving L., and Seymour Feshbach. 1953. "Effects of Fear-arousing Communications." *Journal of Abnormal and Social Psychology* 48:78–92.

Jensen, Arthur R. 1969. "How Much Can We Boost IQ and Scholastic Achievements?" *Harvard Educational Review* 39:1–123.

Jones, Hettie. 1969. "School-Community Relations." In Harold H. Weissman, ed., *Employment and Educational Services,* pp. 136–47. New York, Association Press.

Jones, Stanley E. 1973. "Proxemic Behavior of Black and White First-, Third-, and Fifth-Grade Children." *Journal of Personality and Social Psychology* 25:21–27.

Kadushin, Alfred. 1972. *The Social Work Interview.* New York, Columbia University Press.

Kadushin, Charles. 1966. "The Friends and Supporters of Psychotherapy: on Social Circles in Urban Life." *American Sociological Review* 31:786–802.

Kahn, Alfred J. 1966. *Neighborhood Information Center*. New York, Columbia University School of Social Work.

—— 1973. *Social Policy and Social Services*. New York, Random House.

Kaplan, Abraham. 1964. *The Conduct of Inquiry*. San Francisco, Chandler.

Katz, Elihu. 1957. "The Two-Step Flow of Communication: an Up-to-Date Report on an Hypothesis." *Public Opinion Quarterly* 21:61–78.

Kedem, Alya. 1974. "A Toy Library: an Innovative Service." *Saad (Jerusalem)* 18:58–61.

Keith-Lucas, Alan. 1974. Letter. *Social Work* 19:381–82.

Kelley, Harold H. 1950. "The Warm-cold Variable in First Impressions of Persons." *Journal of Personality* 18:431–39.

Kendall, Katherine. 1958. "Basic Content in Professional Education for Social Work." *International Social Work* (Bombay) 6:29–39.

—— 1973. "Dream or Nightmare? The Future of Social Work." *Journal of Education for Social Work* 9 (Spring):13–23.

Kiesler, Donald J. 1966. "Some Myths of Psychotherapy Research and the Search for a Paradigm." *Psychological Bulletin* 65:110–36.

Kinsey, Alfred C., Wardell B. Pomeroy, and Clyde E. Martin. 1948. *Sexual Behavior in the Human Male*. Philadelphia, Saunders.

Klineberg, Otto. 1938. "Emotional Expression in Chinese Literature." *Journal of Abnormal and Social Psychology* 33:517–20.

Kluckhohn, Clyde. 1958. "Have There Been Discernible Shifts in American Values During the Past Generation?" In Eltin E. Morison, ed., *The American Style*, pp. 145–217. New York, Harper and Bros.

—— 1962. *Culture and Behavior*. New York, Free Press.

Kohn, Melvin L. 1963. "Social Class and Parent-Child Relationship: an Interpretation." In Rose L. Coser, ed., *Life Cycle and Achievement in America*, pp. 21–42. New York, Harper & Row.

—— 1969. *Class and Conformity: a Study in Values*. Homewood, Ill., Dorsey Press.

Komarovsky, Mira. 1964. *Blue-Collar Marriage*. New York, Random House.

Konopka, Gisela. 1963. *Social Group Work: a Helping Process*. Englewood Cliffs, N.J., Prentice-Hall.

Lastrucci, Carlo L. 1963. *The Scientific Approach*. Cambridge, Mass., Schenkman.

Leissner, Aryeh. 1969. *Street Club Work in Tel Aviv and New York*. London, Longmans, Green.

Levenger, George. 1960. "Continuance in Casework and Other Helping Relationships." *Social Work* 5(3):40–51.

Levine, Rachel A. 1970. "Consumer Participation in Planning and Evaluation of Mental Health Services." *Social Work* 15(2):41–46.

Levy, Charles S. 1973. "The Value Base of Social Work." *Journal of Education for Social Work* 9(Winter):34–42.

Lewin, Kurt. 1943. "Forces behind Food Habits and Methods of Change." *Bulletin of the National Research Council*, No. 108.

—— 1948. *Resolving Social Conflict*. New York, Harper & Bros.

Lipset, Seymour M. 1961. "A Change in American Character." In Seymour M. Lipset and Ludwig Loewenthal, eds., *Culture and Social Character*. New York, Free Press.

Loewenberg, Frank M. 1968. "Social Workers and Indigenous Nonprofessionals: Some Structural Dilemmas." *Social Work* 13(3):65–71.

—— and Ralph Dolgoff, eds. 1972. *The Practice of Social Intervention*. Itasca, Ill., Peacock Publishers.

Macarov, David. 1974. "Client-Worker Agreement: Necessity, Desideratum or Dogma." *Social Work Today* (London) 4:773–76.

—— and Naomi Golan. 1973. "Congruence between Social Worker's Purposes and Activities." *Saad* (Jerusalem) 17:3–9.

McCroskey, Jack C., C. E. Larson, and M. L. Knapp. 1971. *An Introduction to Interpersonal Communication*. Englewood Cliffs, N.J., Prentice-Hall.

McLeod, Donna L., and Henry J. Meyer. 1967. "A Study of the Values of Social Workers." In Edwin J. Thomas, ed., *Behavioral Science for Social Workers*, pp. 401–16. New York, Free Press.

MacMahon, James T. 1964. "The Working Class Psychiatric Patient: a Clinical View." In Frank Riessman *et al.*, eds., *Mental Health of the Poor*, pp. 283–303. New York, Free Press.

Maluccio, Anthony. 1974. "Action as a Tool in Casework Practice." *Social Casework* 55:30–35.

Marris, Peter, and Martin Rein. 1967. *Dilemmas of Social Reform*. New York, Atherton.

Mayer, John E., and Noel Timms. 1970. *The Client Speaks*. London, Routledge and Kegan Paul.

Mehrabian Albert. 1968. "Communication without Words." *Psychology Today* 2:53–55.

Mendes, Richard H. P. 1974. "Theory Heroes and Theory Villains." In John M. Romanyshyn, ed., *Social Science and Social Welfare*, pp. 70–85. New York, Council on Social Work Education.

Menzel, Herbert, and Elihu Katz. 1955. "Social Relations and Innovation in the Medical Profession: the Epidemiology of a New Drug." *Public Opinion Quarterly* 19:337–52.

Michels, Robert. 1959. *Political Parties*. Trans. by Eden and Cedar Paul. New York, Dover.

Middleman, Ruth R., and Gale Goldberg. 1974. *Social Service Delivery: a Structural Approach to Social Work Practice*. New York, Columbia University Press.

Miller, Daniel R., and Guy E. Swanson. 1960. *Inner Conflict and Defense*. New York, Henry Holt.

Miller, Emily. 1973. "Treatment of a Communal Family." *Social Casework* 54:331–41.

Miller, Henry. 1968. "Value Dilemmas in Social Casework." *Social Work* 13(1):27–33.

Mills, C. Wright. 1943. "The Professional Ideology of Social Pathologists." *American Journal of Sociology* 49:165–80.

Moles, Oliver, Robert F. Hess, and Daniel Fascione. 1968. "Who Knows Where to Get Public Assistance?" *Welfare in Review* 6:8–13.

Moynihan, Daniel P. 1969. *Maximum Feasible Misunderstanding*. New York, Free Press.

Mullen, Edward J. 1968. "Casework Communications." *Social Casework* 49:546–55.

——, James R. Dumpson, and Associates. 1972. *Evaluation of Social Intervention*. San Francisco, Jossey-Bass.

"National Assessment of Writing." 1970. *Report on Educational Research* 2:8–9.

National Association of Social Workers. 1958. "Working Definition of Social Work Practice." *Social Work* 3(2):5–9.

——, Ad Hoc Committee on Advocacy. 1969. "The Social Worker as Advocate: Champion of Social Victims." *Social Work* 14(2):16–22.

Neugeboren, Bernard. 1970. "Opportunity-centered Social Work." *Social Work* 15(2):47–52.

Newman, Edward, and Jerry Turem. 1974. "The Crisis of Accountability." *Social Work* 19:5–16.

Northen, Helen. 1969. *Social Work with Groups*. New York, Columbia University Press.

Panitch, Arnold. 1974. "Advocacy in Practice." *Social Work* 19:322–26.

Parsons, Talcott. 1960. *Structure and Process in Modern Society*. New York, Free Press.

—— 1970. *Social Structure and Personality*. New York, Free Press.

Peabody, Robert L. 1964. *Organizational Authority*. New York, Atherton.

Perlman, Helen H. 1957. *Social Casework: a Problem-solving Process*. Chicago, University of Chicago Press.

—— 1960. "Intake and Some Role Considerations." *Social Casework* 41:171–77.

—— 1965. "Self-determination: Reality or Illusion?" *Social Service Review* 39:410–22.

—— 1966. "Social Work Method: a Review of the Past Decade." *Social Work* 10(4):166–78.

—— 1968. *Persona: Social Role and Personality*. Chicago, University of Chicago Press.

—— 1970. "The Problem-solving Model in Social Casework." In Robert W. Roberts and Robert H. Nee, eds., *Theories of Social Casework*, pp. 129–79. Chicago, University of Chicago Press.

Pew, Miriam L., David C. Speer, and James Williams. 1973. "Group Counseling for Offenders." *Social Work* 18(1):74–79.

Piliaven, Irving. 1968. "Restructuring Social Services." *Social Work* 13(1):34–41.

Piven, Frances Fox, and Richard A. Cloward. 1971. *Regulating the Poor: the Functions of Public Welfare*. New York, Vintage Books.

Polsky, Howard. 1962. *Cottage Six: the Social System of Delinquent Boys in Residential Treatment.* New York, Russell Sage Foundation.

Pritchard, Colin. 1973. "Nature versus Nurture? Review of Genetic Factors in Mental Disorders." *Social Work Today* (London) 4:566–70.

Pumphrey, Muriel W. 1959. *The Teaching of Values and Ethics in Social Work Education.* New York, Council on Social Work Education.

—— 1973. "Lasting and Outmoded Concepts in the Caseworker's Heritage." *Social Casework* 54:259–67.

Rapoport, Lydia. 1970. "Crisis Intervention as a Mode of Brief Treatment." In Robert W. Roberts and Robert H. Nee, eds., *Theories of Social Casework,* pp. 265–311. Chicago, University of Chicago Press.

Reid, William J. 1967. "Characteristics of Casework Intervention." *Welfare in Review* 5:11–18.

—— and Laura Epstein. 1972. *Task-centered Casework.* New York, Columbia University Press.

—— and Barbara L. Shapiro. 1969. "Client Reactions to Advice." *Social Service Review* 43:165–73.

—— and Ann W. Shyne. 1969. *Brief and Extended Casework.* New York, Columbia University Press.

Reynolds, Bertha C. 1964. "The Social Caseworker on an Uncharted Journey." *Social Work* 9(4):13–17.

Richmond, Mary E. 1917. *Social Diagnosis.* New York, Russell Sage Foundation.

—— 1930. *The Long View.* New York, Russell Sage Foundation.

Ripple, Lilian. 1955. "Motivation, Capacity, and Opportunity as Related to the Use of Casework Service: Theoretical Base and Plan of Study." *Social Service Review* 29:172–93.

—— and Ernestina Alexander. 1956. "Motivation, Capacity, and Opportunity as Related to the Use of Casework Service: Nature of the Client's Problem." *Social Service Review* 30:38–54.

Rogers, Carl R. 1951. *Client-centered Therapy.* Boston, Houghton Mifflin.

Rosen, Aaron, and Ronda S. Connaway. 1969. "Public Welfare, Social Work, and Social Work Education." *Social Work* 14(2):87–94.

Rosenberg, Marvin, and Ralph Brody. 1974. *Systems Serving People: a Breakthrough in Service Delivery.* Cleveland, School of Applied Social Sciences, Case Western Reserve University.

Rosenthal, Robert, and Lenore Jacobson. 1968. "Self-fulfilling Prophecies in the Classroom: Teachers' Expectations as Unintended Determinants of Pupils' Intellectual Competence." In Martin Deutsch, Irwin Katz, and Arthur R. Jensen, eds., *Social Class, Race and Psychological Development,* pp. 219–53. New York, Holt, Rinehart & Winston.

Russell, Bertrand, 1927. *Philosophy.* New York, Norton.

Sample, William C. 1967. "The Findings on Client Change." *Social Service Review* 41:137–51.

Sandifer, Myron G., Anthony Hordern, and Lynda M. Green. 1970. "The

Psychiatric Interview: the Impact of the First Three Minutes." *American Journal of Psychiatry* 126:968–73.

Schild, Sylvia. 1966. "The Challenging Opportunity for Social Workers in Genetics." *Social Work* 11(2):22–28.

—— 1972. "Genetic Counseling." In *Encyclopedia of Social Work,* pp. 471–76. New York, National Association of Social Workers.

Schmidt, Julianna T. 1969. "The Use of Purpose in Casework Practice." *Social Work* 14(1):77–84.

Schubert, Margaret. 1972. *Interviewing in Social Work Practice: an Introduction.* New York, Council on Social Work Education.

Schwartz, Edward E. 1967. "The Field Experiment: Background, Plans, and Selected Findings." *Social Service Review* 41:115–36.

Seabury, Brett A. 1971. "Arrangement of Physical Space in Social Work Settings." *Social Work* 16(4):43–49.

Segal, Arthur. 1970. "Workers' Perception of Mentally Disabled Clients: Effect on Service Delivery." *Social Work* 15(3):39–46.

Segal, Steven P. 1972. "Research on the Outcome of Social Work Therapeutic Interventions: a Review of the Literature." *Journal of Health and Social Behavior* 13:3–17.

Shannon, Barbara E. 1970. "Implications of White Racism for Social Work Practice." *Social Casework* 51:270–76.

Shapiro, Jeffrey G., and Therese Voog. 1969. "Effect of the Inherently Helpful Person on Student Academic Achievement." *Journal of Counseling Psychology* 16:505–9.

Sherif, Muzafer, and Carolyn W. Sherif. 1964. *Reference Groups: Explorations into Conformity and Deviation of Adolescents.* New York, Harper & Row.

Shulman, Lawrence. 1968. *A Casebook of Social Work with Groups.* New York, Council on Social Work Education.

Silverman, Phyllis. 1970. "A Re-examination of the Intake Procedure." *Social Casework* 51:625–34.

Simmel, Georg. 1950. *The Sociology of Georg Simmel.* Trans. by Kurt H. Wolff. Glencoe, Ill., Free Press.

—— 1955. *Conflict.* Trans. by Kurt H. Wolff. Glencoe, Ill., Free Press.

Simon, Bernece K. 1970. "Social Casework Theory: an Overview." In Robert W. Roberts and Robert H. Need, eds., *Theories of Social Casework,* pp. 353–94. Chicago, University of Chicago Press.

Smalley, Ruth E. 1970. "The Functional Approach to Casework Practice." In Robert W. Roberts and Robert H. Nee, eds., *Theories of Social Casework,* pp. 77–128. Chicago, University of Chicago Press.

Spergel, Irving. 1966. *Street Gang Work: Theory and Practice.* Garden City, N.Y., Anchor Books.

Strodtbeck, Fred L. 1951. "Husband-Wife Interaction over Revealed Differences." *American Sociological Review* 16:468–73.

Thomas, Edwin J., ed. 1967. *The Socio-behavioral Approach and Application to Social Work.* New York, Council on Social Work Education.

Toren, Nina. 1970. *Social Work: the Case of a Semi-Profession.* Beverly Hills, Calif., Sage.

Tropp, Emanuel. 1970. "Authenticity in Teacher-Student Communication." In Marguerite Pohek, ed., *Teaching and Learning in Social Work Education,* pp. 13–26. New York, Council on Social Work Education.

—— 1974. "Three Problematic Concepts: Client, Help, Worker." *Social Casework* 55:19–33.

Truax, Charles B., and Kevin M. Mitchell. 1971. "Research on Certain Therapist Interpersonal Skills in Relation to Process and Outcome." In Allen E. Bergin and Sol L. Garfield, eds., *Handbook of Psychotherapy and Behavior Change,* pp. 299–344. New York, Wiley.

Vail, Susan. 1970. "The Effects of Socio-economic Class, Race, and Level of Experience in Social Workers' Judgments of Clients." *Smith College Studies in Social Work* 40:236–46.

Warfield, Martha J. 1972. "Treatment of a 2-Year-Old in Preparation for Adoption." *Social Casework* 53:341–47.

Wasserman, Henry. 1970. "Early Careers of Professional Social Workers in a Public Child Welfare Agency." *Social Work* 15(1):93–101.

—— 1971. "The Professional Social Worker in a Bureaucracy." *Social Work* 16(1):89–95.

Watzlawick, Paul, Janet H. Beavin, and Don D. Jackson. 1967. *Pragmatics of Human Communication.* New York, Norton.

Webb, Allen, and Patrick V. Riley. 1970. "Effectiveness of Casework with Young Female Probationers." *Social Casework* 51:566–72.

Weber, Max. 1946. *From Max Weber.* Trans. and ed. by H. H. Gerth and C. Wright Mills. New York, Oxford University Press.

—— 1947. The Theory of Social and Economic Organization. Trans. and ed. by A. M. Henderson and Talcott Parsons. New York, Oxford University Press.

Whiteman, Martin B., and Martin Deutsch. 1968. "Social Disadvantage as Related to Intellective and Language Development." In Martin B. Deutsch, Irwin Katz, and Arthur R. Jensen, eds., *Social Class, Race and Psychological Development,* pp. 86–114. New York, Holt.

Whyte, William F. 1955. *Street Corner Society.* 2d ed. Chicago, University of Chicago Press.

Wilensky, Harold L., and Charles N. Lebeaux. 1958. *Industrial Society and Social Welfare.* New York, Russell Sage Foundation.

Williams, Robin M., Jr. 1967. "Individual and Group Values." *The Annals* 371:20–37.

Willis, Frank N., Jr. 1966. "Initial Speaking Distance as a Function of the Speakers' Relationship." *Psychonomic Science* 5:221–22.

Wilson, Gertrude, and Gladys Ryland. 1949. *Social Group Work Practice.* Cambridge, Mass., Houghton Mifflin.

Wolins, Martin. 1969. "Group Care: Friend or Foe." *Social Work* 14(1):35–53.

Yablonsky, Lewis. 1965. *The Tunnel Back: Synanon.* New York, Macmillan.
Younghusband, Eileen L. 1958. *Training for Social Work: Third International Survey.* New York, United Nations.
—— 1967. "The Teacher in Education for Social Work." *Social Service Review* 41:359–70.

Zborowski, Mark. 1969. *People in Pain.* San Francisco, Jossey-Bass.
Zimmerman, Don H. 1969. "Tasks and Troubles: the Practical Bases of Work Activities in a Public Assistance Organization." In Donald A. Hansen, ed., *Explorations in Sociology and Counseling,* pp. 237–66. Boston, Houghton Mifflin.

# Name Index

# Index of
# Exemplars
# and Vignettes

# General Index